Transitions - Liminality as Lived Experience

Marta B. Erdos

Transitions - Liminality as Lived Experience

Springer

Marta B. Erdos
Department of Community and Social Studies,
Faculty of Humanities and Social Sciences
University of Pécs
Pécs, Hungary

ISBN 978-3-031-96006-2 ISBN 978-3-031-96007-9 (eBook)
https://doi.org/10.1007/978-3-031-96007-9

This Springer imprint is published by the registered company Springer Nature Switzerland AG
The registered company address is: Gewerbestrasse 11, 6330 Cham, Switzerland

Preface

This book is about life's *extraordinarily* chaotic and confusing moments, liminal experiences, which may radically change our life. Recurring, global-level crises make studying these lived experiences during the profound transformations a timely challenge. Our favourite metaphor, *depth* to describe not only the challenges but recent developments, suggests intensity and thoroughness; but reaching the depths, the nadir point, is also our conception of *crisis*: hitting the bottom in our individual lives, or in a civilization. This book is a systemic, transdisciplinary attempt to capture several experiences of liminality as shaped by societal and cultural factors.

Liminality, a concept to describe the grey zone of transitions, introduced by Arnold van Gennep in 1909, has become a key area of interest in cultural anthropology, sociology, clinical and developmental psychology, health studies, theology, and philosophy. It has (re) directed scholars' attention to the complex and transdisciplinary domain of the psychosocial and has contributed to the establishment of new and innovative areas, for example, political anthropology or semiotic cultural psychology. The concept has soon found its way into popular culture, which fact, though carries some risks of semantic satiation, does not diminish its scientific significance. On the contrary: our era of uncertainties and the often-aborted attempts to control the 21st-century complexities provides diverse opportunities to experience and study the different facets of liminality. Various forms have been identified, from the original version, transformative liminality to the "as if" version, the playful liminoid as a space for identity explorations, or the (self-)destructive context of arrested transitions: permanent or trickster liminality as described by Horvath and Szakolczai in their recent book in 2020.

Studying liminality is inseparable from studying identity as our conception of the self, a dialectic between continuity and change. We attribute special significance to our own or our group's distinctive existence—from the lived past to the envisioned future. Future visions, as the realm of indispensable hopes, are contingent on the success of meaning making in times of major transformations. Traditionally, human cultures have facilitated such sensemaking, the communal and personal reconstructions of shared meanings via rites of transition to tame the risks and unpredictability. Myths behind the rites informed the participants about how our world worked and what a good life was. In late modernity, the frames for meaning making are less compelling, giving the individual the freedom to choose their identity variations and find their unique responses to life's major questions. Parallel, the frames have become fragmented and incomplete, allowing space not only for unique identity variations, but also for mass-level manipulation and arrested transitions, occasionally transforming the space for meaning making into a vacuum of meaninglessness.

Homo symbolicus is characterized by a species-specific behaviour complex, and our rituals have remained an important element in this complex. We can induce major transformations in our lives and in the natural and cultural environment—now at an unprecedented pace and on a global level. During these adventures, we alternate between the alluring, Shakespearean self-position of the paragon of animals and the less attractive identity conception, quintessence of dust. By using symbols, we construe and segment the processes of the self and of the environment into the ones fostering stability perceived as cosmic order, and those of imbalance and chaos. Restoring and maintaining balance (order) is a central issue both in our civilizations and in our individual lives.

When we transitioned from the holistic worldviews of myths and rites and accepted the Newtonian-Cartesian framework as the new, comprehensive ideology, we substituted systemic approaches with linear logic; but this logic is efficient only when we apply it to the domain of technologies. Globally, we are under the impression that we can tackle the complexities that we have created: the complexities of our globalized economic and political systems and the rapidly expanding and proliferating digital environment. Total control is but an illusion. The enhanced focus on risks and short-term management of the uncertainties and problems we are facing now entail the creation of trickster liminalities, permeating our global lifestyles and colonizing the individuals' private spheres in the service of neoplasmic economic growth and the concentration of political power instead of genuine human development. These phenomena represent disruption, but not (yet) development. Our Western civilization with its individualization and technological developments appear to be far from the cultures of our ancestors, and the types of problems we are struggling with seem very different from the recurrent problems that humans have been struggling with from the onset of civilization; but the fundamental patterns of life transitions are rather similar. These transformations, if not lingering, may indeed bring us better lives. Extending the constructive moments of transformative liminality into more-of-the-same, schismogenetic patterns is an ill-founded approach to human problem solving. Being arrested in the process of transformation and entrapment in liminality have become a common experience, a paradox in late modernity celebrating diversity and chances for positive renewal. The losses we all are experiencing well exceed the gains and may lead us to the nowhere of permanent liminality established for nobodies. Let us hope that today's authoritarian reactions to the paradoxes inherent in transitions are not the only response we humans are capable of.

Studying liminality and identity requires a systemic and transdisciplinary, in-between perspective. In this book, I address liminal experiences and processes by including several global, communal, intersubjective, and personal domains into the analysis. Such an approach provides the author with the benefits of a more holistic view, with the inherent risks that some details that are important from a specific disciplinary perspective will be missing.

The first part with its two chapters introduces the main concepts and theoretical foundations of the book. Chapter 1 comments on the evolutionary potentials and weaknesses of *Homo symbolicus*, the super predator, but not the super carer of Earth. The chapter discusses the main properties of symbolic communication and explores how these features are connected to our constructions on liminal phenomena. Human languaging equips us with exceptional developmental potentials and flexibility but is also conducive to schismogenetic polarization—notions on perfectness and annihilation. Chapter 2 comprises a detailed analysis of the transformation patterns facilitated or impeded by symbolic communication. This systemic approach to deep transformations, using the umbrella term of quantum change, is followed by a brief introductory discussion on liminal experiences, outlining a connection between these experiences and Grof's (1985) birth matrices as prototypical source domains for interpreting major life transitions. Part II, following Stenner's suggestion (2017) is an exploration on several sociopsychological phenomena in our global environment, the ones that contribute to the emergence of liminal hotspots as contexts of entrapment in a limbo state. Chapter 3 is a critical reflection on the global-level changes, mainly from the perspective of generativity frustration brought about by our consumerist lifestyles, which escalate conflicts, support craving, and result in networked alienation. Today's globalized systems are a-mazed, manipulated societies in a continual effort to defend themselves from reflecting on the ongoing environmental, societal, and cultural destructions. These complex transformations are intertwined with and strengthened by the domination of info-communication technologies in mass and interpersonal communication, resulting in the fast colonization and sales of private spheres. This chapter comprises a brief analysis of the recent global-level crisis, the COVID-19 pandemic, which transformed us, the *children* of Enlightenment, into helpless subjects governed by the affectivity of the crisis. People immediately co-created hostile groups of vaccine supporters and vaccine deniers in the new, overarching formation of the therapeutic state diminishing any other aspects of human existence and identity. Chapter 4 discusses some spatial, temporal, and relational changes brought about by the liminality of *onlife*, a term introduced by Floridi (2015) to capture the complexities people experience in the virtual world. The transformation is not governed by the playful liminoid only. Onlife processes establish frequent and occasionally tormenting liminal hotspots while decreasing people's capabilities to cope with the negative emotionality of the hotspots. The next two chapters are about the lived experiences of permanent liminality in Eastern Europe under the communist rule, focussing on the various discursive techniques by which trickster liminality was built and maintained. Chapter 5 contrasts two distinct forms of manipulative discourse, the more traditional and transparent classical form, characteristic of open dictatorships with their well-known consequences: terror, societal-level insanity, and the emergence of powerful counter-discourses; and the hidden callousness and obscurity of a "soft" dictatorship, sustaining the absurdities of permanent liminality but mostly refraining from open aggression. This second form seems to have milder consequences in terms of human lives; but it paralyses critical reflectivity, creativity, and renewal and renders the construction of a counter discourse more difficult. A soft dictatorship is killing one softly: its result is not physical death but identicide, the denial and elimination of previous values as the basis of identity. Chapter 6 is an exploration comprising both the sociopsychological and psychosocial aspects of the destructive soft-system processes. The *Dog's Night Song*, a film by Gábor Bódy (1983), capturing the essence of the lived experience of permanent liminality resulting in the highest rate of suicide globally, eradicates the false nostalgies concerning such psycho-political formations. The 1983 introduction of the film was shortly followed by Bódy's debated suicide in 1985.

Part III is about the psychosocial interface, focussing more on the subjective side, the individual's lived experiences. Chapter 7 draws analogies between psychological crisis and transition rites, exploring the connections between the two seminal theories. Proceeding from the global and the societal levels towards the intersubjective and personal domains, this chapter focuses on the communicative and psychological aspects of the experience, establishing a theoretical link between liminal hotspots and entrapment as an explanatory notion for suicide. In Chap. 8, this is followed by a narrative analysis of a novel, Gárdonyi's *Szunyoghy's Paternoster* (1916) written for the purpose to prevent suicide. Several classical and more recent theoretical developments in suicide research are authentically depicted in the novel, but this is not the crux of the analysis. Gárdonyi delves into how humans may be lost in the domain of symbols, and how such abandonment may lead to the idea of destructing the self. The novel evolves around an important aspect of the life-saving potentials inherent in quantum change, epiphany, and the accompanying insights governing such transformations. Chapter 9 is about the positive, life-sustaining aspects of temporary, *transformative* liminality, the intensity of dialogical moments to facilitate the reconstruction of responses to life's ultimate questions that the individual is struggling with during the transition. Traditional rites fulfilled this function through connecting the person to shared, communal understandings and interpretations on the transcendent dimensions of life. Dialogue is represented as a basic human condition that we are born into, and occasionally must return to.

Deep transformations are part of our lives. Let us embrace these moments—but embrace them with *care*. Our prototypical experiences on liminality are birth and death. Exploring liminal experiences may teach us how to make the best of what is given *in between*.

Pécs, Hungary Marta B. Erdos

Acknowledgements

I am deeply indebted to all the authors for their works that I could read throughout my life. Their thoughts are with me; please accept my apologies for the potential misunderstandings in my interpretations. This book is about my conception of liminality as lived experience, one contribution to the numerous pieces already written—and many others, yet to come.

My mentors and close colleagues have been a continual source of inspiration throughout my career. Balázs Kézdi (1938–2010), my PhD supervisor and professional leader at the crisis intervention centre where I used to work at as a practitioner was the first representative of discursive psychiatry in Hungary. He introduced a theme, psychological crisis, that has become my permanent area of interest.

Gábor Kelemen, a senior researcher and previous chair at our department, could always find the time and energy to find inspiring responses to my questions—and ask me the inspiring questions when needed. His creativity, fresh and open perspective, academic resilience, and his deep interest in social constructionism were special assets in the contemporary academic milieu. As a genuine mentor, he thoughtfully read my early papers. I am grateful for his empowering attitude, resourceful comments, and for teaching me how to live a reflective life as a professional.

I am thankful to György Révész for the revelation that psychology is not about the state socialist collection of empty, ready-to-use ideologies predominant in the early 1980s in Hungary, but a genuine scientific adventure. Endre Fülei-Szántó (1924–1995) could successfully convince me that linguistics is more about people's lives and sociocultural processes than about mere formalisms. Bea Ehmann assisted me in taking my first steps in qualitative research. Özséb Horányi patiently tolerated my strong interest in psychology and (initially) less interest in social communication. I owe special thanks for my relatively good command of English to Béla Tóth, my secondary school teacher of English as a second language.

In 2007, I received a scholarship from the contemporary Leonardo Programme and could spend a few months at Chester College University where I could meet Professor Roger Ellis whose friendship and professional support is one of the greatest gifts in my later adulthood. Identity as a subject is our common area of interest.

Rebeka Javor, my former colleague, a competent and creative co-author in several articles from 2020 on, and a good friend with a strong interest in talent development, has never let me leave my drafts unfinished.

I am most grateful to the anonymous reviewers of the draft of this book for their insightful and encouraging comments. I would also like to express my thanks to Springer's editorial team for their ongoing support.

Bea Lábadi, Associate Dean for Research at the Faculty of Humanities and Social Sciences raised the idea of a potential sabbatical leave in 2023 to assist me with finishing my manuscript. In 2024, the University of Pécs granted me the leave, and my close colleagues took over my teaching assignments. Thank you.

Contents

About the Author

Marta B. Erdos is an Associate Professor at the University of Pécs, Hungary. Her areas of research interest are identity transformations, crisis, and liminality. Throughout her career, she has contributed to laying the foundations for systemic, transdisciplinary research and qualitative approaches in her domestic context. Before commencing her academic career in 2000, she used to work as a mental health counsellor.

Part I
Introduction

Chapter 1
Living in a Dual Environment: *Homo Symbolicus* and Languaging

1.1 Symbols from an Evolutionary Perspective

> "When I use a word," Humpty Dumpty said, in rather a scornful tone, "it means just what I choose it to mean—neither more nor less."
> "The question is," said Alice, "whether you can make words mean so many different things."
> "The question is," said Humpty Dumpty, "which is to be master—that's all."
> Alice was too much puzzled to say anything;
> —Lewis Carroll: Through the Looking Glass

Carroll's short metalogue immerses us into the problems inherent in the domain of symbols—a universe of shared but potentially conflicted and debated meanings, defining privileged and subordinated positions while also confusing the conversing partners. When we are communicating, we are involved in a constant, dialectic process of meaning, conservation, and renewal. Symbols represent a quality or entity—an idea, a process, an event, an action, or an object—by *convention*. These conventions determine meanings for the community and the individual and outline the shared and approved frames for a good life. Thus, conventions are our precious legacy, a source of traditional wisdom but often with a touch of absurdity, deviation, and mischief. These dark features are strengthened in times of community crises and prepare the ground for mass-level delusions, wishful thinking, and a rich collection of defensive dysfunctions and failures in semiosis and sensemaking.

This chapter is an exploration of the potential gains and losses related to symbol use. How have symbols, characteristic of human languaging evolved and become the strongest evolutionary factor in our development? How do we construe the domains of our existence through symbol use, establishing and extending the spatial, temporal, and relational boundaries of our lives? Can we navigate safely in these extended dimensions? How do symbols relate to our exceptional constructive abilities, and how and why does their use occasionally result in cognitive and affective entrapments? How do we co-construct the liminal contexts of the in-between

M. B. Erdos, *Transitions - Liminality as Lived Experience*,
https://doi.org/10.1007/978-3-031-96007-9_1

and betwixt when transitioning from one identity position to another? (Salvatore & Venuleo, 2017; Turner, 1969). What makes *Homo symbolicus* (Savage-Rumbaugh & Fields, 2011) so special?

In the light of recent research results, many of the boundaries that seemed to nicely distinguish between humans and nonhumans have proven more permeable than ever before, and our anthropocentric visions on the presumed, discrete differences have given ways to considering more continuity. Several animals build refined communication strategies to protect themselves or maximize their chances for survival. For example, social animals, especially primates develop a certain degree of *intentionality*, attributing mental states to other participants in their joint social action (Bereczkei, 2016; Savage-Rumbaugh & Fields, 2011). Bonobos, humans' genetic siblings use gestures to refer to complex events occurring in a different temporal and spatial context (Pederson et al., 2009, as cited in Savage-Rumbaugh & Fields, 2011). Their pant-hoots are characterized by *dialects*—group-based and group-identifying variations in language. They use signs (symbols) with not any immediate connections based on causality or similarity between the signifier and the signified. They can reflect on past events and develop not only a sense of self (e.g. recognizing themselves in a mirror as apes would normally do) but an *autobiographical* self with internal personal narratives. They behave in socially appropriate and morally responsible ways as adults (Savage-Rumbaugh & Fields, 2011). We could learn that even dogs have a capacity to analyse lexical meaning and intonation separately, very much in the ways humans do (Andics et al., 2016).

These characteristics are much beyond the traditional ideas on instinctive, emotionally expressive, and automatic stimulus-response communication in animals, and especially in nonhuman primates: "the modern view of non-human primate communication is that it is learned, voluntary, and intentionally referential and rule-governed. Language as communication necessarily implies sociality, or in humans, collectivity" (McGrew, 2011, p. 5).

New evidence for a continuity between humans and other social species stronger than in the Darwinian conception is an uneasy discovery, questioning humans' special position in the ecosystem. Savage-Rumbaugh and Fields (2011) have claimed that the level of awareness of the self that both the humans and the bonobos possess is based on a reflective capacity facilitated by the bifurcation into an observer, a reflective self, and a doer, an agentive self. The agentive self is active in a specific context defined by time, space, and the cultural frameworks for social relations. It is vigilant of its environment, also initiating actions and interactions in the environment. The doer mode enables immediate, quick, and non-reflected responses to environmental challenges. Contrastingly, the reflective mode creates its own spatial and temporal dimensions (Castro-Tejerina & Rosa, 2007, as cited in Savage-Rumbaugh & Fields, 2011). The reflexive self manages the beliefs, fantasies, and reflections, providing the person with a sense of uniqueness and continuity, and facilitates the construction of a life story. The public self's presentation is governed by the person and is reflected by others, building a me-perspective, a subject for internal reflections to smooth social synchronization processes (Csányi, 2000; Harré, 1998; Weinreich, 2004).

When accounting for the differences between human and nonhuman adaptation, Csányi (2000) has suggested abandoning the early single factor focus, i.e. tool use, toolmaking, or language use. He has outlined a systemic, integrative framework, the *human behaviour complex* comprising three main, interrelated constituents: social behaviour patterns, mechanisms for the synchronization of behaviour, and activities of construction (Csányi, 2000, p. 243). Signs and symbols are the critical components of this complex.

Csányi also examined the level of correspondence between the communicating partners. Signals are classified as Type I communication if the level of correspondence is high: for example, when two dogs are using the language of smells they would immediately and automatically understand each other. Between humans and dogs, the initial level of correspondence is often zero, but gradually, the dog will learn how to respond to human language—parallel, its human caretaker will develop more sensitivity to the dog's signals. For us, this Type II communication with low levels of initial correspondence is quite common, as many of the signs we are using are not automatically interpreted and their meaning varies depending on the social context.

Social behaviour patterns include several distinctive traits, such as the formation of closed and dense groups, mechanisms to regulate internal aggression, food sharing among the members other than close relatives, complementary patterns in collaboration, the development of loyalty, and the perception of own group (and not only its members) as a specific entity (Csányi, 2000). We develop a strong sense and image of our own selves and of the group we belong to as *identities*, rooted in our past experiences while also shaping our visions of the future; and we also attribute such autobiographically constructed identities to our others. Synchronization refers to highly developed empathy to map others' emotional states, and to hypnotic susceptibility; hypnosis is a two-way communication process between the hypnotist and the subject (Motzkau, 2009). Synchronization relies on our highly refined mimics, about ten times more variable than in other primates, rhythmic activities (singing and dancing), motives for imitation relatively independently of its immediate goal, education, and obeying to the rules of the group (Csányi, 2000).

The discovery of mirror neurons in social animals was a seminal development in the 1990s (Acharya & Shukla, 2012). These neurons are activated while the individual is executing an action or witnessing an action. Mirror neurons are the neurological basis for imitation and fine-tuned collaboration, also grounding the development of a theory of mind (Szécsi, 2016). Finally, the common-sense slogan that the eyes are the mirror of the soul has proven a valid observation, as connecting through the visual channel has a key role in mirror neural activity. Ongoing studies have confirmed that this huge neural system extends into the somatosensory cortex, thereby facilitating imitation and synchronization (Acharya & Shukla, 2012). Mirror neurons serve as a basis for sympathy through the simulation of a movement, a sensation, or an emotion. This is but a pre-reflective automatism, and empathy is built only when the individual connects the other's perceived sensations, emotions, or actions to their own reflected experiences (Lux, 2010). Mirror neurons facilitate the understanding of each other's actions and the actors' intentions. By enabling recursive embeddings and assisting the appropriate interpretations of gestures in an interaction, mirror neurons play a crucial role in the development of language: "it solves one of the fundamental difficulties for understanding language evolution, that is, how and what is valid for the sender of a message become valid also for the receiver" (Acharya & Shukla, 2012, p. 121). Recursive embeddings open the possibility of a rewind mode, a time travel into the remote past, the accumulation and sharing of experiences to be used in the future, and creatively rearranging past experiences to generate visions of the future. Our motivations are embedded in these visions and enable us to build well-grounded or defensive strategies (Acharya & Shukla, 2012; De Luca Picione & Lozzi, 2021).

Imitation, a key socialization factor, often involves some modification of the original pattern, utilizing the third component of the human behaviour complex, our constructive abilities. These constructive abilities comprise abstraction, toolmaking and usage, and the development of language into a practically infinite domain (Csányi, 2000). Concerning creativity, an important aspect of human communication is the *digital* quality of certain signs, primarily, of our words (Watzlawick et al., 1968). These meaningful units can be combined to construe myriads of new forms and meanings, allowing great flexibility and creativity in language use. From a pragmatic point, the units we use can be conceptual contents referring to objects, events, or abstract notions, and procedural contents, orienting us what to do with these concepts (Moeschler, 2016; Reboul & Moeschler, 2005). Procedural contents guide our subconscious mental operations that are targeted at the conceptual contents, e.g. identifying the speaker in a conversation when hearing "I", or invalidate, that is, try and delete the previously constructed or recalled mental contents when these are combined with negation. The central potentials inherent in procedural contents are to interpret causalities and reconstruct the context of speech without sharing the same physical, temporal, and spatial contexts (Moeschler, 2016).

Thus, we are equipped with special gifts for survival, and these qualities have indeed ensured a special position for us. Synchronization processes enable us to identify our roles, leading to the emergence of longstanding and complementary collaboration patterns and dividing a task into different sub-tasks to be solved by the individual members of the group. Collaboration is consensual and is based on sympathetic identification or empathy. Humans are "constantly monitoring the mind states of their conspecifics" (Csányi, 2000, p. 251). The synchronization of emotions and abstraction together establish the grounds for developing the two main forms of reflectivity: relational reflections and self-reflections (McNamee, 2004). In the possession of all these developments, we can analyse and evaluate the events, actions, and circumstances to build complex strategies and share and store them for future use. This leads to enhanced levels of abstraction and control as well as to the hierarchical but decentralized organization of language, affording much flexibility in strategic planning (Planer, 2023). The *me* perspective, seeing ourselves in the eyes of other group members while collaborating, together with our exceptional reflexive potentials, allow us to *explore, anticipate, and plan* our responses to diverse situations that we have never experienced personally. This is what Savage-Rumbaugh and Fields (2011) have identified as a crucial difference between humans and nonhumans. Interestingly, the very same feature seems a major barrier in the future development of artificial intelligence (Smith, 2024).

Csányi (2000) defined the group as a superorganism, characterized and converged by common ideas and other symbolic constructions (artefacts), common actions, loyalty, and self-denial and sacrifice. The emergence of this superorganism is a systemic change. Our second environment, culture, comes into existence through signs and symbols as a representational reality, comprising physically real or imagined actors, objects, and events. Culture is constantly reconstructed through Type II. communication, a human compulsion that is not just the result of our evolution but also a driving force. Our cultural memes and communication technologies change the usual patterns of sensing and processing information (Csikszentmihalyi, 1996; Floridi, 2015; McLuhan & Fiore, 2012; Planer, 2023; Tari, 2023).

1.2 Communication, Care, and Identity

Savage-Rumbaugh and Fields (2011) point out the salient differences in the developmental pathways of a human baby from those of our closest genetic relatives. Early explanations, the psychoanalytical theories on the human condition beginning with primary frustrations, the baby's inability to cling on to the mother, focussed on humans' loss of body hair and its consequence (Hermann, 1984). Indeed, human infants depend on and welcome close physical connections to their caretakers, but, on both sides, there are barriers to maintain the continuity of the physical contact. Human babies are born with a large head and considerable body fat. Their neck and spine need constant support, further, they have an inborn reflex to move their limbs. Contact must be maintained while the mother is involved in activities other than care and is leaving the baby on the ground. The unity between the human mother and the child is interrupted early but is restored when needed. The baby's vocalizations are an important signal for the mother about the unsettling conditions perceived by the baby (Savage-Rumbaugh & Fields, 2011). This demands sophisticated ways of communication, and the continuous, rapid correction of the mismatches frequent in our flexible communication (Tronick & Cohn, 1989).

Vocalizations will attract the predators, so both the mother and the baby need the protection provided by the group (Savage-Rumbaugh & Fields, 2011). Thus, caretakers must pay extra attention to reducing conflicts and maintaining strong and secure social ties within the group. Recursivity, a precondition for remembering our experiences in the form of a structured narrative, is also a process of *re-membering*: re-establishing and redefining our membership in the community. Castells (1997), analysing various late modern examples, has concluded that our predictions on a peaceful, future global village seems but an illusion: social identity remains a central concern for humans, and the different cultures invariably distinguish between the own members and non-members of the group through their symbols and rituals. We are extremely sensitive about our group level determinants, such as ethnicity, nationality, gender, religion, and professional background. This is reflected by the current proliferation of identity variations and the associated deep societal conflicts when a social group feels their identity threatened. Intergroup competition for the environmental resources is underpinned by identity constructions, and xenophobia appears (Csányi, 2000). Adaptive competition for the resources has evolved into dysfunctional *greed,* a main motive for wars in modernity (Fromm, 1973).

Forming and reconstructing our personal and group-based identities, the central concerns in a rite of passage (Turner, 1969; van Gennep, 1909/2019) are a natural sequel of the human behaviour complex. The development of reflexivity, the 'me' perspective, human's creative potentials, and an ability to mentally navigate in time entail the development of a multifaceted self-concept. The distinction between I, the agentive self, and Me, the public self as reflected by others, and the constant reflections on our own behaviour by the reflexive self, evaluating and managing the discrepancies between the public self and one's own perceptions of self, will ease and fine-tune interpersonal collaboration (Harré, 1998; Savage-Rumbaugh & Fields, 2011; Weinreich, 2004). Consequently, we evaluate our experiences from many different perspectives when we are involved in the meaning-making processes related to a single experience, or in times of major transitions, to the flow of our life. The success of such meaning-making is not only critical to collaboration; the sense of coherence, comprising perceived comprehensibility, meaningfulness, and directionality, orienting us towards value-consistent goals, coupled with perceived manageability of stressful and chaotic events emerge as a key factor in our personal wellbeing (Antonovsky, 1996; Galletta et al., 2019; Lau & Tov, 2023; McAdams, 2006). Establishing coherence—order from chaos—requires interpersonal communication as meaning-making is an intersubjective (social) process.

These evolutionary developments have led to a complex, personal, and unique self-concept, identity. Weinreich's (2004) theory, Identity Structure Analysis (ISA) is a synthesis of seminal earlier notions:

- The psychosocial development theory with a focus on constant explorations and commitments (Erikson, 1968; Marcia, 1966).
- The need to resolve cognitive dissonance, a common result of the ambivalence and uncertainties of our evaluations and decisions (Festinger, 1957)
- The need for organismic valuing (Rogers, 1964)
- A tendency to arrange our world into bipolar constructs (Kelly, 1955)
- And the postmodern theory on the discursive and dialogical nature of self, highlighting the interplay between the agentive, the public, and the reflexive selves (Harré, 1998)

Weinreich also differentiates between the temporal aspects of self (such as past selves and anticipations on our future selves), the self's unique perspective on other important entities, exploratory selves (the self as experienced or envisioned in recurrent or significant states and contexts), and the meta-perspectives of the self, connecting one's public self to one's own ideas about this public self (e.g. "I think that others think that I…") (Weinreich, 2004). Thus, identity is seen as the totality of our self-construals, a continuity rooted in our past, and through our anticipations, setting life's future directions for a personally understood meaningful life. Identifications and contra-identifications with role models are shaped by complex and lengthy socialization processes, incorporating various themes and situations, continually establishing, and resolving the arising conflicts between the incorporated identity elements. We evaluate the people around us and choose role models to identify with their appealing identity elements, while rejecting others through contra-identifications. The resulting polarities, the ideal and contra-ideal selves (Weinreich, 2004) play an important part in our psychology as internal measures for our identity strivings.

1.3 Languaging and Intersubjectivity

Becker (1991) has proposed focusing on language use as a social process more than on language as an abstraction: "Try thinking of it this way: assume that there is no such thing as Language, only continual languaging, an activity of human beings in the world" (Becker, 1991, p. 34). From a structuralist perspective, the idea seems rather provocative. We usually think of human languages as abstract systems described as a structure representing and encoding other, extra-linguistic structures in the physical and social environment, as well as the related contents of the human mind. However, language use or languaging as a form of life is inherently relational and behavioural, inseparable from the human cognition and social activities (Kravchenko, 2021; Maturana et al., 1995). Humans' innate system, a faculty of language is strongly embedded in their social relations (Hauser et al., 2002). The shift from language—an abstract structure and a reification, in this new framework conceived as second-order languaging—to languaging is a key to understanding the nature of symbols and narratives. Languaging, as "an embodied and cognitive technique of sense-making" (Raimondi, 2019, p. 20) captures one's personal and communal experiences. Languaging functions demand complexity, reuniting the words with the body, and liberating people's social and creative potentials (Gurney & Demuro, 2022; Krantz & Pennebaker, 2007). Languaging addresses the entirety of human behaviour complex, like the traditional rites of passage have always done (Turner, 1969; van Gennep, 1909/2019). Thus, languaging is social action—both for its origins and for its consequences (Austin, 1975; Dunbar, 2004; Senft, 2009). Even the most abstract and "objective" scientific description will influence human behaviour, not to mention evocative poems, promises, or prohibitions. As Wittgenstein (1953, section 23) commented on this unity, "the speaking of language is part of an activity, or a form of life".

There is enormous flexibility and resiliency inherent in humans' complex and multimodal communication, comprising gestures, speech, singing, writing, etc. as these are actualized in the social environment to facilitate joint actions through anticipating others' behaviour (Raimondi, 2019). Impairments in languaging (e.g. with severely traumatized persons) will lead to isolation, and deteriorations in well-being (van der Kolk, 2015).

Austin (1975) in his speech act theory has outlined a reflexive relationship between speech and shared realities: speakers do not only represent the reality "out there" but also construe their social realities, establishing a word-to-world or, inversely, a world-to-word direction (Searle, 1979). Humans can create potential, virtual worlds through languaging—utopias or dystopias in the distant future, the Promised Land, or, as it frequently happens in the political discourse, a waste land of unmet promises. Semiosis and symbol use are inseparable from sociocultural practices (Turner, 1974). The constructed realities are not arbitrary language-games, but are the conventional games people play, and as such, they must be adjusted to certain rules or conventions: the grammars (Wittgenstein, 1953). These grammars, determined by the cultural traditions, comprise the felicity conditions of the discourse (Austin, 1975).

Re-presenting the environment and sharing true or false statements, the results of our observations, was seen as the predominant linguistic function in the positivist era. Importantly, representation enables us to communicate across the different situations, travelling relatively freely in time and space, and to adopt different perspectives, including our own potential future positions (Csányi, 2000). Representation is a precondition both for abstractions and narratives. In the paradigmatic mode, we utilize the potentials inherent in analysis and logic to build an abstract system of categories and identify their relations. The narrative mode is about authenticity and the complexities of personal meaning (Bruner, 2004). Narratives have a distinguished role not only in identity construction but also in the interpretation of new situations and responding to these by the appropriate actions (McAdams, 1993; Szécsi, 2020). We spend considerable time on building our narrative identity and capture our "lived time" in a personal narrative (Bruner, 2004, p. 12.). Narrating our lives inherently requires reflexivity, assuming the double roles of the narrator and the hero of the story. The lived narrative is not identical with our life story: the latter is also shaped by the psychological realities of future fantasies and suppressed experiences (Bruner, 2004; Hänninen, 2004). Thus, languaging is much more than about representing the perceived realities "out there".

For most of the time, we use communication to manage our social lives, express hierarchy, and bonding, optimize group collaboration, and resolve conflicts (Dunbar, 2004). The term "phatic" to describe the power of languaging to maintain community ties and build identities was first used by Malinowski (1923), who conducted his ethnographic studies in an era when the immense power of language to shape social realities was considered only secondary to representation.

1.4 Symbols and Interpreters

Horányi (1999, 2007) in his participation theory of communication focussed on the evolutionary gains inherent in human communication, understood as a state in which the necessary competencies—as readiness or fitness for problem solving—are accessible. Communication as participation enables the members of a group to interpret, co-construct, and reconstruct the meanings they live by. Horányi has distinguished between the different levels of signification, mainly between the "brute", physical, and symbolic significations. Horányi's participation theory is grounded in the Peircean tradition in semiotics. In this framework, a sign gains its meaning in relation to a previous sign in an infinite semiosis and the interpreters reconstruct the meaning from a set of potentialities (Atkin, 2023). Salvatore refers to this quality as the difference between Signification in Presentia (actual use of the sign) and Signification in Absentia (potential, latent meanings) (Reho & Salvatore, 2024). Salvatore et al. (2021) in their integrative Semiotic Cultural Psychology Theory outline nine key, interrelated tenets of semiosis:

- Interpretative *mediation* of reality from a specific perspective.
- *Triadicity*, comprising the recursive relationship between the sign and the interpreter's response, in addition to the dyad of the signifier and signified.
- *Embodiment,* highlighting the relationship between the dynamic patters of representations and sensorimotor activity.
- *Inferential* nature referring to our anticipations concerning the environment.
- *Self-referentiality* implying that to anticipate events, we must endow our experiences with meaning.
- And our meanings are (at least partly) *hierarchically* organized, belonging to different levels.
- The authors, referring to the Peircean idea of a semiotic chain, conclude that *affects*, if interpreted, are also signs.
- Affectivity serves as a motivation for sharing the signs with others: they are *embedded* in our culture.
- And are related to social practices as *performativity* of signs.

While it is a common characteristic of all the types of signs that they refer to something else, the connections between the signifier and the signified are different. These connections can be established via similarity (iconic signs), physical law, e.g. causality (indexes), and the conventions of use, as with symbols (Atkin, 2023). These conventions are rooted in a community's shared experiences and knowledge but are not always easy to detect; further, they are subject to change in relation to the interpreters' individual actions, representations, and interests. The etymology of *symbola* is revealing about the characteristics of a symbol. In ancient Greece, a clay tablet was used by the contracting parties to enter into an agreement. The tablet was broken, and the pieces (symbola) were given to the parties, who were aware of the existence of the other parts but could not possess the whole. The agreement came in force through commun(icat)ion (Airey & O'Connell, 2005; Horányi, 1999). A symbol cannot exist without an interpreting human community: its meaning resides within the community and is also constitutive of that community. A symbol hints at an invisible part and implies that the individual-level interpretations are neither exhaustive nor uniform; they cannot be. This is what establishes the bivalence of meaning: symbols (and, more generally, signs) have a directly perceivable and a latent side (Salvatore & Venuleo, 2017). It may also imply that something that was once well-known for the participants of a communicative act may be missing and can only be reconstructed through involvement in the repeated restorative activities (e.g. rituals, formal education, etc.) of the culture bearers.

Recent discoveries concerning the continuity in communication patterns and signification processes in the animal kingdom lay a particular emphasis on humans' symbol use. Symbols are an interface between the personal and the social domains. Sharing the meanings through learning and constant community reconstructions are a prerequisite for the symbol to operate. Symbol use has its constraints, both as for their interpretations and for the social actions they facilitate or prohibit (Zittoun et al., 2003).

The meaning of the term changes across the different disciplines and theories. In art and psychotherapy, symbols are usually understood as signs related to unconscious, cosmic, archaic, and transcendental–spiritual contents, possibly connected to social taboos or to the mystical archetypes of the collective unconscious, guiding our personal identity development in times of crises (Campbell, 2008; Jung, 2012; Weatherly, 2015). In this view, a symbol is a concrete entity referring to a complex and abstract, partly unknown, unknowable, and sacred signified. Mechanisms as displacement and condensation, uniting the multiple layers of meaning are central to this conceptualization. From this holistic perspective, symbols refer to the shared transcendental knowledge of an interpreting community, comprising the emotional and embodied (sensorimotor) patterns of the experience, and as such, play an important part in marking and interpreting life transitions in the accompanying rites.

The two traditions, the psychological–anthropological and the semiotic conception of symbols might be a source of confusion: for Jung (2012), many of the signs that Peirce (Atkin, 2023) would consider a symbol would simply count as a sign. What is understood as a symbol in the psychological or anthropological tradition, for example, motherland, terra mater (Eliade, 1961) is commonly identified as a metaphor in linguistics (Sargsyan, 2021). While the Jungian perspective highlights the importance of humans' relations to cosmic, collective, and often unconscious domains represented in the different archetypes, Peirce's conceptualization, attaching signification processes to social conventions, focuses more on humans' constructive and collaborative abilities.

Peirce (in Atkin, 2023) elaborated on his semiotic theory and concluded that many variations exist by combining the elements of his system, differentiating between the types according to the interpretant, the object, and the vehicle of the sign. The final version, introducing 66 different types in the model, has never been fully elaborated (Atkin, 2023).

The following example may illuminate some of the problems inherent in this typology: a boy complained that the sound of the wind chimes did not resemble the sound of the wind, as he had erroneously expected. For a correct interpretation, we need specific knowledge, a dynamic model of the world, a context model to reveal the type and degree of correspondence between the object, the signified, and the signifier as the basis for transferability (Tileaga, 2011; van Dijk, 2013, 2014). We must know if wind chimes are supposed to make a sound like the wind (iconic signs of the wind), are activated only when the wind is blowing, or the aliens are coming as in the film *Signs* by Shyamalan (2002) (indexical), if there is a common agreement that they are operated by humans to predict high wind (a version of the Peircean symbolic) or they reveal the will of some supernatural power (symbolic both in the Jungian and the Peircean sense). But in all these cases, there is an agreement to name wind chimes wind chimes in English (Peircean symbolic). The use of the word is based solely on the convention of the interpreting community. In conclusion, wind chime as a *word,* a label is entirely symbolic; the sound can be considered indexical as its operation is caused by the wind; and at least partly iconic as wind chimes echo, if not the sound, but the natural rhythm of the wind; and wind chimes also resemble a musical instrument, potentially referring to other objects in this class. Wind chimes as an object-sign, however, also has its Jungian symbolic qualities, as they remind us of our deep connectedness to nature and cosmic powers.

Language, a distinguished domain of social actions and relations, is largely symbolic (with the rare exceptions of onomatopoeic words). Cultural conventions governing the meaning of a symbol are defined by use: "For a large class of cases—though not for all—in which we employ the word "meaning" it can be defined thus: the meaning of a word is its use in the language" (Wittgenstein, 1953, section 43). Use varies between the speakers, as their reflections on the world through language are shaped by their diverse experiences, and by their envisioned future interests. Thus, we can never mean precisely the same—speakers' language use always involves a degree of difference, of heteroglossia (Bakhtin, 1984a). To cope with ambiguities and uncertainties in meaning, and use these for enriching our shared meanings, we use symbols to comment on the use of symbols. These meta-functions are characteristic of human communication, a system to maximize reflexivity; and every utterance is inherently *relational* as it has an addressee, even if not physically present.

Even with the differences inherent in the varied contexts and interpreters, participants' consensus governs the use of a word and imposes constraints on the potential meanings. If the deviation from the conventions is salient, and the constraints as the *boundaries of meaning* are dissolved, then the usual explanation lies in individual- or collective-level insanity. My favourite example to this feature goes back to the early 1990s in Hungary, only a few years after the system change. Naturally, the transition did not result in an immediate and substantial change in people's mindsets. I was a member of a group of parents, protesting a municipality decision to close a nearby school. The decision-makers frequently asked our group to try and find a "compromise", what we did, proposing to establish a community-funded, NGO-run institution for the locals. At a certain point, the repeated negotiations, however, made it clear that "compromise" was not meant in the sense that is codified in a thesaurus, but belonged to the specific Hungarian dialect of the prevailing state socialist "Newspeak" with its twisted "political correctness" of vagueness, ambiguities, and sometimes emptiness of meaning, transferring a latent, powerful, distorted, and hegemonic (monosemic) meaning ("we expect you to obey our orders and stop protesting immediately"). Symbols enable us to construe, interpret, and manage the liminal settings when the disruptions in the previously untroubled experience of ordinary life demand alterations in the semiotic chain as "meanings cease to be taken for granted" (Zittoun et al., 2003, p. 415). Symbol use, however, does not only transform the existing social forms but can also contribute to the fruitless repetition of unsustainable patterns of an arrested transition.

1.5 Metaphors, Representation, and Re-Creation

Van Boeckel has referred to Bateson's notions in the film *An Ecology of Mind* (2010) as follows: "Metaphor is the language of relationships, the language of natural systems, in which there is room to communicate in spectrums of possibility" (van Boeckel, 2011, p. 3). The holistic, relational, and revealing complexity of metaphors make them central not only to our language but also to human cognition (Lakoff, 1993). Metaphors play a key role in transitions. By connecting languaging to vivid imagery in an embodied process, they mobilize right hemisphere functions and convey the deep emotional contents of a transformation (Kövecses, 2003). Metaphors are often multimodal, with their verbal contents accompanied by nonverbal elements, such as gestures, mimics, or visual signs (Forceville, 2009).

Early conceptions by linguists and philosophers were evolving around some "primary" or "simple" ways of formulating our messages and saw metaphors as verbal elements characterized by high levels of mediacy, expressing some complication (e.g. Searle, 1993). Studies in psycholinguistics and cognition have challenged this view (Glucksberg & Keysar, 1993; Lakoff, 1993). The cognitive theory of metaphor has claimed that metaphor use involves structural mappings between the different conceptual domains, a source domain and a target domain, a semiotic process central to our cognition. In this conception, there are no "dead" metaphors, just the conventional ones that are so common that we are hardly ever conscious of the mappings when we are using them—these are the metaphors we live by, think by, and feel by. Metaphors assist us to depict our emotions, experiences, and abstractions that cannot be sensed directly and/or are transcendent. There are higher order mappings, root metaphors, such as, for example, DEEP TRANSFORMATION IS BIRTH, and if we adhere to these shared and basic conceptualizations, then the individual and unique variations will be understood easily.

The aptitude to connect the different domains of experiences and use a source domain to capture the meaning of a new experience, the target domain, is present early in life. I was taking my little daughter to the nursery on a fall day—she was about one and a half years old in those days, using small children's telegram style for communication. It was late in the morning, and I showed her the moon that was still visible in the sky. She commented on the extraordinary event by demanding to switch the moon off. She immediately used the source domain of a forgotten light to interpret the unusual phenomenon and proposed an action to restore order.

Drawing analogies and understanding a new phenomenon or a hardly comprehensible abstraction in terms of a relevant source domain are the general characteristics of human thinking (Lakoff, 1993; Lakoff & Johnson, 1980). Metaphors capture many different, occasionally even *contrasting* layers of meaning and unite them in a framework that mobilizes not only the thoughts and affects but entire scripts of a narrative to prepare and enable an appropriate action. Thus, metaphors can reintegrate the polarities, inherent in the digital features of language use bringing about a simplified yes-no, black and white type of reality, into a more comprehensive representation. Reconnecting the verbal representations of experiences to the body through metaphors is another important feature: metaphors are *embodied*, and therefore they can convey deep emotional contents (Lakoff, 2012). Our lived experiences are processed and verbalized, and this creates a distance from the original experience, but metaphors also have the evocative power to preserve the original valence. Without metaphors, there is no genuine reflection.

Metaphors, however, do not only reveal the truth but may also hide some of the truth—not because of their complexity, but because of our contextual and personal constraints in interpretation. We infer meanings and shape our beliefs with respect to the overall guiding principle, collaboration, to the speaker's role and position and our own disposition (Grice, 1975). When hearing "Juliet is the Sun" from her true lover, Romeo, then we associate this statement with the triumph of light over darkness as the most accessible, ready-to-use cultural interpretation. We adopt an appealing and comfortable semiotic chain without any disruptions or alternative pathways. Juliet ends the night of the soul and the power of evil, she is the source of life, bright and beautiful. We may neglect that the sun is a source of lethal danger for the one who dares to approach it or is even trying to reach for it—in the play, breaking not only the loyalty to one's family of origin, but also the rules of medieval, esoteric romantic love. The positive interpretations are deeply rooted in human cultures, but they may change parallel to changing experiences.

The significance of metaphors during life transitions lies in their power to grasp complex and holistic experiences, comprising the embodied impressions and ambiguities in meaning, and assisting the management of emotions by absorbing and expressing the affective load—and even comprising basic scripts for action. Metaphors resist the true or false dichotomies of left hemisphere logic. They are evaluated by their adequacy, depth, and richness to describe the experience (B. Erdős, 2006; Kövecses, 2003; Lakoff & Johnson, 1980; Lakoff, 1993; Rácz & Kaló, 2009; Rohovit, 1960). Polysemy facilitates capturing the ambivalence, paradoxes, and ambiguities that people encounter during a profound transition.

1.6 Burke's *Definition of Man*

Kenneth Burke, a philosopher in the cold war era, the decades bearing regretful similarities to our contemporary global contexts, focussed on humans' strong disposition to, and the consequences of symbol use in his *Definition on Man* (1963, p. 507):

> Man is the symbol-using (symbol-making, symbol-misusing) animal, inventor of the negative (or moralized by the negative), separated from his natural condition by instruments of his own making, goaded by the spirit of hierarchy (or moved by the sense of order) and rotten with perfection.

While Burke notes that by sophisticated language use, we can solve problems that other species cannot, he also captures some unwanted consequences that *Homo Symbolicus* must face. At a first glance, this human-made, symbolic environment may seem more controllable than our natural environment. The idea that we can rule this secondary environment *because* we have created is alluring—but it is not true. As the ointment itself gets increasingly complex and attractive, more and more flies will breed. We may lose our way in these double, physical (or as Burke defines it, animalistic), and symbolic environments. Occasionally, we mistake the symbolic for the physical, the thing itself for its representation, eating the menu card and not the meal (Bateson, 1972). At times, we forget that symbolic-level misrepresentations may well have their consequences in the physical reality, as the Thomas Theorem has concluded (Merton, 1995). Burke (1963) mentions a salient example, "hexing", the actual death brought about solely by the victim's beliefs. To raise a hexing example from the "rationalism" of late modernity, consider a grave financial setback stimulated by the investors' shared beliefs, spreading rapidly through the Internet, and resulting in both strategically planned, and unforeseen consequences. The symbolic domain can easily turn into a labyrinth, a web not only connecting but also entrapping its users (Geertz, 1973).

1.6.1 Inventor of the Negative

Occasional confusions in our dual environment are intrinsically connected to negation: "There is an implied sense of negativity in the ability to use words at all. For to use them properly, we must know that they are not the things they stand for" (Burke, 1963, p. 501). As language is a combination of digital and analogue signs, our meanings inherently imply the opposite as a potentiality hiding in the shadow (Gergen et al., 2001). Partly, we live in a yes-no, 1–0 type of linguistic universe, condemned to defend ourselves against the perceived uncertainties involved in this controversy.

Humans' frequent use of negative structures has long been a theme of interest in several disciplines. Clearly, the negative is not merely a question in logic or linguistics: as a source of paradox and a means of expressing ambivalence and destruction, it has its utmost relevance in the construction of liminal contexts and experiences. Pennebaker et al. (2003) have concluded that about half of what we say when we are speaking are function words. The use of function words—or, using again the term of relevance theory, procedural contents (Moeschler, 2016)—is not pre-planned, and it cannot be: they are automatically selected in a conversation, and their recall is poor as compared to that of the conceptual contents. (How many negative structures could you find in this chapter so far?) Procedural contents, though they may go unnoticed and seem insignificant, have an immense role in a conversation as they orient us in time, space, and relationships—in other words, guide us in the *shared physical and social realities* of the communicating partners. A basic difference between what are seen as adaptive, healthy behaviours and psychotic, seriously ill states is exactly the appropriateness of this orientation. These words are often *embodied* contents: to interpret a demonstrative or personal pronoun we must anchor the meaning in our body spatially and relationally (e.g. "I" or "you" can refer to oneself and to another speaker's self; we can include all the speakers or exclude some, etc.) (Lakoff, 2012). Whether the use of procedural contents is determined by personality traits, situational constraints, role expectations, or, probably, by the combination of all these factors, is still an open question (Stelzer et al., 2019).

Harré (2004), referring to Wittgenstein, claims that negation makes sense only if we can imagine a situation in which the statement is not true. His first example describes a natural phenomenon, "ice floats on water", but the second one, using the mutually exclusive *labels* of some physical objects is a paradox, a challenge to our imagination "Nothing can be red and green all over at once" (Harré, 2004, p. 1444). While the first utterance referring to the physical environment is meaningful, and, in many cases, is a useful and valid description, the second one represents a strange loop, a dead end in the symbolic universe and in human thinking. The use of negative structures, enabled by our verbal systems as symbolic and digital sign systems (1 = positive, existing, 0 = negative, missing or not existing anymore) facilitates the construction of grammatical and intelligible, nonetheless puzzling statements, inviting the recipients, guided by the urge to collaborate and consider meaning on a meta-level, to consider why, and in what contexts this statement can be relevant.

Burke (1963) related the negative primarily to the *delete mode* of unfulfilled expectations but noted that this was only one possible type of the negative. With simple prohibitions, no abstractions, paradoxes, or alternative interpretations based on pragmatic rules impede our understandings. However, the negative is also a way to express our choices between potential *alternatives*: not this one but that one. This feature is central to our identity reconstruction processes, a combination of identifications and counter-identifications (wanting to be like/not wanting to be like, Weinreich, 2004). Most groups increase their cohesion by telling who they are *not*—and, if hostility is fuelled to manipulate and exploit the group, they may even miss to disclose who they are and who they want to be.

This disconfirmation, termed as chronotopic or ambivalent by Bakhtin (1984a), results in distinctions that segment the perceived reality into taxonomies and oppositions, where extreme polarization or splitting is a possibility—a peculiar zero-sum game in human languaging. A second type, abstract negation (Bakhtin, 1984b) as annihilation, is not about one's choices between the alternatives, but the zero results of the game. It constitutes a closed universe, and often the destruction of one's own, previously precious identity or identity element (as none, nobody, never, etc).

Negation, both the delete mode and the ambivalent type, leading to the polarization of meaning opens a special dimension for the construction of liminality. The medieval story, *Historia Nemine* as a mock hagiography (Bakhtin, 1984a), was popular in the Middle Ages when regulated alternations between the sacred and the profane, the structure and antistructure constituted the order of life. Both *Historia Nemine* and the mock sermon *Saint Nobody* (sint Neimand, Parsons & Jongenelen, 2010) are specific language games rooted in liminal settings and rendered possible through the playful, relativizing, and destructive aspects of negation. The distinction between the procedural and conceptual contents are conflated in these literary pieces and the negative is transferred into the powerful position of a subject: Nobody (Nemo) is regarded as a *person* under the name Nobody. In the stories, Nobody is the absolute ruler, he is granted eternal life, and is practically almighty as he can do as he pleases. No laws, rules, or conventions apply to him: "Nemo was honoured by Jesus, who ordered his followers to "salute Nobody by the way" (Luke 10:4). He is immortal, since Ecclesiastes 9:4 attests that "Nobody liveth forever" (Parsons & Jongenelen, 2010, p. 96).

Through these humorous and rule-breaking stories in the Middle Ages, people were confronted with moments of chaos in meaning, and were experiencing the characteristic reversals of the antistructure: "… virtue and sin—and even good and evil—are made to exchange places" (Parsons & Jongenelen, 2010, p. 100). This is the world of the medieval carnival, where the rules of daily life have been *temporarily* suspended (Bakhtin, 1984b). The dissolution of the societal boundaries (e.g. the roi pour rire in the medieval France), depicting the *extremities* of the human body or the *destruction* of the body, the reversal of spatial directions, particularly height/up, representing the divine, and abyss/down, the underworld and risks, are typical manifestations of the grotesque. Negation is associated with ultimate freedoms and power; but not with the divine quality endowed with the power of creation (Horvath & Szakolczai, 2020). Thus, negation can represent only the liminal destructions, but not the reconstructions.

Negation, with its relation to liminality, also resists simple logic. Applying the traditional logical rules to comprehend negative statements while disregarding our conventions manifested in pragmatic rules can be misleading. There is always an asymmetry present in the negative. Colston (1999) in his study has concluded that most people would judge the meaning of "not good" as "bad", but "not bad" does not equal to "good" as it overwrites our previous, positive expectations on "good". Further, in a conversation, using straightforward negative statements would often be considered as impolite, while the negation of the positive statement is regarded more appropriate. The increased level of immediacy, using a more complicated form instead of a simple one usually refers to an emotional, social, or interpersonal complication, or the speaker's wish to distance from the central meaning, e.g. a forbidden theme or supressed aggression (Wiener & Mehrabian, 1968). Using negative structures is one way to speak about *social taboos*.

1.6.2 Rotten with Perfection

In his *Definition*, Burke (1963, p. 508) connects symbol use to the idea of perfection, rooted in the bipolarity and polarization of meaning: "There is a principle of perfection implicit in the nature of symbol-systems; and in keeping with his nature as symbol-using animal, man is moved by this principle". Perfection cannot prevail in nature—it would stop evolution, and, in the end, all forms of life. Honorific "perfection", however, is not exclusively a human striving. In the animal kingdom, this is known as runaway selection (Bateson, 1972; Bereczkei, 2016), a costly and risky strategy favouring only a few individuals, the most resourceful ones whose survival is constantly threatened by their own attractive but exaggerated features. The balance between the potential gains and losses is delicate and upsets easily. From a systemic perspective, this is s*chismogenesis* (Bateson, 1972; Horvath & Szakolczai, 2020; Szakolczai, 2015): repeated but dysfunctional positive feedbacks in a system, which lead to a desired but malfunctional state of "perfection". If these processes are not interrupted, then they will result in an overall rigidity, and the consequential escalation of risks.

Human attraction to perfection—to enhancement and extremes—is associated with the dread of uncertainties and control. De Luca Picione and Lozzi (2021) note that we tend to perceive patterns where there are none; we are attracted to sharp contours as a perceptual wiring for establishing boundaries, and thus, polarization; and develop an attachment to "reliable" inanimate objects. In times of deep transformations, we reduce chaos and ambiguity by paranoicization to identify the enemies responsible for the chaos; prefer pessimistic but stable and predictable scenarios; and rely on rigid hierarchies.

The value of "perfection" has been challenged by Winnicott (1960) who pointed out that "good enough" is much better than "perfect". The unattainable and unrealistic goal to reach perfection results in deep sufferings, and not necessarily on individual or interpersonal levels only. Burke (1963) raised several examples of "perfectness", both in the honorific and ironic senses (p. 511), including the Nazi ideologies connecting the idea of perfection with the negative, resulting in mass-level destructions up to the point of genocide.

Burke developed a pessimistic view about our future. In his view, we tend to underestimate the power of symbols in capturing and creating our environmental realities. He finished his essay with a caustic version of a nursery jingle, proceeding from the axe ("If all the trees were one tree…") to the threat of intercontinental ballistic missiles. A powerful warning on human "progress" that is still valid today.

1.7 Conclusion

Symbol use, including language as a refined symbolic system, is the most powerful tool we possess to construe and leave our knowledge as a legacy for the future generations. Symbols enable us to live and collaborate relatively peacefully in large groups and facilitate temporary identification with other people's perspectives. We construe our identities as the continuity, uniqueness, and significance of our existence by using symbols. With all these benefits, symbol use has its dark side, and we are not always aware of the boundaries and transgressions. The violations, usually the results of a polarized perspective of "perfection", do not necessarily have their immediate consequences urging instant corrections. We may end up with personal or community-level delusions and maintain false identities. This may happen because we are not able to grasp all the complexities of our physical and cultural environments and have a strong preference for certainty. Collaboration demands predictability; therefore, we prefer to construe stability, especially if these constructions are intertwined with the idea of steady progress (Gergen & Gergen, 1983). Using world-to-word matches facilitated by humans' elaborated symbol use and constructive capacities, we can enduringly maintain an illusionary context. Change, however, is continuous. Disregarding irrelevant events is a feasible strategy but taking no notice of the ones that will have a deep impact on our lives is not.

With a strong aptitude to manipulate and reshape our environment and focus mainly on linear cause-and-effect chains, *Homo symbolicus* could optimize their survival skills by controlling many aspects of the environment. Consequently, humans do not perceive themselves in unity with their environment as much as other species (McGrew, 2011)—and this kind of separation has its seamier side. Setting and managing the boundaries between an organism and its environment is a must, but symbol use may result in excessively rigid boundaries through polarization, or, on the contrary, enmeshes the boundaries where more clarity would be needed. Such distortions are a source of additional risks in an era of deep transformations. When experiencing global-level transformations, it is worth remembering that languaging and symbol use is originated in care.

References

Acharya, S., & Shukla, S. (2012). Mirror neurons: Enigma of the metaphysical modular brain. *Journal of Natural Science, Biology and Medicine, 3*(2), 118–118. https://doi.org/10.4103/0976-9668.101878

Airey, R., & O'Connell, M. (2005). *The complete encyclopaedia of signs & symbols*. Hermes House.

Andics, A., Gábor, A., Gácsi, M., Faragó, T., Szabó, D., & Miklósi, A. (2016). Neural mechanisms for lexical processing in dogs. *Science, 353*(6303), 1030–1032. https://www.science.org/doi/10.1126/science.aaf3777

Antonovsky, A. (1996). The salutogenic model as a theory to guide health promotion. *Health Promotion International, 11*(1), 11–18. https://doi.org/10.1093/heapro/11.1.11

Atkin, A. (2023). Peirce's theory of signs. In E. N. Zalta & U. Nodelman (Eds.), *The Stanford encyclopaedia of philosophy* (Spring 2023 edition). https://plato.stanford.edu/archives/spr2023/entries/peirce-semiotics/.

Austin, J. L. (1975). *How to do things with words*. Harvard University Press.

B. Erdős, M. (2006). *A nyelvben élő kapcsolat: egy öngyilkosság-megelőző sürgősségi telefonszolgálat beszélgetéseinek vizsgálata. [The language bond: explorations of calls in a suicide prevention hotline]*. Typotex Kft.

Bakhtin, M. (1984a). *Problems of Dostoevsky's poetics*. University of Minnesota Press.

Bakhtin, M. (1984b). *Rabelais and his world*. Indiana University Press.

Bateson, G. (1972). *Steps to an ecology of mind. Collected essays in anthropology, psychiatry, evolution, and epistemology*. Jason Aronson.

Becker, A. L. (1991). Language and languaging. *Language & Communication, 11*(1–2), 33–35. https://doi.org/10.1016/0271-5309(91)90013-L

Bereczkei, T. (2016). *Machiavellizmus: A megtévesztés pszichológiája [Machiavellism. The psychology of deception]*. Typotex.

Bruner, J. (2004). Life as narrative. *Social research: An international quarterly, 71*(3), 691–710.

Burke, K. (1963). Definition of man. *The Hudson Review, 16*(4), 491–514. http://www.jstor.org/stable/3848123

Campbell, J. (2008). *The hero with a thousand faces*. New World Library.

Castells, M. (1997). *The information age: Economy, society, and culture. Volume II: The power of identity*. Blackwell.

Colston, H. L. (1999). "Not good" is "bad" but "not bad" is not "good": An analysis of three accounts of negation asymmetry. *Discourse Processes, 28*(3), 237–256. https://doi.org/10.1080/01638539909545083

Csányi, V. (2000). The 'human behavior complex' and the compulsion of communication: Key factors of human evolution. *Semiotica, 128*(3/4), 243–258. https://doi.org/10.1515/semi.2000.128.3-4.243

Csikszentmihalyi, M. (1996). *Creativity. Flow and the psychology of discovery and invention*. HarperCollins Publishers.

De Luca Picione, R., & Lozzi, U. (2021). Uncertainty as a constitutive condition of human experience. An extensive review of the paradoxes and complexities of sensemaking processes in the face of uncertainty crisis. *International Journal of Psychoanalysis and Education: Subject, Action & Society, 1*(2), 14–53. https://doi.org/10.32111/SAS.2021.1.2.2

Dunbar, R. I. M. (2004). Gossip in evolutionary perspective. *Review of General Psychology, 8*(2), 100–110. https://doi.org/10.1037/1089-2680.8.2.100

Eliade, M. (1961). *The sacred and the profane: The nature of religion*. Harper & Row.

Erikson, E. H. (1968). *Identity: Youth and crisis*. Norton.

Festinger, L. (1957). *A theory of cognitive dissonance*. Stanford University Press.

Floridi, L. (Ed.). (2015). *The onlife manifesto. Being human in a hyperconnected era*. Springer. https://doi.org/10.1007/978-3-319-04093-6

Forceville, C. (2009). Chapter 2. Non-verbal and multimodal metaphor in a cognitivist framework: Agendas for research. In C. Forceville & E. Urios-Aparisi (Eds.), *Multimodal metaphor* (pp. 19–44). De Gruyter Mouton. https://doi.org/10.1515/9783110215366.1.19

Fromm, E. (1973). *The anatomy of human destructiveness*. Holt, Rinehart and Winston.

Galletta, M., Cherchi, M., Cocco, A., Lai, G., Manca, V., Pau, M., Tatti, F., Zambon, G., Deidda, S., Origa, P., Massa, E., Cossu, E., Boi, F., & Contu, P. (2019). Sense of coherence and physical health-related quality of life in Italian chronic patients: The mediating role of the mental component. *BMJ Open, 9*(9), e030001. https://doi.org/10.1136/bmjopen-2019-030001

Geertz, C. (1973). *The interpretation of cultures*. Basic Books.

Gergen, K. J., & Gergen, M. M. (1983). Narratives of the self. In T. R. Sarbin & K. E. Scheibe (Eds.), *Studies in social identity* (pp. 254–273). Praeger.

Gergen, K. J., McNamee, S., & Barrett, F. J. (2001). Toward transformative dialogue. *International Journal of Public Administration, 24*(7–8), 679–707. https://doi.org/10.1081/PAD-100104770

Glucksberg, S., & Keysar, B. (1993). How metaphors work. In A. Ortony (Ed.), *Metaphor and thought* (pp. 401–424). Cambridge University Press.

Grice, H. P. (1975). Logic and conversation. In D. Davidson (Ed.), *The logic of grammar* (pp. 64-75). Encino, Calif.: Dickenson Pub. Co.

Gurney, L., & Demuro, E. (2022). *Exploring languaging through an ontological register*. https://www.natcult.net/wp-content/uploads/2022/03/OTOC2022gurneydemuro.pdf

Hänninen, V. (2004). A model of narrative circulation. *Narrative Inquiry, 14*(1), 69–85. https://doi.org/10.1075/ni.14.1.04han

Harré, R. (1998). *The singular self*. Sage.

Harré, R. (2004). Discursive psychology and the boundaries of sense. *Organization Studies, 25*(8), 1435–1453. https://doi.org/10.1177/0170840604046351

Hauser, M. D., Chomsky, N., & Fitch, W. T. (2002). The faculty of language: What is it, who has it, and how did it evolve? *Science (New York, N.Y.), 298*(5598), 1569–1579. https://doi.org/10.1126/science.298.5598.1569

Hermann, I. (1984). *Az ember ősi ösztönei [Humans' ancient instincts]*. Magvető.

Horányi, Ö. (1999). A kommunikációról [On communication]. In I. Béres & Ö. Horányi (Eds.), *Társadalmi kommunikáció* (pp. 22–34). Osiris.
Horányi, Ö. (2007). A kommunikáció participációra alapozott felfogásáról [Communication as participation]. In Ö. Horányi (Ed.), *A kommunikáció mint participáció* (pp. 246–264). AKTI-Typotex.
Horvath, A., & Szakolczai, A. (2020). *The political sociology and anthropology of evil: Tricksterology*. Routledge.
Jung, C. G. (2012). *Man and his symbols*. Bantam.
Kelly, G. A. (1955). *The psychology of personal constructs. Vol. 1. A theory of personality*. W. W. Norton.
Kövecses, Z. (2003). *Metaphor and emotion: Language, culture, and body in human feeling*. Cambridge University Press.
Krantz, A. M., & Pennebaker, J. W. (2007). Expressive dance, writing, trauma, and health: When words have a body. In I. A. Serlin, J. Sonke-Henderson, R. Brandman, & J. Graham-Pole (Eds.), *Whole person healthcare. Vol. 3. The arts and health* (pp. 201–229). Praeger Publishers.
Kravchenko, A. V. (2021). Information technologies, literacy, and cognitive development: An eco-linguistic view. *Language Sciences, 84*, 101368. https://doi.org/10.1016/j.langsci.2021.101368
Lakoff, G. (1993). The contemporary theory of metaphor. In A. Ortony (Ed.), *Metaphor and thought* (pp. 202–252). Cambridge University Press.
Lakoff, G. (2012). Explaining embodied cognition results. *Topics in Cognitive Science, 4*(4), 773–785. https://doi.org/10.1111/j.1756-8765.2012.01222.x
Lakoff, G., & Johnson, M. (1980). *Metaphors we live by*. University of Chicago Press.
Lau, C. Y. H., & Tov, W. (2023). Effects of positive reappraisal and self-distancing on the meaningfulness of everyday negative events. *Frontiers in Psychology, 14*, 1093412. https://doi.org/10.3389/fpsyg.2023.1093412
Lux, M. (2010). The magic of encounter: The person-centered approach and the neurosciences. *Person-Centered and Experiential Psychotherapies, 9*(4), 274–289. https://doi.org/10.1080/14779757.2010.9689072
Malinowski, B. (1923). The problem of meaning in primitive languages. In C. K. Ogden & I. A. Richards (Eds.), *The meaning of meaning. Supplement I* (pp. 296–336). Kegan Paul.
Marcia, J. E. (1966). Development and validation of ego-identity status. *Journal of Personality and Social Psychology, 3*(5), 551.
Maturana, H., Mpodozis, J., & Letelier, J. C. (1995). Brain, language, and the origin of human mental functions. *Biological Research, 28*(1), 15–26.
McAdams, D. P. (1993). *The stories we live by: Personal myths and the making of the self*. William Morrow &.
McAdams, D. P. (2006). The problem of narrative coherence. *Journal of Constructivist Psychology, 19*(2), 109–125. https://doi.org/10.1080/10720530500508720
McGrew, W. C. (2011). Pan symbolicus. In C. S. Henshilwood & F. D'Errico (Eds.), *Homo symbolicus: The dawn of language, imagination and spirituality* (pp. 1–12). John Benjamins Publishing Company.
McLuhan, M., & Fiore, Q. (2012). *Médiamasszázs [The medium is the massage]*. Typotex.
McNamee, S. (2004). Critical moments as "transformations". *Negotiation Journal, 20*(2), 269–274. https://doi.org/10.1111/j.1571-9979.2004.00022.x
Merton, R. K. (1995). The Thomas theorem and the Matthews effect. *Social Forces, 74*(2), 379–424.
Moeschler, J. (2016). Where is procedural meaning located? Evidence from discourse connectives and tenses. *Lingua, 175–176*, 122–138. https://doi.org/10.1016/j.lingua.2015.11.006
Motzkau, J. F. (2009). Exploring the transdisciplinary trajectory of suggestibility. *Subjectivity, 27*(1), 172–194. https://doi.org/10.1057/sub.2009.3
Parsons, B., & Jongenelen, B. (2010). "The sermon on saint nobody": A verse translation of a Middle Dutch Parodic Sermon. *Journal of American Folklore, 123*(487), 92–107. https://doi.org/10.5406/jamerfolk.123.487.0092

Pennebaker, J. W., Mehl, M. R., & Niederhoffer, K. G. (2003). Psychological aspects of natural language. Use: Our words, our selves. *Annual Review of Psychology, 54*, 547–577. https://doi.org/10.1146/annurev.psych.54.101601.145041

Planer, R. J. (2023). The evolution of hierarchically structured communication. *Frontiers in Psychology, 14*, 1224324. https://doi.org/10.3389/fpsyg.2023.1224324

Rácz, J., & Kaló, Z. (2009). Metaforák és pszichoaktív anyaghasználat. *Korunk, 20*(7), 14–22. http://epa.oszk.hu/00400/00458/00151/indexfc29.html

Raimondi, V. (2019). The bio-logic of languaging and its epistemological background. *Language Sciences, 71*, 19–26. https://doi.org/10.1016/j.langsci.2018.03.003

Reboul, A., & Moeschler, J. (2005). *A társalgás cselei. Bevezetés a pragmatikába [Tricks in conversation. Introduction to pragmatics]*. Osiris Kiadó.

Reho, M., & Salvatore, S. (2024). Redefining meaning: A micro-genetic model of the constitution of experience. *Integrative Psychological & Behavioral Science, 58*(3), 828–835. https://doi.org/10.1007/s12124-024-09849-5

Rogers, C. R. (1964). Toward a modern approach to values: The valuing process in the mature person. *The Journal of Abnormal and Social Psychology, 68*(2), 160–167. https://doi.org/10.1037/h0046419

Rohovit, D. D. (1960). Metaphor and mind: A re-evaluation of metaphor theory. *American Imago, 17*(3), 289–309. http://www.jstor.org/stable/26301741

Salvatore, S., Palmieri, A., Cordella, B., & Iuso, S. (2021). The decay of signs' semiotic value: A cultural psychology interpretation of the contemporary social scenario. *Culture & Psychology, 27*(4), 539–561. https://doi.org/10.1177/1354067X2110272767

Salvatore, S., & Venuleo, C. (2017). Liminal transitions in a semiotic key: The mutual in-feeding between present and past. *Theory & Psychology, 27*(2), 215–230. https://doi.org/10.1177/0959354317692889

Sargsyan, M. A. (2021). Metaphor in semiotics: Foundations, embodiments, analysis. *Studia Semiotyczne, 35*(1), 55–72. https://doi.org/10.26333/sts.xxxv1.04

Savage-Rumbaugh, E. S., & Fields, W. M. (2011). The evolution and the rise of human language: Carry the baby. In C. S. Henshilwood & F. D'Errico (Eds.), *Homo symbolicus: The dawn of language, imagination and spirituality* (pp. 13–48). John Benjamins Publishing Company.

Searle, J. R. (1979). *Expression and meaning*. Cambridge University Press.

Searle, J. R. (1993). Metaphor. In A. Ortony (Ed.), *Metaphor and thought* (pp. 83–111). Cambridge University Press.

Senft, G. (2009). Phatic communion. In G. Senft, J. Östman, & J. Verschueren (Eds.), *Culture and language use, handbook of pragmatics, highlights* (Vol. 2, pp. 226–233). John Benjamins Publishing.

Shyamalan, M. N. (Director) (2002). *Signs* (Film). Touchstone Pictures, Blinding Edge Pictures & The Kennedy/Marshall Company.

Smith, B. (2024). LLMs and practical knowledge—What is intelligence? In K. Nyíri (Ed.), *Envisioning an electrifying future. Perspectives on visual learning* (Vol. 6, pp. 19–26). Hungarian Academy of Sciences—University of Pécs. https://www.researchgate.net/publication/387312058_Envisioning_an_Electrifying_Future

Stelzer, E. M., Atkinson, C., O'Connor, M. F., & Croft, A. (2019). Gender differences in grief narrative construction: A myth or reality? *European Journal of Psychotraumatology, 10*(1), 1688130. https://doi.org/10.1080/20008198.2019.1688130

Szakolczai, Á. (2015). Marginalitás és liminalitás. *Regio, 23*(2), 6–29. https://regio.tk.hu/wp-content/uploads/SZAKOLCZAI_2015_2_6_29.pdf

Szécsi, G. (2016). *Média és társadalom az információ korában: Kommunikációfilozófiai adalékok a mediatizáció fogalmához [Media and society in the information age. Notes on mediation from the perspective of the philosophy of communication]*. Akadémia Kiadó.

Szécsi, G. (2020). *A történetekbe zárt elme: Adalékok a narrativitás filozófiájához [The mind captured in stories. Complementary notions to the philosophy of narrative]*. Akadémiai Kiadó.

Tari, A. (2023). Manipulált képek és videók lélektana—a valóság kitágítása, avagy az illúziók valóságba emelése [The pychology of manipulated images and videos—extending realities or reifying illusions]. In P. Aczél & Á. Veszelszki (Eds.), *Deepfake: A valótlan valóság* (pp. 233–252). Gondolat.

Tileaga, C. (2011). Context, mental models and discourse analysis. *Journal of SocioLinguistics, 15*(1), 124–134. https://doi.org/10.1111/j.1467-9841.2010.00475.x

Tronick, E. Z., & Cohn, J. F. (1989). Infant-mother face-to-face interaction: Age and gender differences in coordination and the occurrence of miscoordination. *Child Development, 60*(1), 85–92. https://doi.org/10.2307/1131074

Turner, V. W. (1969). *The ritual process: Structure and anti-structure*. Aldine Transaction, University of New York Press.

Turner, V. W. (1974). Liminal to liminoid, in play, flow, and ritual: An essay in comparative symbology. *Rice University Studies, 60*(3), 53–92. https://hdl.handle.net/1911/63159

van Boeckel, J. (2011). *"When we find meaning in art, our thinking is most in sync with nature". A Review of An Ecology of Mind - The Gregory Bateson Documentary*. https://www.academia.edu/12919745/_When_we_find_meaning_in_art_our_thinking_is_most_in_sync_with_nature_A_Review_of_An_Ecology_of_Mind_The_Gregory_Bateson_Documentary

van der Kolk, B. (2015). *The body keeps the score: Brain, mind, and body in the healing of trauma*. Penguin Books.

Van Dijk, T. A. (2013). The field of epistemic discourse analysis. *Discourse Studies, 15*(5), 497–499. https://doi.org/10.1177/1461445613501448

Van Dijk, T. A. (2014). Discourse-cognition-society: Current state and prospects of the socio-cognitive approach to discourse. In C. Hart & P. Cap (Eds.), *Contemporary studies in critical discourse analysis* (pp. 121–146). Bloomsbury.

Van Gennep, A. (1909/2019). *The rites of passage*. University of Chicago Press.

Watzlawick, P., Bavelas, J. B., & Jackson, D. D. (1968). *Pragmatics of human communication: A study of interactional patterns, pathologies and paradoxes*. Faber & Faber.

Weatherly, J. (2015). The chariot of the hero: Myth and metaphor in Campbell. In K. Golden (Ed.), *Uses of comparative mythology (RLE myth)* (pp. 141–151). Routledge.

Weinreich, P. (2004). Identity structure analysis. In P. Weinreich & W. Saunderson (Eds.), *Analysing identity: Cross-cultural, societal and clinical contexts* (pp. 7–76). Routledge.

Wiener, M., & Mehrabian, A. (1968). *Language within language: Immediacy, a channel in verbal communication*. Ardent Media.

Winnicott, D. W. (1960). The theory of the parent-infant relationship. *International Journal of Psychoanalysis, 41*(6), 585–595.

Wittgenstein, L. (1953). *Philosophical investigations*. Basil Blackwell.

Zittoun, T., Duveen, G., Gillespie, A., Ivinson, G., & Psaltis, C. (2003). The use of symbolic resources in developmental transitions. *Culture & Psychology, 9*(4), 415–448. https://doi.org/10.1177/1354067X0394006

Chapter 2
Transitions from a Systemic Perspective: Quantum Change and Liminality

2.1 Interpreting Transitions

Humans often think of themselves as rational beings whose controlled choices between the potential alternatives during transformations are motivated by cool reason. Several early theories with different epistemological and disciplinary backgrounds have challenged this conception (e.g. Aronson, 1973; Bateson, 1972; Drapela, 1995). Beliefs about the immense power of reason and conscious control about human decisions still prevail (Resnicow & Page, 2008). The authors argue that pervasive change is more like a quantum event, and as such, it is not based on the linear, cause-and-effect chains of events. These chains as directionalities are constructed only retrospectively in our narratives. The concept of linear causality, however, has a distinguished position in human thinking (Lakoff, 2014). Thus, classical physics has remained the preferred scientific framework, serving as a model discipline for several other fields, while quantum physics, exceeding and questioning the simple causalities we are able to capture in our everyday world, has not gained such popularity.

Now we know that matter is but one potential state of a particle—the other is wave. Matter is about structures, and wave ("antistructure") is about energies and processes. As Ponte and Schäfer (2013, p. 601) concluded, anything that "wasn't matter didn't matter" in the Newtonian framework. Matter, energy, and information, the third one as the organizing principle or form in a system, are inseparable qualities (Stonier, 1996).

> At the foundation of the visible world we find Entities, which always appear to us as Elementary Things, when we interact with them. However, when they are on their own, they become waves. As waves, they have lost all mass, and they have become pure forms, patterns of information, something mindlike or thoughtlike. Accordingly, we can call the units of existence at the foundation of the world "ETs", meaning Elementary Things, of Elementary Thoughts; or, simply, EntiTies. (Ponte & Schäfer, 2013, p. 604–605)

M. B. Erdos, *Transitions - Liminality as Lived Experience*,
https://doi.org/10.1007/978-3-031-96007-9_2

From the perspective of quantum physics, the "material" world is composed of probability fields, in which information defines the relations and overall patterns. When a complex adaptive system (CAS) is undergoing a deep transformation, these probability fields are perceived as *chaos* with their increasing and unpredictable perplexities. Contrastingly, we recognize the patterns that seem stable enough as culturally acceptable, desirable, safe, and solid order, relatively free from uncertainties or ambiguities (Resnicow & Page, 2008). We introduce cultural practices and cognitive-affective manoeuvres to navigate from the disturbing uncertainties towards a conceived order and regain control through rituals (De Luca Picione & Lozzi, 2021). Cultural practices, however, may also dictate an opposite direction by misusing symbols and proceeding towards the mere *imitation* of order, leading people towards the sustained chaos of permanent liminality (Szakolczai, 2001).

When managing the uncertainties, information as an organizing principle, a resource for the construction of the meaning of transitions by focussing on certain aspects while neglecting others becomes of key importance (Stonier, 1996). All living systems are epistemological systems that exchange information with their environment. This idea serves as a foundation for Bateson's (1972) conception on change. Information, as a system's organizing principle, turns into a processed and transferred *message* to be interpreted, and finally gains *meaning* as the sense of one's experiences if it is compared to previous schemes and is evaluated for its utility and creative potentials (De Luca Picione & Lozzi, 2021; Stonier, 1996). Meaning-making is a narrative, intersubjective, and culturally embedded process; and meanings are central to our identity (De Luca Picione & Lozzi, 2021). Knowledge and meanings are grounded in our experiences and extend into the physical and affective domains (Taylor, 2001).

Learning, the management of information and message, is governed by species- and individual-level adaptation processes. In Bateson's (1972) framework, simple transfers are 0 learning—automatically receiving or discarding environmental information. Most species do not change the automatic patterns of zero learning polished by a long evolutionary process, but humans may occasionally decide to intervene and focus on something that gains extra significance through a constructive act, such as meditation, a self-induced change in the state of consciousness. We may end up in *paradoxes* when trying to transform a simple, spontaneous response into a voluntary action, a controlled choice between non-existing alternatives. If you are being photographed and are *instructed* to smile, the result is often a miserable grimace, and the confusion will be evident to the observer. A genuine smile is the result of evoking some happy moments in your life.

Humans and several other species memorize the repeatedly occurring contexts that are either rewarding or risky; and remember the ones that do not frequently occur but are of vital significance (e.g. the contexts of major threats, up to the level of flashback memories). Naturally occurring examples of classical conditioning are Learning I, changing our behaviour in a familiar context, for example, responding to a phone call (Bateson, 1972).

Occasionally, the environment undergoes a substantial change, and the rules that we have derived as former, trustable guarantees for attaining the desirable levels of safety and growth do not work any longer. We enter a new and unpredictable environment, not knowing the rules, risks, and benefits. These are the bifurcation points where the different future scenarios cannot be evaluated for their inherent risks or resources and the continuity of our experiences is disrupted. The wish to anticipate and control future uncertainties motivates humans' extensive and flexible semiosis in a continual search for new meaning (De Luca Picione & Lozzi, 2021). Symbols gain their immense power to echo in "people's minds and hearts" because they are born in liminal moments of high affectivity and are anchored in sudden and deep transformative experiences (Wydra, 2012, p. 50).

Learning II or deutero-learning (Bateson, 1972) is a contextual change, which is often predicted by obscure signs, the indicators of the increasing imbalance in the previous system. These signs foretell the forthcoming turn and soon the tipping point is reached where the change becomes irreversible. Encountering second-order changes, Learning II during the individual-level transitions and societal transformations is risky and difficult; self-deception, motivated by the appealing but non-adaptive illusion of sustained safety may occur. Disregarding the important contextual cues is how "self-deception" comes into existence, as "the self's former inattention to an unpalatable truth about which the person becomes uncomfortably aware" (Weinreich, 2004 p. 37). The paradox of self-deception is that the deceiver and the deceived are the same, and the very act of repression should also be repressed, leading to an infinite cycle of repressions. Intuition about the truth is there but the information is subject to defensive selection (Høgh-Olesen, 2024).

Learning II is rare in the animal kingdom. Bateson (1972) commented on a case of a dolphin. She had realized that she had to invent a new type of behaviour instead of repeating the previous patterns if she wanted a reward—and acted accordingly. Similarly, Burke (1963) wrote about a wren, inventing a way to de-bird her nest when her offspring was reluctant to leave the comfortable environment. These are but the exceptions to the rule. Considering our species specific constructive abilities and symbol use, Learning II is a recurrent experience in a human's life course. We have a strong tendency and an elaborate symbolic system at our disposal to represent and tame such changes and leave them as a legacy for the species (Henshilwood & D'Errico, 2011; McAdams, 2018). Myths and heroes' stories, so popular in every culture, are about the deep transformations, severely disrupting the usual flow of life. We have invented rituals and social institutions to minimize its risks while maximizing the possible gains.

In their seminal work on change, Watzlawick et al. (1974), reformulating Bateson's original epistemological model, differentiated between the difficulties or tasks requiring common solutions, utilizing a set of already existing alternatives (or just learning how to live with the issue) and second-order levels, the problems as "impasses, deadlocks, knots, [binds], etc., which are created and maintained through the mishandling of difficulties" (Watzlawick et al., 1974, pp. 38–39). Changing the perspective and introducing contextual level responses to the demanding second-order transformations are represented in our popular riddles and jokes, taming the unpredictable and relieving the tensions of such challenges. Watzlawick et al. (1974) refer to the nine-dot problem as an illustration on the utility and need of a systemic approach. The solution involves transgressing the previously "existing" (perceived) boundaries that are established by our conventional, Gestalt-based information processing. The problem is inherent in our perception but not in the situation. Connecting nine dots with four straight lines without lifting our pencil seems difficult only because we have an in-built perceptual schema of a *square.* Statistically, focusing more on a salient figure than an empty space, the background, serves us well. This strategy has been refined during the millions of years when, for example, our ancestors had to identify the sabretooth cat in the bush and run as fast as possible. It was much more useful than changing the perspective and meditating on the alternative meaning of the patchy images of stripes and spots. Runaway was a task for the agentive and not the reflective self. Cultural practices still strengthen such preference for figures: as kids, we are trained to solve connect-the-dots puzzles to reach the safe and conforming level of Learning I, and enjoy the community rewards of the learning process (Kershaw & Ohlsson, 2001).

In the original version, the nine dots forming a "square" seem the more relevant information, and the background, the empty space that would provide us with the solution goes unnoticed. In Fig. 2.1, the nine-dot puzzle is combined with another figure suggesting an alternative boundary, serving as a delicate prompt.

Gregory Bateson often invited his readers to change their perspectives and integrate art as a holistic, more natural way of comprehension and learning (van Boeckel, 2011). His metalogues, in which the context and the relational patterns are just as important as the contents, are typical examples of this perspective shift, questioning common-sense, evident beliefs. He argued that the continuity of our environment (reality) is segmented only from our human point of view. The segmentation of selves-in-environments designates the agents and recipients of actions, the beginnings and ends, the figures and backgrounds—and we usually miss the pattern that connects:

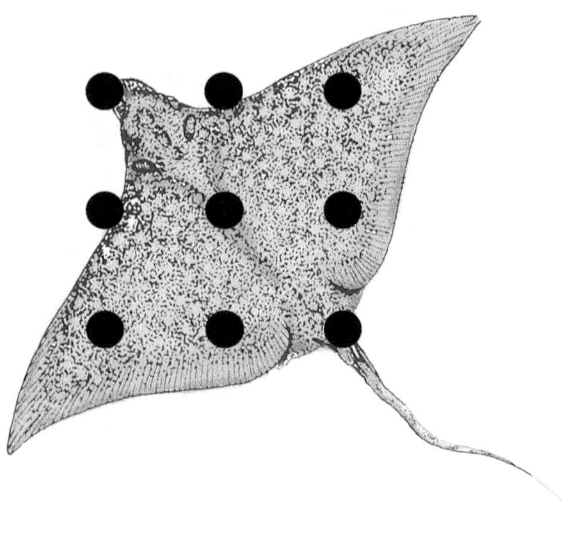

Fig. 2.1 A variation of the nine-dot problem (Credit: Kitti Bognar, 2025). *Note:* The figure of *Sting Ray* by P. S. Foresman (Source: Wikimedia Commons [https://commons.wikimedia.org/wiki/File:Sting_Ray_(PSF).png] [in the public domain]) was slightly modified

> You have probably been taught that you have five fingers. That is, on the whole, incorrect. It is the way language subdivides things into things. Probably the biological truth is that in the growth of this thing—in your embryology, which you scarcely remember—what was important was not five, but four relations between pairs of fingers (Gregory Bateson in An Ecology of Mind, cit. by van Boeckel, 2011, p. 3)

Fundamental, contextual transformations seem unexpected and paradoxical: we experience a disruption in the continuity and safety of our previous schemes. The playfulness inherent in the above riddles, demanding a shift in perspectives, may entirely disappear when we are experiencing the contextual-level changes in our social life, as it has happened recently during the Covid-19 pandemic. We must follow an abductive logic, which is more about probabilities than "verified" truth. Without workable solutions, we are entrapped in the dead end of more-of-the-same efforts. Rittel and Webber (1973; also in Greco & Stenner, 2017) have proposed to distinguish between tame and wicked problems. Wicked problems challenge the traditional ways of problem resolution, are hard to define, tend to recur, and require reflexivity. The transitions between the different states or *forms-of-process*—identity reconstruction or culture change—are specific types of wicked problems (Greco & Stenner, 2017).

Many of the wicked problems we must face are rooted in double-bind relations, leading to an unresolvable and highly destructive impasse. In a double-bind context, a strict order is given to a subject by an authority possessing the resources for, or the right to decide about the individual's survival—but obeying the order will be sanctioned. The inescapable and severe sanction is communicated at another, usually more abstract and obscure level. Obeying *and* not obeying the order are equally vital but commenting on or transforming the situation does not seem viable for the subject. The double bind[1] is usually a recurring situation, forming a context from which escape appears impossible (Bateson, 1972). Second order, contextual change is necessary when the previous, mistargeted attempts at problem-solving have not resolved the issue.

Watzlawick et al. (1974) have outlined three different problem-sustaining procedures that will worsen the situation but are facilitated by the malleability and polarizing features inherent in human sign use. The first one involves trying to solve a "problem" that cannot be solved. With our utopistic visions, we may end up finding ourselves "rotten with perfection" (Burke, 1963, p. 507): for example, while strivings to establish more equitable conditions in a community is a noble and fruitful effort, the idea to institute "perfect" equity has resulted in terror and destructions throughout history. The idea of a society "perfectly" free from psychotropic substance use has led to the invention of organized crime and mafia wars in the United States in the 1920s. Ambitious utopias, however, have always been popular in the political discourse: the *National Strategy Against Illegal Drugs (2013–2020)* (Resolution H/11798, 2013, p. 34.) envisions a "drug-free Hungary by 2020", mentioning that in the light of the previous tendencies, this may seem an unrealistic,

---

[1] For a discursive approach on double bind, see *Chap. 5, Authoritarian Discourses*.

nevertheless worthy goal that should be pursued in the interest of future generations. What we would need instead of "perfection" is good enough: more equity (much more than we are experiencing now globally) and considerable reductions in harmful substance use. A variation of the previous problem-not-solving strategy is to seek a solution to a problem that does not even exist (Watzlawick et al., 1974). Here we may echo Reynolds' (2014) classical question in evaluation: to what problem is the specific plan, proposal, or project a solution?

The second way of problem mishandling is to provide a solution at an inappropriate level, e.g. trying more of an ineffective measure. In some countries, it is still very popular to "inform" people about the harms and risks involved in their behaviour, that is, offering a rational approach to a complex problem involving emotional and social components, demanding a systemic approach and a more comprehensive procedure. Before secularization, the response was targeted at the "morals" of the victims, usually resulting in a blaming-the-victim situation. Such single-minded measures are usually popular among the wider public who want something to be done, but, in most cases, only in the discursive domain (the menu card), which would leave their financial resources (the meal) unaffected.

Finally, there are the problems that are not constructed as problems but are naturalized in the public discourse. Silencing these demanding problems usually result in more votes in political life than the narrow and bumpy roads to actual problem-solving. Currently, the use of illicit drugs is on the increase in Hungary and the country has long been struggling with severe problems of alcohol misuse. The notable similarities between these two patterns are a silenced fact. Ineffective punitive measures are taken at supply reduction to combat illicit drug use, while the pubs, the "soul of the village" may apply for government support (Barta, 2025).

2.2 Deep Transformations and Complex Adaptive Systems

Theoretically, Bateson's (1972) learning levels could be continued to infinity: Learning II is followed by the next levels. Though symbol use facilitates recursivity, our capacities to fully capture these meta-levels are delimited. We encounter deep challenges even when attempting to understand Learning III. This context, as a change in the sets of sets is often related to transcendental-spiritual domains: the ultimate meaning of one's own life, of human life on Earth, and of the cosmic order (Kelemen & B. Erdos, 2010). In rites and myths, this level is inherently present, assisting us in tackling the deepest challenges in life. On such occasions, our prior knowledge, which serves us reasonably well in solving everyday tasks, may prevent us from finding a solution for the vicissitudes triggering *quantum change* (C'de Baca & Wilbourne, 2004; Miller, 2004). Quantum change is a term to capture the deep transformations of both Learning II and Learning III. The metaphor is rooted in quantum physics and describes a phenomenon when an electron, *receiving extra energies, deviates from its usual orbit to an expanded one*.

Post-Newtonian quantum physics resulted in a continuous epistemological transition from the determined to the indetermined, from the perceptions of boundaries and differences to the perceptions of unity (McDonald, 2008)—from the stability of structures to forms-of-processes, as Stenner (2017) has proposed. Thus, quantum physics represents a paradigmatic shift from the material to the nonmaterial, from structures to processes, and from matter to thought-like patterns of information (Ponte & Schäfer, 2013; Stonier, 1996). These discoveries have influenced other disciplines, though they have not altered their prevailing scientific paradigms yet. For example, Jung and Pauli worked together to identify a new, acausal principle of nature to explain for both physical and psychological phenomena (Butzer, 2021; Hocoy, 2012). In this new framework, Ponte and Schäfer (2013) suggest a new interpretation for the spiritual–transcendent level of Learning III: one's insights and acceptance of cosmic interconnectedness, including the connectedness of the human mind to a cosmic (mindlike) system.

Quantum change occurs suddenly and unexpectedly, and it has a pervasive and lasting impact on the system—with humans, on one's identity. This fundamental transformation has an irreversible impact on our view of the world and of our own self (C'de Baca & Wilbourne, 2004; Miller, 2004). People experiencing quantum change describe it as a holistic, all-embracing transformation that can be grasped on an intuitive level only. The change is deeply emotional and remains very vivid, even after several decades (C'de Baca & Wilbourne, 2004). In times of crises, the meaning of a sign is not stable anymore. It changes during the deep transformations and new, potential meanings are co-constructed or disclosed. Meaning reconstruction is motivated by the strong affective activation inherent in the change (De Luca Picione & Lozzi, 2021). The emerging new perspectives question the significance of the existing boundaries and, parallel, open a space of potentialities.

Resnicow and Page (2008) have studied the changes in people's health behaviour in the risky moments in life. They claim that transformation in human behaviour (or identity) in these threatening moments is nonlinear, is a quantum event sensitive to initial conditions, and as such, is difficult to predict. This difficulty comes from the complexities of system experiencing the transformation. Humans as complex adaptive systems (CASs) are open and dynamic organizations, in which the components are interacting nonlinearly, and the results of these interactions cannot be predicted by simply adding up the initial components. Complexity neither means chaos nor a 100% predictability: such systems have developed specific routes to respond immediately to common problems in the environment but also have the potential to work out novel solutions by changing the original pathways organized around the previous, specialized attractors, if necessary (Csermely, 2005; Csermely, 2018).

CASs are autopoietic systems involved in continuous self-organizing, renewal, and reproduction, characterized by systemic causation patterns (Bussolari & Goodell, 2009; Lakoff, 2014; Maturana et al., 1995; Resnicow & Page, 2008). With humans, the initial conditions include a variety of factors from the individual genetics, lifestyles, motivations, knowledge, attitudes, and states to the characteristics of the target behaviour and of the societal–symbolic context—these together leading to an uncontrollably large number of permutations (Resnicow & Page, 2008).

However, path dependency in these complex systems, brought about by continuous, undisturbed positive feedback mechanisms, will determine the outcomes and magnify the impact of the initial conditions. When path dependency is present in a system, there are certain trigger points, also named tipping points or lever points. Arrival at these points entails that there is no way back anymore; but before reaching the tipping point, alternatives are present, and decisions can be made (Resnicow & Page, 2008). The initial conditions of the system, the previous events, as well as the order of these events will determine the tipping point. In symbolic (cultural) systems, we encounter many examples of path dependence. The tipping points are depicted as dramatic events in myths, tales, and in our personal narratives about our life crises. Though these are decisive moments, they are not without any precedents. Often, in the larger context of complex transformations, we are simply blind or *blinded* by blinkers of manipulation and self-deception to the patterns evolving at a slower pace and perceive the results of the culminating processes as abrupt changes. This questions not only our capacity to rationally evaluate but also to control all the aspects of quantum changes and act appropriately. Extreme sensitivity to initial conditions, also known as the butterfly effect—when minor inputs lead to huge, disproportionate differences in the outcomes and render identifying the tipping points difficult—makes the attempts at control a mission impossible. Global-level examples for deep transformations in complex adaptive systems include climate change, epidemics, financial and military crises, digitalization, and the dilemmas concerning the use of artificial intelligence. Erroneously, the climate change was communicated as an expected 2 °C rise in average temperature. Now we have first-hand experiences on the behaviour of a changing system transforming from one state into another. It is the abrupt changes between the extremes, and the "unexpected" synergies that make the change so threatening and not the "warming", suggesting an essentially *positive* metaphorical script. ("Warmth" is traditionally associated with positive qualities.) We have experienced a financial crisis in 2008, an element in a predictable but not widely acknowledged future series. We have suffered from the health, societal, and economic impacts of a pandemic, and now we are living in the shadow of a potential world war. "Unexpected" demographic changes in the population (either decline, or growth) are challenging many societies.

These examples are illuminative of how our predictions, the illusions concerning human control may fail. We end up in the whirlpool of crises: the interactions within a system where dramatic changes take place are too complex to predict and govern. This gives us the impression that events happen to us, and not by us, leading to a loss of control experience. To grasp the complexities and develop trust and hope, people proceed from the paradoxes and unexpected solutions of Learning II to the spiritual domains of Learning III—traditionally, within the frameworks of a rite.

2.3 Transformative Rites and the Birth Experience

Cultures have created their social institutions to tame wicked problems, cope with the uncertainties and risks inherent in quantum changes and guide their members through the deep transformations in life. Rites restore continuity, stability, and meaning (De Luca Picione & Lozzi, 2021). The rite-of-passage theory about the universal processes of deep transformations was formulated by van Gennep in 1909 (2019) and later enriched by Turner (1969). A rite mimics the processes of creation: after leaving behind the previous complexities, new and hopefully more adaptive forms arise. The first element is the pre-liminal separation from earlier states, roles, and identities, and then the individual or a group (e.g. a group of initiands) progresses into a liminal context, the zone of the in-between where the new knowledge necessary for the fulfilment of the new position can be acquired, and new motivations and dispositions are being formed. New to the initiands; but these are the traditional elements of a rich cultural reservoir, renewed for the community during the rite and loaded with personalized meaning for the initiand in the ritual context. Liminality enables the participants to experience a temporary freedom from structural constraints: they are neither in the previous social positions nor in the new ones. Liminality is characterized by these new, daunting freedoms and the associated ambivalence; but energies are also released in the process. The third, concluding post-liminal phase is reincorporation or reintegration: the community will celebrate and validate the person's achievements, and their new positions acquired within the community. The transformation is risky, and there are no full guarantees for success. Degradation ceremonies also change one's status, but for the worse, and may lead to longstanding marginalization or excommunication (Garfinkel, 1956).

The prototype of a transition rite is our birth process. There is continuity between intrauterine life and life after birth, but the change is immense. The third-order transformation permeates practically all the domains of our existence: breathing, sensing, moving, feeding, and belonging. All our senses are challenged and stressed by the new environment where the perception of light, gravitation, and sound abruptly changes. The new experiences concerning gravitation—our first experiences on "heavy" and "falling"—serve as a key source domain for metaphorical mappings to describe subsequent life crises and difficulties (Lakoff & Johnson, 1980; McNamee, 1992). On such occasions, the solution is usually holding on to someone, as this must also happen right after our birth. Birth is a basic metaphor for successful, substantial transformations as second birth or rebirth, a quantum change, when the world before and the world after are incommensurable (see also *Chap. 7, The Psychosocial Crisis as a Liminal Experience*).

Grof (1985, 1988) has argued that traditional drug use during the rituals opens a risky gate leading to our suppressed birth experiences. Such rituals in their archaic form correspond to the renewal of life and the recreation of birth, a sacred event, as an exemplification of creation (Eliade, 1961). Traditionally, the birth process used to involve vital risks for both the child and the mother, and these risks, tamed and diminished but not fully eliminated, reoccur in the sacred environment of the initiation rites. Newborn babies look like tired travellers entering an undiscovered world. However, infants' experiences of the previous environment and of the phases of their birth journey, described by Grof (1985) as birth perinatal matrices (BPMs) may significantly differ. According to Grof, patients' recollections during the therapeutic use of LSD, a hallucinogen, informative of the contents of their unconscious affective memory, reveal the early somatic traumatization that potentially sustains ill states in adult life. The early trauma is translated into embodied memories, and the physical, unconscious, and embodied qualities are transferred into the symbolic, psychological domain (Grof, 1985; Riedlinger & Riedlinger, 1986). Grof has identified experience-specific images emerging during the therapeutic sessions and related one's subsequent mental problems to these specific experiences during the birth process.

BPM 1 is about a "good" or a "bad" womb. The mother's abortion attempts, illnesses, stressful states, or accidents will define this status in a continuum of "heaven" and "hell" as the two endpoints. Depending on these earliest somatic experiences, this can be the origin of oceanic feelings and cosmic unity, or paranoid ideations and cosmic engulfment. In this framework, psychosis, hypochondria, and hysterical hallucinosis are the consequences of the "bad womb" experience (Grof, 1985).

BPM 2 is about the somatically experienced, unequivocal signs of the imminent transition. The powerful contractions while the cervix is still closed are our primary experiences of entrapment and helplessness, evoking great sufferings with the tormenting impression that the experience *will never end*. This is an impression of being stuck in a hazardous situation—in an agony. In this large-scale natural "double bind", progress must be made but it is impossible. Such transient or, in some cases, extended experiences are characteristic of liminality. The baby's heart rate is elevated during the contractions, indicating the immense somatic stress and the first impressions of *anxiety*. The mother is experiencing a parallel sensation: the pain elicited by the contractions is relatively short but is deep, and it is at the focus of attention. In some cultures, this is considered as a *sacred* punishment for Eve's part in the "original sin". The perception of time changes significantly: time shrinks and extends, following the rhythm of the contractions. Grof (1985) has noted that our images of death, hell, as well as impressions of meaninglessness, absurdity, and apocalyptic visions are rooted in these experiences. The many potential disturbances in later life related to this phase are breathing difficulties, depression, irrational inferiority feelings, hypochondria, schizophrenic psychosis, as well as alcohol and drug addiction.

In the subsequent phase, BPM 3, the cervix is open, but the foetus's progress in the birth canal is slow and painful. This phase is probably our first somatic experience on the *heavy burdens* and the entangling *whirlpool* of a life crisis, as progress is made outside the womb where the amniotic fluid previously diminished the impact of gravitation. The umbilical cord, a source of supply for the foetus's vital needs, may turn into a source of danger, in some unfortunate cases, even strangling the baby. Vital struggles begin, encoded in one's memories as the somatic-level grounding impressions for war, aggression, or rough flight. Several cultural patterns associated with liminality and antistructure, such as the carnival, orgies/wild parties are related to this phase, resulting in a variety of potential psychopathologies. BPM 3 is also related to one's sexuality, and the delivery of own children.

In BPM 4, the tension reaches its peak, and the tormenting experience is followed by an immediate relief. The space suddenly expands, and new sensations follow. The radical changes in the environment, changing the basic sensory experiences of light, sounds, movements, and touch are all occurring in this phase. These are associated with one's subsequent experiences of radiant light (also a common near-death experience), bright colours, sensory enhancement, and grandiosity. The phase is concluded by the umbilical crisis, putting an end to the previous ways of obtaining oxygen and nourishments.[2] This phase is associated with death, rebirth, and redemption (Grof, 1985, 1988).

Though the birth experience is beyond conscious recall, deep and repeated traumas in later life may activate the somatic experiences along with some "primitive awareness" or "experiential content" (Riedlinger & Riedlinger, 1986, p. 21), framing the transition experiences.

2.4 Experiencing Liminality

Experience is a key concept in a transition; in fact, an experience is transition: "the sequential order of a rite of passage is the sequence of lived experience" (Szakolczai, 2009, p. 147). Thus, an experience is much beyond sensing or a mere impression. It involves our entire existence.

Lived experience has become a central concept in qualitative studies with their primary interest in the moments of change in life. Gergen (2013) has proposed a working definition for experience, emphasizing its power to shape personal values and ideologies. An experience is the result of the vital, adaptive, or maladaptive interactions between the ongoing environmental processes and the individual. Davey (2015) reflects on the philosophical traditions of the term by pointing out the distinction between *Erlebnis* and *Erfahrung* by Gadamer. While *Erlebnis* is ineffable and can be described as a psychologically (also emotionally) intensive encounter with some significant entity or event, *Erfahrung* is the type of reflected experience that the individual or the community can construe in a recursive interpretative process, a hermeneutical circle. Farin (2021, p. 466) defines the lived experience as an insightful moment, "a condition of being affected by the surrounding world in such a way that the present situation is revealed in its specific meaning for the one who is affected".

The birth experience is indeed an experience in the sense that it affects the totality of our existence. However, another key aspect, the consciousness of the event, at least in the usual sense, is missing. The embodied sensations, deeply affecting our

[2] The modern medical team used a quasi-ritual technological element, clamping and cutting the cord as soon as possible—until it turned out that nature knows better (Uwins & Hutchon, 2014).

future lives, cannot build into one's narrative as *meaningful episodes*. In a rite of transition, the lived, pre-reflective experiences and perceptual-level sensations are matched to an appropriate cultural interpretative framework and are transformed into a *reflected experience*, as a new element of our identity. There is a reflexive relationship between meaning and experience: sensing is transformed into experience through meaning-making, and meanings are enriched by one's experiences.

Personal experiences are the representations of transformative events that are anchored in time, space, and personal relationships; even if no one else is present physically, the experience gains its significance in the context of our relationships. They are anchored, but not always deeply: at times, pre-reflective experiences are dissociated from the original context and live their own lives as flashbacks, separating the person from the actual environment and create an impasse in the flow of life (Stenner, 2017; van der Kolk, 2015). Thus, an experience can hide in the realm of not-yet-said (Rober, 2002). Reflected experiences are integrated into the life story, creating places of significance, structuring our time both personally and communally, and orienting us in our relationships. Thus, an experience becomes a building block in the life narrative, with its holistic logic and strong emotionality, motivating us to grasp the gradually unfolding complexities of human life.

When the separation from the previous environment takes place together with the invalidation of past identity elements, the person experiencing the transition enters the chaos of liminality, a time-space, a chronotope (Bakhtin, 1984) that separates *and* connects the distinct forms of process:

> …suddenly, the taken for granted order of things becomes suspended, previous expectations are no longer met, people become uncertain and disoriented, as if trapped in the 'in between'—neither here, nor there, no longer in the past, not yet in the future—which, somehow, must be solved (Szakolczai, 2024, no. 1126)

Thus, the participants in a rite are neither part of the previous settings nor of the new ones; but they have their memories abridging the previous contexts, and their future anticipations that rely on other community members' personal narratives who have already had the experience, as well as on the shared myths and tales of the community.

There are two types of characteristic experiences inherent in liminality. *Unconditional waiting* as a concept was introduced by Berguno (2001) in his analysis on a scene in Joseph Konrad's *The Shadow-Line*, a development novel. In a key scene in the novel, the sailors suffering from a fever are stuck in their voyage and they must wait for the wind to come. It does not arrive, and they cannot do anything either to move the ship. Unconditional waiting—an experience somatically and mentally embedded in BPM 2—is the acceptance of the person's own, total helplessness and loss of control, accompanied by deep anxieties. Experiencing *entrapment* involves the danger of dissociation and self-destruction (Williams & Pollock, 2001). In Konrad's novel, powers higher than the self—Nature or God—decide about the continuation of life's journey. The total loss of control also gives rise to *supernatural* explanations by the crew: possibly, the ship is haunted by the evil spirit of a previous captain. In this liminal zone, the boundaries between this world and the other world temporarily and disorderly dissolve. Unconditional waiting as part of the disorder culminates in a tipping point where decisions are made, and paralysation finally comes to an end. Things get into motion (as in BPM 3), and those undergoing the transformation must cope with the challenges, respond to the risks, and take the opportunities by quickly choosing an alternative that seems the best of the available options. The function of these struggles is to prove that they are worthy of their new position, have the knowledge, skills, and appropriate attitudes to fulfil their new roles.

One of Victor Turner's (1969) major contributions to van Gennep's (1909/2019) original idea was his elaboration on communitas, a special social context that appears not only during the traditional rites but also in late modern settings. Communitas is a community's temporary detachment from the usual structures of social life, bringing about the *antistructure* with its characteristic reversals, chaos, ambiguities, and paradoxes. The antistructure provides a space for the transient manifestations of humankind's ideas on equity, liberty, and fraternity. The moments of communitas give us the chance to reflect on the very foundations of our social life both personally and communally: on the norms and values as well as taken-for-granted realities, as, for example, it happened during the medieval carnivals (Bakhtin, 1984). These reflections urge us to reconstruct the value base of our community. Maintaining a balance between communitas, fostering renewal and development, and structure, as predictability and stability inherent in the institutionalized ways of life, is essential. When the balance is upset, then the consequences are miserable, as, for example, the lasting chaos, terror, and the subsequent absolutism in conclusion of the French Revolution, or the permanent liminality of communist dictatorships (Wydra, 2012). Kephart and Zellner (1991) noted that experimenting with the artificial extension of antistructure through hippie lifestyles in the 1970s resulted in an increasing respect for the traditional values and lifestyles by the hippies' children.

On the other hand, laying too much emphasis on structure alone leads to community-level burnout and "depression", understood as loss of motivation, hopes, and future visions. Creative energies and the ability to respond to environmental challenges are lost, together with the values serving as a basis for identity (O'Connor, 2021). Here, cool reason wants to triumph over the emotions but usually with little success. Chasing the perfection of rationality usually leads to absurdities. Care and empathy, humans' precious elements of their survival toolkit, are lost in the overemphasized institutional settings.

A widow, a few weeks after her husband's death, still immersed in the many administrative duties and the regular visits to the authorized institutions, was dreaming about her late husband, which is quite common in these weeks. However, her dream was somewhat unusual. Her deceased husband asked her to fill in a form for him. He claimed that without this form, he would not be allowed to enter the other world. Here, we can identify the late modern traces of ancient customs to assist the dead enter the underworld by executing some ritual action or sacrifice. We can also witness the *desacralization of the transition*, emptying the previous traditions, while *sacralising bureaucratic trivialities*. A dream, of course, has many different layers and interpretations. One potential interpretation—beyond the evident message about the difficulties of the transition—is that in the specific cultural context, more attention is paid to rules and paperwork than to the psychological realities of grief. In this setting, the primary emphasis on administrative issues seems a collective defence against the acknowledgement of the known endpoint of all human transitions: our mortality.

Antistructure is the traditional transformative mode of human communities. In late modernity, eliminating the traditional forms by giving ways to other variations compatible with consumerism as the leading ideology, transformative liminality is but one option. The term liminoid was introduced by Turner (1974, p. 65; 1982) to identify "industrial leisure genres" the ambiguous, playful, and potentially creative spaces in the recreational domain of one's choice where there are not any strict obligations or guarantees for the transformation of one's social position. Transitioning between the different positions or alternative selves is not necessarily a purpose but a potentiality (Daskalaki & Simosi, 2018; Turner, 1982). Thus, the liminoid is a space for psychosocial moratorium (Erikson, 1968), where people can freely continue their explorations and experimentations with potential identity variants, reflect on, and play with their ideas without taking any serious commitments. The liminoid, however, is also a context for identity diffusion, where uncertainties and affectivity are present, but deep explorations, as "identity work" are missing.

Today's contexts are neither restricted to transformative liminality with its inherent obligations; nor to the recreational, but not necessarily *re-creational* liminoid. As Szakolczai (2017) has argued, liminality has become a master word in the social sciences. Though the overuse of a term always entails the risks of semantic satiation, efforts to describe the multitude of liminal contexts and the emerging phenomena may undeniably add to our understandings of liminality. Attributes as permanent, endless or trickster (Horvath & Szakolczai, 2020; Szakolczai, 2001, 2017), limbo, ambiguous, or perpetual (Scott et al., 2022), under-institutionalized or self-guided (Hsu & Gao, 2022), focusing on the margins and boundaries, networked (Soncul & Bollmer, 2020), enduring (Greco & Stenner, 2017), extended (Beech, 2011), cyclic-permanent (Appau et al., 2020), perpetual (Winkler & Kristensen, 2021), and chronic (Mimoun & Bardhi, 2022) have appeared to describe the many possible faces of liminality.

Traditional, transformative liminal occupational fields focussing on care, wellbeing, truth, justice, and spirituality are now reinterpreted in terms of business and profits, "monetising the suffering and unhappiness of others" (Benţa, 2021, p. 108). The medieval sale of indulgencies or charlatans' promising mixtures were the early and sanctioned attempts at such commodification. Today, the problem is not so much the quality and effectiveness of the interventions anymore but the unilateral shift of focus from humans to business.

Technological advances bring about new contexts where liminality is experienced, but without the accessible cultural frameworks assisting the interpretations. This phenomenon is salient in the health sector where life-threatening conditions occur, and people encounter several non-traditional experiences and moral dilemmas related to birth and death (McKechnie et al., 2010). For example, liminal lives come into being during an in vitro fertilization process (IVF), raising ethical concerns about embryo culture experimentation (Squier, 2004). The patients perceive "embryos in a malleable and constantly changing way": from the fertilized eggs (in vitro), the frozen "by-products" of the IVF procedure to a future child (in vivo) (Vicsek et al., 2021, p. 149). Preterm birth may result in life-threatening conditions for the infant whose survival depends on medical technologies, and parents' transitioning to their new roles and identities is arrested (Monostori et al., 2024). Little et al. (1998) interpret cancer patients' experiences of loss of control, disorientation, and uncertainties in terms of liminality. The authors introduce the notion of suspended liminality to describe the patients' experiences in the subsequent adaptation stage, indicating a state on the boundary that separates them from the usual way of life. Residential care homes for older people may be characterized by the disempowering features of permanent liminality, often with unnecessary restrictions and surveillance, exposing older people to iatrogenic liminality that prevents them from maintaining meaningful relationships (Cook et al., 2021).

Most of the above descriptions refer to a condition in which reaching a new, distinct state is not possible or the process leads only to repeated, unsuccessful cycles as self-referential strange loops in the social system. Studying the uniqueness and sensitivity of the lived experiences concerning the losses and transformations are a subject of several contemporary research projects (e.g. Eatough & Smith, 2017). Shared aspects of the transformation may invariably appear in formal institutional contexts, in the marginal settings of the criminal justice system, or in the extended or transformative liminality of psychiatric care. Recovering persons experience a deep identity transformation, successfully progressing from ill states into healthy ones (Kelemen & B. Erdos, 2010). They are released from the trap of extended liminality characterized by unmanageable affectivity and isolation and are advancing towards transformative liminality and reintegration.

In this book, I focus mainly on the lived experiences related to transformative, and permanent or trickster liminality, emphasizing their characteristic differences. By transformative liminality, I mean in-betweenness in the traditional sense with its habitual struggles and surrenders, finally leading to a new identity state. Permanent or trickster liminality is a manipulative and destructive version, making the chaos inherent in communitas a norm, and deliberately sustaining a transient formation (Szakolczai, 2001, 2017). Permanent liminality facilitates the abuse of power and results in the creation of fake identities. It relegates spirituality and invalidates a community's visions and hopes through its permanent absurdities that replace the genuine human values. Occasionally, I refer to Turner's (1982) term, liminoid; as well as to extended liminality to describe a state where the abuse of power and the suspension of normality is not a prominent feature (yet), but neither the minimum predictability of temporary transformative liminality nor the playfulness and creative character of the liminoid prevail.

2.5 Liminal Hotspots

Van Gennep (1909/2019) attempted to introduce his idea in an era when the Newtonian–Cartesian spell dominated and focussing on processes instead of structures was considered a deviance from the dominant scientific paradigm (Szakolczai, 2009). The paradigm change brought about by quantum physics describes a world in a constant transformation with its different patterns of change between two endpoints of a continuum: the forms perceived as stable, cosmic order and the chaos surrounding a quantum change. Construing the transition as occurring between these two perceived endpoints and interpreting information as the organizing principle of a dynamically changing system demand more emphasis on meaning-making (Greco & Stenner, 2017; Stenner, 2017).

Transitioning may involve being suspended or entrapped in liminality, and on such occasions, *liminal hotpots* come into existence. Greco and Stenner (2017, p. 147) describe a liminal hotspot as "an occasion characterized by the experience of being trapped in the interstitial dimension between different forms-of-process, and in the situation of ontological indeterminacy". It is an impasse, an entrapment in a limbo state as in BPM 2, characterized by chaos and high affectivity, keeping the previously adaptive but now dysfunctional identity elements alive (Salvatore & Venuleo, 2017). Affectivity refers to a psychological turmoil, a combination of emotional overheat and ambivalence, and the resulting, enhanced *suggestibility* (Greco & Stenner, 2017; Motzkau, 2009; Stenner, 2017). A paradox of the psychosocial is that this suggestibility has its life-saving potential in times of crises, and for the very same reasons, it is also central to group-level manipulation.

Liminal hotspots are the isolating contexts characteristic of our era with its rapid transformations that pervade the globalized world. They lead to the instability of previous forms and boundaries, and culminate in recurrent crises, transforming the former, functional discourses of utility into expressive triggers of affective activation (Salvatore et al., 2021). The predominance of affectivity facilitates self-deception, operated at pre-reflective levels to exclude potentially troubling contents (Høgh-Olesen, 2024). Thus, sustaining liminal hotspots as a power strategy relies on a dysfunctional mass-level defence against a danger signal, the dread of unconstrained transitions, facilitating the abuse and expropriation of the arrested transformation processes. To end entrapment in a liminal hotspot and enter transformative liminality, first the affective semantic scenario belonging to the previous condition must be suspended (Salvatore & Venuleo, 2017).

Challenges to remove the barriers and manage the transition are of varied intensity: Greco and Stenner (2017) identify minimally liminal hotspots where relatively simple spatial or temporal adjustments can solve the issue. Here, pattern shift involves a deliberate choice within the available alternatives. These minimally liminal hotspots are our daily experiences and are the common results of our modern communication technologies, dissolving the previous spatial or temporal boundaries and disrupting the continuity of the experience but leaving our identities relatively unaffected. The maximum variation is a more permanent and tormenting inability to manage the transition. This is the crisis experience: here, the relational rearrangements are at the focus of the transformation.

Maintaining a liminal hotspot establishes either extended or permanent liminality. In extended liminality, though the transformation is arrested, viable alternatives can be created through the relational reconstructions. The person experiencing the transition is aware that the turning point has been reached, and once the decisions are made in the unpredictable and volatile environment, the trap of the hotspot will open. Entrapment with no escape (Williams & Pollock, 2001) is not restricted to, but is inherent in the destructive and longstanding forms of permanent liminality, usually extending to the macro-levels of culture (Szakolczai, 2001, 2017). In these settings, the individual does not perceive any genuine opportunities for change as cultural and relational rearrangements do not seem feasible anymore.

2.6 Time and Space in Liminality

The core meaning, threshold (limen), is a place that separates and connects places and times that are normally construed as different. Though experiencing liminality equals to experiencing ambiguities and chaos, traditionally, the limen was clearly indicated by ritual (symbolic) markers (Banfield, 2022). The limen is to warn the members of a community that they are about to enter the world of transformations, and the threshold is leading them from the stable mundane zones to sacred dimensions. Transformative liminality facilitates the momentary immersion in the supernatural order of unity and then returning to the intelligible cultural order, while permanent liminality represents the paralysing zone of a ditch, or even abyss, and not a limen: you cannot stay where you are, but there is no way out either.

Traditionally, one's lifeworld comprised consecrated versus profane places and times. Sacred people, for example, priests, shamans, and witches were to commute between the liminal zones and guide other members of community upon entering liminality (Eliade, 1961). This has changed in modernity: Foucault (1967) pointed out that Galilei's discovery has substantially changed and relativized the archaic and polarized constructions on space, consisting of the sacred and the profane, as well as the safe and the unprotected domains. He described two different types of liminal space. Utopia is an imaginary land of perfection in the symbolic realm, representing the desired contrast of perfection to existing imperfect realities. Heterotopia is a transformative space anchored both in the symbolic and the physical realities—as, for example, the space of a mirror (are *you* in the mirror?), or the distinguished spaces of knowledge construction as the library or a university. Heterotopia is a counter site, questioning the existing structures, disconnecting but also uniting the different places and even times. Entering such heterotopias is often regulated by a ritual. The context of a rite is a crisis-heterotopy, a context for substantial transformations—a context that separates and connects. Contrarily, heterotopies of deviation are the contexts of permanent liminality or marginalization. These are the spaces for those who do not fit into the community, break the norms, and are considered a threat to society (Foucault, 1967).

Our conception of time and the diverse temporal perspectives are the products of humans' reflective mode. When witnessing a series of environmental changes, reflecting on our past experiences, and envisioning possible future alternatives, we are well aware of the significance of time. Still, we do not have any direct capacity, e.g. a specific sensory organ with the related awareness of its operations, to sense time (Lakoff, 1993). We only sense events and actions, including our own mental activities and the changes in our body. To capture time, we use basic metaphors that operate through spatial concepts, such as time as a container that can be partially empty or full (spending time) or as a linear spatial movement, emphasizing directionality and goal-orientation when time passes (Lakoff, 1993; Lakoff & Johnson, 1980). We distinguish between the many different conceptions of time and match these to our experiences: for example, a fixed moment or duration identified in the flow of time, an event happening in *illo tempore* (Eliade, 1961); or the differentiation between chronos, the devouring time, the time that is spent, and kairos, the right moment for transformative action (Hartog, 2021). Liminal phenomena, for example, being arrested in a liminal hotspot and condemned to unconditional waiting, and then being involved in the struggles to reach the next stage are outside the usual chronology of life and are related to kairotic moments as the time of potentialities, risks, and transformations (Hartog, 2021). We do not only segment time into different domains but also attach our personal evaluations and perceptions on control to these temporal domains (Zimbardo & Boyd, 2015). Fate resides in the present-fatalistic worldview of liminality with no control over the future. Present-hedonistic moments are an inherent quality of the liminoid. An accomplished transition rite requires changes between the temporal perspectives, involving our ambivalent evaluations on the past and a choice between the future orientations.

Bakhtin's (1981) concept, the chronotope characterizes the temporal and spatial unity as a holistic perspective of the context for significant, transformative events in the life narrative. The chronotope is a specific circumstance where time thickens, and space becomes intensive. The two dimensions cannot be separated anymore as they establish an integrated whole as one meaningful frame. The chronotope is manifested as the context of a genuine transformative action, often a significant encounter or a turning point in a story. As Bakhtin noted, the temporal aspects are revealed in, and are connected to space, and spatial characteristics are conceived via time. The scene when Odysseus, a wanderer in alien worlds, and living in adventurous times, is holding firmly to a fig tree at Charybdis after a series of misfortune, losing everything but his life, now completely isolated, arrested in his journey and struggling hard to survive, is a prototypical example of a transformative liminal chronotope. The spot is right above the navel of Earth in the sea, a transition point, the immense whirlpool threatening to flood the whole world. This is neither the sea, nor the earth—rather, a gate and a boundary. Odysseus, formerly known as a king and triumphant warrior, is now trying to save his bare life, waiting only for the hoped reappearance of the remnants of his raft when the natural cycle of the whirlpool brings the decisive moment for action. This is happening at sunrise, neither the daylight nor the night (Hammond, 2007). This chronotope, the time and space together make up the reality of an outcast's ultimate liminality, of a man who was cursed by the God of the Sea.

2.7 Conclusion

We experience the physical world around us as relatively stable, with its objects nicely demarcated by solid boundaries, though it is in constant motion, changing between forms-of-process, rather than between structures (Greco & Stenner, 2017). This perceived constancy seems useful as it suggests reassuring predictability and opens the space for planned and synchronized actions. Humans as social beings must successfully coordinate their activities, and collaborate to survive, and for this reason, be predictable. Thus, ambivalence and diffusion are not welcomed in human cultures. However, the inescapable transformations triggered by our personal and social development and by the need to adapt to environmental changes require temporary immersion in transformative liminality. Expelling these liminal moments could give rise to non-adaptive rigidity and defensiveness ("depression" and "paranoia"). Maintaining liminality through schismogenetic feedback would result in approximately the same. Both states are barriers to our adaptation and growth, imposing severe limitations on humans' genuine creative-constructive capacities.

Recursivity opens the door for meta-level abstractions, facilitating our mental travels in time. We remember, reconstruct, and narrate our past, and not only envision but, guided by our deepest wishes or the worries shaped by our past experiences, also try to predict the future. By inhabiting these temporal dimensions, we can construe our identity. The deconstruction and reconstruction of identity can only take place in a liminal context, serving as a boundary and a bridge, separating, and connecting the previous realities to be remembered, explored, and reflected, and future, hopeful realities to be experienced. Such continuity is essential to maintain a constructive identity variant free from the torments of self-deprecation, diffusion, or defensiveness (Erikson, 1968; Weinreich, 2004).

Assisted by our languaging and guided by the dread of uncertainties, we prefer to focus on linear causalities in an ecological system; and we face difficulties when attempting to capture the patterns characteristic of complex adaptive systems (De Luca Picione & Lozzi, 2021; Lakoff, 2014; Resnicow & Page, 2008). This feature makes liminal balancing on the boundaries a strenuous mission during large-scale transformations.

References

Appau, S., Ozanne, J. L., & Klein, J. (2020). Understanding difficult consumer transitions: The in/dividual consumer in permanent liminality. *Journal of Consumer Research, 47*(2), 167. https://doi.org/10.1093/jcr/ucaa010

Aronson, E. (1973). The rationalizing animal. *Psychology Today, 6*(5), 46–52.

Bakhtin, M. (1981). *The dialogic imagination* (Forms of time and of the chronotope in the novel) (pp. 84–258). University Texas Press.

Bakhtin, M. (1984). *Rabelais and his world*. Indiana University Press.

Banfield, J. (2022). From liminal spaces to the spatialities of liminality. *Area, 54*, 610–617. https://doi.org/10.1111/area.12791

Barta, L. (2025, February 26). Nagy Márton megmentené a falu lelkét, indul a kocsmaprogram [Márton Nagy to save the soul of the village. Pub projects are starting]. *Index* https://index.hu/gazdasag/2025/02/26/nagy-marton-allami-tamogatas-kocsma-borozo-bar-nemzetgazdasagi-miniszterium/

Bateson, G. (1972). *Steps to an ecology of mind. Collected essays in anthropology, psychiatry, evolution, and epistemology*. Jason Aronson.

Beech, N. (2011). Liminality and the practices of identity reconstruction. *Human Relations, 64*(2), 285–302. https://doi.org/10.1177/0018726710371235

Benţa, M. I. (2021). The firefighter effect: Social pathology and corruption in liminal occupations. *International Political Anthropology, 14*(2), 103–111. https://doi.org/10.5281/zenodo.5721730

Berguno, G. (2001). The phenomenology of waiting. *Journal of the Society for Existential Analysis, 12*(2), 154–159.

Burke, K. (1963). Definition of man. *The Hudson Review, 16*(4), 491–514. http://www.jstor.org/stable/3848123

Bussolari, C. J., & Goodell, J. A. (2009). Chaos theory as a model for life transitions counseling: Nonlinear dynamics and life's changes. *Journal of Counseling & Development, 87*(1), 98–107. https://doi.org/10.1002/j.1556-6678.2009.tb00555.x

Butzer, B. (2021). Does synchronicity point us towards the fundamental nature of consciousness?: An exploration of psychology, ontology, and research prospects. *Journal of Consciousness Studies, 28*(3–4), 29–54.

C'de Baca, J., & Wilbourne, P. (2004). Quantum change: Ten years later. *Journal of Clinical Psychology, 60*(5), 531–541. https://doi.org/10.1002/jclp.20006

Cook, C., Henrickson, M., Atefi, N., Schouten, V., & Mcdonald, S. (2021). Iatrogenic loneliness and loss of intimacy in residential care. *Nursing Ethics, 28*(6), 911–923. https://doi.org/10.1177/0969733020983394

Csermely, P. (2005). *A rejtett hálózatok ereje [the power of hidden networks]*. Vince Kiadó.

Csermely, P. (2018). A demokrácia mint a túlélés többmilliárd éves evolúciós eszköze [Democracy as a successful evolutionary survival strategy]. *Magyar Tudomány, 179*(5), 615–623. https://doi.org/10.1556/2065.179.2018.5.3

Daskalaki, M., & Simosi, M. (2018). Unemployment as a liminoid phenomenon: Identity trajectories in times of crisis. *Human Relations, 71*(9), 1153–1178. https://doi.org/10.1177/0018726717737824

Davey, N. (2015). Lived experience. In N. Keane & C. Lawn (Eds.), *A companion to hermeneutics* (pp. 326–332). Wiley-Blackwell. https://doi.org/10.1002/9781118529812.ch38

De Luca Picione, R., & Lozzi, U. (2021). Uncertainty as a constitutive condition of human experience. An extensive review of the paradoxes and complexities of sensemaking processes in the face of uncertainty crisis. *International Journal of Psychoanalysis and Education: Subject, Action & Society, 1*(2), 14–53. https://doi.org/10.32111/SAS.2021.1.2.2

Drapela, V. J. (1995). *A review of personality theories* (Chapter 2. Psychoanalytic theory: Siegmund Freud) (pp. 10–23). Charles C. Thomas Publisher.

Eatough, V., & Smith, J. A. (2017). Interpretative phenomenological analysis. In C. Willig & W. Stainton-Rogers (Eds.), *Handbook of qualitative psychology* (2nd ed., pp. 193–211). Sage.

Eliade, M. (1961). *The sacred and the profane: The nature of religion*. Harper & Row.

Erikson, E. H. (1968). *Identity: Youth and crisis*. Norton.

Farin, I. (2021). Lived experience (erlebnis). In M. A. Wrathall (Ed.), *The Cambridge Heidegger Lexicon* (pp. 466–467). Cambridge University Press.

Foresman, P. S. (2020). *Sting ray (drawing)*. Wikimedia Commons. https://commons.wikimedia.org/wiki/File:Sting_Ray_(PSF).png

Foucault, M. (1967) Más terekről [Other spaces]. (Transl. M. Erhardt). *Exindex*. https://exindex.hu/hu/nem-tema/mas-terekrol-1967/

Garfinkel, H. (1956). Conditions of successful degradation ceremonies. *American Journal of Sociology, 61*(5), 420–424. https://doi.org/10.1086/221800

Gergen, M. (2013). Qualitative methods in feminist psychology. In C. Willing & W. Stainton-Rogers (Eds.), *The Sage handbook of qualitative research in psychology* (pp. 208–295). Sage.

Greco, M., & Stenner, P. (2017). From paradox to pattern shift: Conceptualising liminal hotspots and their affective dynamics. *Theory & Psychology, 27*(2), 147–166. https://doi.org/10.1177/0959354317693120

Grof, S. (1985). *Beyond the brain: Birth, death, and transcendence in psychotherapy*. State University of New York.

Grof, S. (1988). *The adventure of self-discovery. Dimensions of consciousness and new perspectives in psychotherapy and inner exploration*. SUNY Press.

H/11798. számú országgyűlési határozati javaslat a Nemzeti Drogellenes Stratégiáról 2013–2020 Tiszta tudat, józanság, küzdelem a kábítószer-bűnözés ellen. (2013, July) [Parliamentary resolution proposal no H/11798. on The National Strategy Against Drugs, 2013–2020, Clean minds, sobriety and fighting against drug-related crimes] https://drogproblemak.hu/wp-content/uploads/2022/02/11798.pdf

Hammond, R. M. (2007). *Cosmological motifs and themes in the Odyssey of Homer, with some antecedents in Minoan and Mycenaean iconography*. Doctoral Dissertation, Open University. Open Research Online. https://doi.org/10.21954/ou.ro.0000fa33.

Hartog, F. (2021). Chronos, kairos, krisis: The genesis of western time. *History and Theory, 60*, 425–439. https://doi.org/10.1111/hith.12218

Henshilwood, C. S., & D'Errico, F. (2011). Middle Stone Age engravings and their significance to the debate on the emergence of symbolic material culture. In C. S. Henshilwood & F. D'Errico (Eds.), *Homo symbolicus: The dawn of language, imagination and spirituality* (pp. 75–96). John Benjamins Publishing Company.

Hocoy, D. (2012). Sixty years later: The enduring allure of synchronicity. *Journal of Humanistic Psychology, 52*(4), 467–478. https://doi.org/10.1177/0022167812436427

Høgh-Olesen, H. (2024). Inside the mind of the self-deceiver: Foundational issues in relation to human defences and "the unconscious". *Human Arenas*. (Advance online publication). https://doi.org/10.1007/s42087-024-00458-7

Horvath, A., & Szakolczai, A. (2020). *The political sociology and anthropology of evil: Tricksterology*. Routledge.

Hsu, S., & Gao, J. H. H. (2022). From under-institutionalized to self-guided Liminality: The role of situational meaning-making. In *Proceedings of the eighty-second annual meeting of the academy of management*. Academy of Management. https://doi.org/10.5465/AMBPP.2022.113

Kelemen, G., & B. Erdos, M. (2010). Health learning as identity learning in the therapeutic community. *Addiktológia: Addictologia Hungarica, 9*(3), 216–225.

Kephart, W. M., & Zellner, W. W. (1991). *Extraordinary groups: An examination of unconventional life-styles*. St. Martin's Press.

Kershaw, T. C., & Ohlsson, S. (2001). Training for insight: The case of the nine-dot problem. In *Proceedings of the annual meeting of the cognitive science society* (Vol. 23). https://escholarship.org/uc/item/9g3432x1

Lakoff, G. (1993). The contemporary theory of metaphor. In A. Ortony (Ed.), *Metaphor and thought* (pp. 202–252). Cambridge University Press.

Lakoff, G. (2014). *The all new don't think of an elephant!: Know your values and frame the debate*. Chelsea Green Publishing.

Lakoff, G., & Johnson, M. (1980). *Metaphors we live by*. University of Chicago Press.

Little, M., Jordens, C. F., Paul, K., Montgomery, K., & Philipson, B. (1998). Liminality: A major category of the experience of cancer illness. *Social Science & Medicine (1982), 47*(10), 1485–1494. https://doi.org/10.1016/s0277-9536(98)00248-2

McDonald M. G., (2008). The nature of epiphanic experience. *Journal of Humanistic Psychology 48*(1), 89–115. https://doi.org/10.1177/0022167807311878

Maturana, H., Mpodozis, J., & Letelier, J. C. (1995). Brain, language and the origin of human mental functions. *Biological Research, 28*(1), 15–15.

McAdams, D. P. (2018). "I am what survives me". Generativity and the self. In J. A. Frey & C. Vogler (Eds.), *Self-transcendence and virtue. Perspectives form psychology, philosophy and theology* (pp. 251–273). Routledge.

McKechnie, R., Jaye, C., & MacLeod, R. (2010). The liminality of palliative care. *Sites: A Journal of Social Anthropology and Cultural Studies, 7*(2), 9–29. https://doi.org/10.11157/sites-vol7iss2id158

McNamee, S. (1992). Reconstructing identity: The communal construction of crisis. In S. McNamee & K. Gergen (Eds.), *Therapy as social construction* (pp. 186–199). Sage.

Miller, W. R. (2004). The phenomenon of quantum change. *Journal of Clinical Psychology, 60*(5), 453–460. https://doi.org/10.1002/jclp.20000

Mimoun, L., & Bardhi, F. (2022). Chronic consumer liminality: Being flexible in precarious times. *Journal of Consumer Research, 49*(3), 496–519. https://doi.org/10.1093/jcr/ucab073

Monostori, D., Lampek, K., & Erdos, M. B. (2024). "Lost in space and time": Fathers' experiences of preterm birth. *European Journal of Psychotherapy & Counselling, 26*(3–4), 333–351. https://doi.org/10.1080/13642537.2024.2355957

Motzkau, J. (2009). Exploring the transdisciplinary trajectory of suggestibility. *Subjectivity, 27*(1), 172–194. https://doi.org/10.1057/sub.2009.3

O'Connor, P. (2021). Civilisational complexity and elite decay. *International Political Anthropology, 14*(2), 157–173. https://doi.org/10.5281/zenodo.5721822

Ponte, D. V., & Schäfer, L. (2013). Carl Gustav Jung, quantum physics and the spiritual mind: A mystical vision of the twenty-first century. *Behavioral Sciences (Basel, Switzerland), 3*(4), 601–618. https://doi.org/10.3390/bs3040601

Resnicow, K., & Page, S. E. (2008). Embracing chaos and complexity: A quantum change for public health. *American Journal of Public Health, 98*(8), 1382–1389. https://doi.org/10.2105/AJPH.2007.129460

Reynolds, M. (2014). Equity-focused developmental evaluation using critical systems thinking. *Evaluation, 20*(1), 75–95. https://doi.org/10.1177/1356389013516054

Riedlinger, T., & Riedlinger, J. (1986). Taking birth trauma seriously. *Medical Hypotheses, 19*(1), 15–25. https://doi.org/10.1016/0306-9877(86)90133-7

Rittel, H. W., & Webber, M. M. (1973). Dilemmas in a general theory of planning. *Policy Sciences, 4*(2), 155–169. https://doi.org/10.1007/BF01405730

Rober, P. (2002). Constructive hypothesizing, dialogic understanding and the therapist's inner conversation: Some ideas about knowing and not knowing in the family therapy session. *Journal of Marital and Family Therapy, 28*(4), 467–478. https://doi.org/10.1111/j.1752-0606.2002.tb00371.x

Salvatore, S., Palmieri, A., Cordella, B., & Iuso, S. (2021). The decay of signs' semiotic value: A cultural psychology interpretation of the contemporary social scenario. *Culture & Psychology, 27*(4), 539–561. https://doi.org/10.1177/1354067X211027276

Salvatore, S., & Venuleo, C. (2017). Liminal transitions in a semiotic key: The mutual infeeding between present and past. *Theory & Psychology, 27*(2), 215–230. https://doi.org/10.1177/0959354317692889

Scott, S., Jakobsen, T. S., Rye, J. F., & Visser, M. A. (2022). Labour migration, precarious work and liminality. *Work in the Global Economy, 2*(1), 27–45. https://doi.org/10.1332/273241721X16471891313746

Soncul, Y., & Bollmer, G. (2020). Networked liminality. *Parallax, 26*(1), 1–8. https://doi.org/10.1080/13534645.2019.1685775

Squier, S. M. (2004). *Liminal lives: Imagining the human at the frontiers of biomedicine*. Duke University Press.

Stenner, P. (2017). *Liminality and experience. A transdisciplinary approach to the psychosocial*. Palgrave Macmillan.

Stonier, T. (1996). Information as a basic property of the universe. *Biosystems, 38*(2–3), 135–140. https://doi.org/10.1016/0303-2647(96)88368-7

Szakolczai, A. (2001). In a permanent state of transition: Theorizing the East-European condition. *Journal for Theory and Practice of Liminal Phenomena, 1*(1) http://limen.mi2.hr/limen1-2001/arpad_szakolczai.html

Szakolczai, A. (2009). Liminality and experience: Structuring transitory situations and transformative events. *International Political Anthropology, 2*(1), 141–172.

Szakolczai, A. (2017). Permanent (trickster) liminality: The reasons of the heart and of the mind. *Theory & Psychology, 27*(2), 231–248. https://doi.org/10.1177/0959354317694095

Szakolczai, A. (2024). An epistemology of revelation. *Religions, 15*(9), 1126. https://doi.org/10.3390/rel15091126

Taylor, E. W. (2001). Transformative learning theory: A neurobiological perspective of the role of emotions and unconscious ways of knowing. *International Journal of Lifelong Education, 20*(3), 218–236. https://doi.org/10.1080/02601370110036064

Turner, V. W. (1969). *The ritual process: Structure and anti-structure*. Aldine Transaction, University of New York Press.

Turner, V. W. (1974). Liminal to liminoid, in play, flow, and ritual: An essay in comparative symbology. *Rice University Studies, 60*(3), 53–92. https://hdl.handle.net/1911/63159

Turner, V. W. (1982). *From ritual to theatre*. PAJ Publications.

Uwins, C, & Hutchon, D. (2014). Delayed umbilical cord clamping after childbirth: potential benefits to baby's health. *Pediatric Health, Medicine and Therapeutics, 2014*(5), 161–171.

van Boeckel, J. (2011). *"When we find meaning in art, our thinking is most in sync with nature" A Review of An Ecology of Mind - The Gregory Bateson Documentary*. https://www.academia.edu/12919745/_When_we_find_meaning_in_art_our_thinking_is_most_in_sync_with_nature_A_Review_of_An_Ecology_of_Mind_The_Gregory_Bateson_Documentary

Van Gennep, A. (1909/2019). The rites of passage. University of Chicago Press.

van der Kolk, B. (2015). *The body keeps the score: Brain, mind, and body in the healing of trauma*. Penguin Books.

Vicsek, L., Sándor, J., & Bauer, Z. (2021). The human embryo: Mapping patients' ethical decisions in Hungary. *Intersections. East European Journal of Society and Politics, 7*(2), 149–169. https://doi.org/10.17356/ieejsp.v7i2.780

Watzlawick, P., Weakland, J. H., & Fisch, R. (1974). *Change: Principles of problem formation and problem resolution*. W. W. Norton.

Weinreich, P. (2004). Identity structure analysis. In P. Weinreich & W. Saunderson (Eds.), *Analysing identity: Cross-cultural, societal and clinical contexts* (pp. 7–76). Routledge.

Williams, J. M. G., & Pollock, L. R. (2001). Psychological aspects of the suicidal process. In K. Van Heeringen (Ed.), *Understanding suicidal behaviour* (pp. 76–94). John Wiley and Sons.

Winkler, I., & Kristensen, M. L. (2021). Trapped in limbo: Academics' identity negotiation in conditions of perpetual liminality. *Qualitative Research in Organizations and Management: An International Journal, 16*(2), 332–349. https://doi.org/10.1108/QROM-09-2020-2023

Wydra, H. (2012). The power of symbols—Communism and beyond. *International Journal of Politics, Culture, and Society, 25*(1–3), 49–69. https://doi.org/10.1007/s10767-011-9116-x

Zimbardo, P. G., & Boyd, J. N. (2015). Putting time in perspective: A valid, reliable individual-differences metric. In M. Stolarski, N. Fieulaine, & W. van Beek (Eds.), *Time perspective theory; review, research and application: Essays in honor of Philip G. Zimbardo* (pp. 17–55). Springer International Publishing/Springer Nature.

Part II
Explorations of the Sociopsychological: Liminal Hotspots, Permanent Liminality, and the Rise of the Trickster

Chapter 3
Liminal Experiences in Late Modernity. A-Mazed Societies and Institutionalized Craving

3.1 Odysseus in Extended Liminality

Odysseus is a prototypical liminal hero, spending 10 years lost in extended liminality, hoping to recover his lost identity elements as the King of Ithaca, a husband, and a father. His eternal story mirrors several contemporary problems, the ones caused by exclusive reliance on *techné* in the resolution of life's complications, or the risks inherent in a leader's hubris.

During his adventurous, often tormenting, search for his identity, Odysseus is repeatedly captured in the threatening, unknown outer space, the margins—a space representing the dangers of liminality for the traveller (Bauman, 1998). Odysseus is alternately confronted with vital struggles, trying not only his wits, but also his skills as a warrior to the extremes, and with occasional, demoralizing entrapment in the contexts where unconditional waiting (Berguno, 2001) and the accompanying sensation of loss of control prevail. As a fallible human being, he is often helpless before the powers of revengeful gods and goddesses, who represent both human virtues and malevolence (McAdams, 1985). Odysseus, however, is eager to experience the totality of human existence through his adventures and pass the ultimate boundaries that ordinary men cannot. This feature, and his cunningness represent the trickster aspects of his identity, which he must abandon to reach reincorporation into his community.

Craving, sensation-seeking, and enhancement, concepts that we often use today to describe an addict's behaviour, are the major sources of his crew's sufferings and death. Odysseus as an astute leader takes precautions against the predictable risks, and with Athene's goodwill, he can foresee many of the threats. Still his men are at their own peril. Careful balancing between the risks, precautions, and courageous actions is Odysseus's main strength during his adventures. However, as it is with heroes, he is making a fatal mistake. His trick, the trojan horse to win the war is not yet a source of lasting misfortune. Being captured in extended liminality is

M. B. Erdos, *Transitions - Liminality as Lived Experience*,
https://doi.org/10.1007/978-3-031-96007-9_3

Odysseus's punishment for his hubris, the self-centred celebration of his own wits and strengths while forgetting about human vulnerabilities to the forces that are more powerful than any human being. Concerning such hubris and its cure, surrender, I am focussing on four key scenes as important turning points, in which the liminal loss of social identity is a central theme.

Entrapped by Polyphemes, Poseidon's one-eyed cyclops son, Odysseus identifies himself as the liminal *Nobody*, expressing total surrender and freedom[1] from the usual obligations of social life. Telling one's name is a symbolic action of giving the other party control over the person, and the resulting troubles are frequently represented in myths and tales all over the world. Odysseus, when identifying himself as Nobody, does not only choose the safety of liminal anonymity but also using the polysemic potentials inherent in the word. When the man-eater cyclops is complaining of Nobody hurting him, he receives no help. The trick seems to work well, and Odysseus is ready to make sail with the remaining crew, but he is overestimating the safety of his ship, a liminal home for the contemporary voyager. At this point, he exchanges the shelter of anonymity for warriors' glory. Hubris takes over him, and he tells the blinded Polyphemos his name. Retaliation is quick: stepping out of liminal namelessness proves a fatal error for many of his fellows who are killed immediately by a rock thrown on the ship by Polyphemes. Hurting Poseidon, God of the Sea that all of them depend on, and even advertising the act puts Odysseus into a radically different position and transforms him into a *homo sacer*, a source of peril for the community (Horvath & Szakolczai, 2020). He is to spend many more years voyaging. *Odysseus has failed through his victory.*

Slowly he is learning the lesson and begins to inhabit his liminal anonymity, accepting his loss of status in the subsequent escapes. When arriving at Phaeacia as a shipwreck, he looks like a *monster*, and his human nature is recognized only by Nausicaa, the king's daughter. Hubris and nostalgia conquer him again and he uncovers his previous identity as a triumphant warrior. Saving and helping him results in the collective punishment of the sailors of Phaeacia by the God of Sea.

After spending 10 years in the liminality of his long voyage, he is finally allowed to return home under the strong protection of Athene. His patroness encourages him to disguise his most important identity elements—techné, warrior skills and cunning. He is masked as a beggar before returning home. The beggar as a character represents marginalization, as well as the uncertainties and polarities inherent in one's identity. Gods and kings are often disguised as beggars to test and try the people they are visiting. This role for Odysseus, however, is more than the hero's unrecognized arrival, a recurrent element in myths and tales (Campbell, 2008; Propp, 1999). Odysseus must experience a ritual reversal again and learn a deeper lesson of the shadows in his identity through surrender. Experiencing helplessness and humiliation helps him combat his hubris, which, coupled with his exceptional talents, is a danger to him and his people.

[1] For more details on *Historia Nemine*, see Chap. 1, *Living in a Dual Environment. Homo Symbolicus and Languaging.*

He must fight for his royal position, proving that he is worthy of reclaiming his lost identity, but he is not yet forgiven and cannot fulfil his role in the sacred order of his community. The hero's journey to integration has not come to an end yet. His final trial is not a heroic act, but an exercise in full surrender. His pilgrimage should last until he, now a *stranger*, has reached a land where people know nothing of the sea, the home of the voyager and adventurer, and mistake the oar he is carrying—the symbol of his previous identity and of his connections to the sea—for a winnowing shovel. Performing a ritual, a sacrifice to Poseidon is a final act of accepting the loss. Solely this act, as an atonement with the father (Campbell, 2008), can liberate him from the malevolence and persecution of the God of the Sea. Finally, Odysseus can win a meaningful life, and find home and peace through experiencing the loss of his central identity element as a voyager and adventurer. Total surrender is the precondition for reconciliation, and for living a new life as a master of two worlds (Campbell, 2008). Odysseus must sacrifice the identity part that kept him entrapped in liminality. He is *triumphant only after the loss*. The road to reintegration is finally open, and he can find the peace of a good life. He is free to live according to his social roles as a responsible king, a husband, and a father.

A myth, manifested in its ritual enactment and narrative framework, is a recurrent reminder for the community that we must acknowledge the existence of greater powers than ourselves. When venturing into the spiritual domains of human existence, we enter the symbolic universe of ecological–systemic thinking—to use a contemporary term for old wisdoms. The idea was quite evident for our ancestors, but it has been challenged by our technical civilization. Currently, techné, a materialistic and mechanistic approach, prevails over gnosis (Grof, 1985; Gyulai, 2012). Ponte and Schäfer (2013) argue that Darwin's theory, following the Newtonian materialism, has changed the broad focus of our culture.

Though the Darwinian ideas are still in use to underpin today's economic and societal ideologies, our story does not seem to be about the survival of the fittest anymore: the road we are currently taking raises very serious questions. Attributing an utmost importance to material resources and increasing one's own possessions at all costs are seen as the ultimate meaning in life. These enhanced consumerist features are accompanied with the symptoms of an inflated ego: aggression and greed. This cultural change, conducive to utterly competitive, schismogenetic processes, never breaking the increasing spirals of acquisition, segregates the seemingly "globalized" and "networked" people and societies, and leads, as such processes (ab) normally do, to escalating conflicts and the proliferation of hostile identity definitions in all areas of life (Szakolczai, 2015). Techné is the non-reflected knowledge about the hows without philosopher kings' other virtues as the indispensable sources for balanced development (Bloom, 2020):

> Three further constructs partially overlap *episteme* and *techne*—*arête* (excellence or virtue in living), *phronesis* (practical/moral wisdom), and *eudaimonia* (happiness via flourishing within a polity, with friendship a significant component) (…) philosopher kings would necessarily excel in these types of knowledge and through them excel in ruling a society (Bloom, 2020, p. 628).

In ancient times, techné was also understood as *tricking* the gods, like, in the possession of his trickster identity elements, the cunning Odysseus occasionally did. While technology is indeed useful, if not accompanied by personal and cultural awareness and efforts to search for some redemptive wisdom of the whys, of the *meanings, as a long-term and evidence-based survival strategy* tested by human evolution, then it imposes a risk to our adaptation, wellbeing, and even existence.

Science, and here I mean the STEM areas only, is seen as our best friend and strong ally to economic and political successes in the contemporary global context, provided it does not cross the boundaries set by the Newtonian–Cartesian–Darwinian spell (Yearworth et al., 2010). Generally, this attitude is more conservative than innovative. Physics has always been considered a model science for several disciplines, but it has long transcended the Newtonian worldview, so practical in our everyday life on Earth, but not in a larger, cosmic context. Thus, our "enlightened" ideologies are governed more by interest-driven attitudes than scientific facts, and "progress" seems to be determined more by the non-reflected and skewed powers of the symbolic domain than the powers of nature that STEM branches are dedicated to study.

In the possession of our strong constructive potentials, we are continuously struggling to transform both our natural and cultural environments. In this framework, however, constructiveness is accompanied by the illusion of *full* human control, as reflected, for example, by visions on geoengineering, or the artificial human womb meant for people as machines. We underestimate the complexity of our environments, relying on a comfortably linear, cause-and-effect type of thinking instead of systems-based thinking (Lakoff, 2014; Yearworth et al., 2010). In the complexity of the globalized world, more-of-the-same solutions based on the same preconceptions, will lead to deepening problems. From a systemic perspective, the idea of all-embracing human control is nothing but a shared fallacy, as no part of a system can control the entire system (Bateson, 1972). Freud (1917) referred to our masked disappointments and doubts concerning the anthropocentric celebrations of humans' superior status as narcissistic traumas: the trauma of not occupying a central position in the solar system, not to mention the Universe; the principle of genetic continuity confirmed by Darwin; and, finally, Freud's own idea questioning the all-encompassing power of rationality. Late modernity has added another candidate to the original list: technological developments as the means of effective risk management and adaptation. With our complex human-made systems, such as the global economy or the Internet, we must give a thought or two to our favourite obsession: control. Will more of the same, that is, more developed technologies introduced in the hope of increasing control, solve the crises we are currently facing?

3.2 Regressing from Reflexive Modernity to A-Mazed Societies

After World War II, Jean Monnet, one of the founding fathers of European collaboration, identified a dynamic that shaped the political life and future visions in Europe: that of fear and hope (Van Beek, 2008). In the contemporary liminal contexts, sharp contrasts are envisioned between the threats and the positive future scripts concerning globalization, consumerism, and new technologies—from utterly hopeless scenarios to delusional bright visions.

From the majority's perspective, globalization is perhaps the largest scale double bind ever, forcing, and at the same time, impeding or sanctioning mobility. As Beck (1992) has noted, globalization connects people on the whole planet, but also arranges them into social layers or even castes, strengthening their identity conflicts. There are the groups that may enjoy the new opportunities and the ones who pay the price. Those who are deprived of the new freedoms or even of their basic needs, are almost as "localised", soil-bound as the helots in ancient Sparta—not by the force of law but by the imminent force of finances, the very same force that requires mobility.

Global corporations are insensitive to the environmental and social costs, as these can be transferred to places that seem far away enough to escape the detrimental consequences. In the Middle Ages, landlords, to some extent, were compelled to take care of their property for they needed the people living in the locality to produce more wealth (Bauman, 1998). Today's leading regimes have a lot in common with medieval sanjak-beys in Eastern Europe during the Ottoman rule. Sanjak-beys' temporary and mobile positions made them rather greedy, which increased the levels of exploitation in the occupied areas. They robbed the people of their resources and then left, letting the locals cope with the consequences: starvation, plagues, and hopelessness in a waste land amidst the crisis and chaos of the margins.

We are ordered by the global economy to act, but our actions are sanctioned (Bauman, 1998); either by the competitors themselves, or by the ecosystem that changes independently of human delusions, fallacies, and oppositions. We are facing recurrent problems, but without a reasonable escape (Lanyi, 2022). The global economy is being fed by humans' craving, and consequently, now we live our lives maintaining a sustainability paradox: enhanced consumption, the very act that makes the global ecological system unsustainable keeps the symbolic system of the economy alive and working (Hayward, 2016). The double bind is established by the duality of our environments, and today's complex sustainability problems are probably the worst of the wicked problems we have ever faced, as they call into question the very foundations of human civilization:

> If we were a biological accident initially, and may at some point become an extinct species, and the processes of the expanding universe operate independent of our desires, beliefs, and values, then the meanings we experience, however full of sound and fury, may ultimately be momentary and, in the end, signify nothing (Hocoy, 2012, p. 469).

The politics of unsustainability and the parallel commercialization of sustainability ideas, often reduced to the introduction of marketable "green" commodities, may question the truth involved in the sustainability discourses (Blühdorn, 2017; Lanyi, 2022).

Recently, capitalism as a concept has attracted several new attributes as predatory, vampire, or surveillance, the first two referring to new forms of exploitation with less restraints than ever before, and to its related death economy of ecological destructions (Kennedy, 2017, 2020). The third notion, surveillance capitalism describes a form bringing about the colonization and control of private experiences to raise the profits (Zuboff, 2019). For the largest companies and banks, globalization and electronic communication have resulted in *unlimited* freedoms. Corporations maintain *anonymity* and communicate via automated messages, neither responding to, nor taking the responsibility for the problems they are creating, and for the common resources they are wasting. This version of capitalism is deregulated and disengaged (Kennedy, 2020). Seeming inconsistencies between deregulation and surveillance are resolved by Szakolczai (2020), who described today's formations as the collusion of the police state and fairground economy, connecting the carnivalesque features to strict surveillance in a permanent apocalyptic context. Such inconsistencies are central to permanent liminality. Ben̦ta (2021) has introduced a new term, firestarter capitalism to describe the liminal features sustaining a context of controversies and eliminating the reasonable limitations on greed.

Unlimited greed has its consequences. Regional differences in terms of income, political power, and environmental harms causing incurable chronic diseases are increasing. We experience a decline in between-country inequality due to the growing performance of emerging Asian economies, most importantly, China—but within the countries, inequality between people is on the increase, and 71% of the global population lives in the countries with worsening trends. Parallel, the concentration of wealth and the rise of the *undeserving rich* continued: in 2018, the 26 richest persons owned as much wealth as the 3.8 billion poorest persons globally (United Nations, n.d.). While there is a steady growth in life expectancy globally, in 2022, a person born in North America could expect about 16 more years than a person born in Africa. In Hong Kong, life expectancy is about 86 years, and in Nigeria, it is only about 55 (Richter, 2023). Exploitation, and its consequence, poverty, brings about an unstable and chaotic environment, the whirlpool of a global crisis.

Corporate irresponsibility—taking the profits and leaving the destructions behind—is not only about the physical harms anymore. Parallel to this, manipulation pushes the majority into a cognitive trap, a more subtle form of victimization and colonization that extends to all the important spheres of life (Deetz, 1992). Globalization is problematic exactly because it remains *unreflected* (Bauman, 1998). Shortly after the Chernobyl catastrophe, Beck (1992) described an emerging globalized pattern, *reflexive modernity*, claiming that we entered an era when we were forced to face the impact of global-level human-made, unforeseen, and incalculable catastrophes. Still, on a global level, we do not. The Chernobyl disaster followed four decades after the use of nuclear bombs in Hiroshima and Nagasaki.

Since 1945, we have been aware that we have the scaring power to extinguish life on Earth. We can destroy life, but we cannot create life.

Reflexive modernity promised a potentially optimistic scenario by introducing new forms of solidarity. In this positive scenario, science, politics, and economy, having learnt the lessons of risk societies, would work for a better future (Beck, 1992). Today's deepening sustainability problems question the optimistic scheme. Risk societies, with their incalculability, have become the societies of *not knowing* (Gross, 2016). Reflection is painful. Risks are being solved (if at all) at a much slower pace than they are being created. Soon it turned out that globalized risks—"riskification" (Gross, 2016, p. 390)—is a distinguished economic and political product. Notions of predatory capitalism are hardly ever challenged, though unpredictable *adverse impacts* of the technology–pharmakon have grown into a permanent problem in science and technology (Aczél, 2024). Several of today's beliefs are stemmed in modernity, e. g. what is good for the economy must be good for the people; what is newer is always better; resources are infinite and all we must do is to discover and exploit them; and technological development is identical with human progress. Recent examples try to tackle the complexities that are beyond our true potentials: geoengineering will solve the problems of climate change; should the biosphere of Earth collapse, we will be able to move to another planet and adapt to its biosphere (if any), or "terraform" it, etc.

In the shadow of these propagated utopistic scenarios, there are the deep worries pushing us into a defensive position of "hear no evil, see no evil, speak no evil". In relation to this attitude, concepts as "self-jeopardy society" by Sørensen and Christiansen (2013, p. 14, cit. by Gross, 2016, p. 387) and the "nescience" of unknown ignorance, not knowing what we could know but do not know have emerged (Gross, 2016, p. 388). The meaning of *risk* is losing its functionality through the myriads of repetitions in the discourse (Gross, 2016). Thus, the shared basis for common reflections has been lost, but the compelling and free-floating negative affects have remained. A new transition into *a-mazed societies* is being formed, where globalization, craving, and manipulation, longstanding features of consumer societies are now intertwined with the deep impact of info-communication technologies (ICTs), radically and rapidly changing human psychologics and societies. Today's societies are a-mazed because people are subject to refined or brute forms of exploitation through mass-level manipulation, finding themselves entrapped in a maze; and this e-based and e-convenient maze is much more amazing—attractive, addictive, and indefinite—than its early forerunners, the medieval bear-beatings were. Today, *circenses* are granted, but *panem* might be missing for many.

Beck (1992) has claimed that social ills, such as unemployment and poverty, do not affect people as a social class anymore. Problems are related more to the individual phases of life, and are conceived as one's individual problem, resulting in isolation and in the blaming of the victims. Beck's powerful metaphor of the ghost station refers to ineffective but forced "reintegration strategies" through education, offering the opportunity to get on a train that is already crowded or is taking one nowhere. The next generation is often invited to irrational, absurd and disappointing career pathways (Beck, 1992).

3.3 Consumer Societies, Craving, and Control

In the Middle Ages, people were educated to free themselves from the seven cardinal sins: pride, greed, wrath, envy, lust, gluttony, and sloth to become worthy of God's grace, though, as always, not everyone took these moral obligations seriously. From time to time, carnivals, the institutionalized forms of liminality, suspended the prevailing order, and people were immersed into the reversed patterns of the antistructure of a feast, transgressing the boundaries of the established social positions and entering a context of opposites, of the anti-structure. This liberation from the hierarchies of a "monolithically serious and gloomy" (Bakhtin, 1984a, p. 129), dogmatic order was legitimate but *temporary,* safeguarded by strict boundaries: the profane, obscene, and ambivalent carnivalesque milieu. This way, values did not only serve the purposes of hypocritical discipline but also worked as a gentle reminder for the lucky ones that their position is not *eternal,* and disruptions happen. In this setting, the extraordinary, the antistructure connecting the spaces, times, and people previously separated, was predictably alternating with the ordinary way of life (Bakhtin, 1984b). Though carnivalesque patterns are undoubtedly present in our culture, their meaning has changed, from the re-creational to recreational. Previous boundaries between the ordinary and the extraordinary have become blurred.

In the early capitalist systems, the medieval values seen as God's order, some transcendent qualities, were slowly exchanged for productivity, creativity, and utility (Bauman, 2005). We celebrated the rapidly expanding technological developments as ultimate proofs of human talents and constructive potentials. A new and destructive myth was introduced about humans' capability to rule the "blind" forces of nature through these new technologies, as if *Homo Symbolicus* was not part of its environment but some superordinate being.

In present-day consumer societies, the values of early capitalism are not the priorities anymore. These virtues do not maintain craving, the force governing today's *limitless* economic growth effectively. They appear only in the double discourse directed at the social castes with limited resources, who are expected to be useful and productive only to be able to increase their share in consumption. The least lucky ones, the have-nots, are invariably expected to adhere to the medieval virtues and resign themselves to exclusion from consumerist happiness. Adam Smith's idea on the invisible hand, directing the economy towards progress and welfare, is often cited as a cornerstone of (neo)liberal ideologies. However, enthusiastic summaries tend to dismiss at least one crucial aspect, that the lasting success of such a self-regulating system depends on a human virtue, *solidarity* (sympathy) with others (Horvath, 1997). Without this virtue, and with the anonymous irresponsibility and extreme manipulation by the market, the benevolent invisible hand, as some symbolic, social Darwinist evolutionary force, will turn into the hand of the trickster, expropriating and destroying the common good.

The foundations for the consumer discourse were laid in the 1950s to transfer us to the postmodern by the 1980s (Brown, 2015). Now we celebrate the consumer-friendly, trickster-type *reversals* of all the medieval and even some early capitalist virtues. If we did not have new desires and needs, then the current economy, together with the contemporary world order, would collapse (Hayward, 2016). Thus, transformative, temporary liminality is exchanged for the consumer-friendly versions: the playful liminoid with its creative potentials but no guarantees for reintegration (Turner, 1974, 1982), or the more destructive patterns of permanent or trickster liminality (Horvath & Szakolczai, 2020; Szakolczai, 2001, 2015, 2017). People's constructive abilities are canalized into consumer activities. As Firat (1991) has noted, previously, the goods were produced by the people, but in the tricky, reversed scenario of post-industrial consumer societies, people's identities have become the products of the commodities, services, and, more recently, the data or message they purchase. In this setting, enhanced hedonism prevails over eudaimonia. Hedonism, as we understand it today, is the individual's freedom from sufferings, pursuing an easy and comfortable way of life and experiencing liberties in pleasure-seeking. Its moderate forms, prevailing in the ancient Greek cultures have been exchanged for the extremities of consumerism (Deci & Ryan, 2008; Lubics et al., 2024; Mekler & Hornbæk, 2016). Though consumption is an action that characterizes every human society, in late modernity, consumption is at the centre of human life. It is the market that defines the values of the society, and people's hierarchical positions (Bauman, 1998; Hayward, 2016). The Latin word *consumo* has several meanings, including to destroy, to wear away, to kill, to make smaller, to reduce to nothing, to weaken severely, to wear down, to devour, to employ, to spend, to exhaust the possibilities, and to *waste* (Glare, 1982). Thus, the word fully captures what is currently happening in our natural and cultural environment.

Erikson (1968) pointed out that every society will develop its specific character pathology, embodied in a trickster-type caricature, like an image in a funhouse mirror. The character, endowed with the sincerity of the clown, represents the underlying negative character structure, the shadow self of the society's heroes. Addiction is the global-level grand narrative and a way of life in late modern consumer societies (B. Erdos, 2014). The addict, chasing but never getting satisfaction, unable to tolerate pain, obsessed with control, and existing in a simulated hyperreality is the sad parody of the ideal consumer. Discourses of addiction are intertwined with the discourses of risk, for example, harm reduction, requiring constant monitoring of both the risks and the subject carrying the hazards. The war on drugs as a societal mission represents a mass-level projective identification, e.g. criminalizing a pattern, excessive consumption, which is strongly supported by the actual value system of these societies (Buda, 2009; B. Erdos, 2014; Firat, 1991; Reith, 2004).

Consumer societies must increase craving; and craving does not lead to satisfaction but to more craving (Bauman, 1998). Craving is beyond control, as the addicts entering the 12-step recovery movements (e.g. Anonymous Alcoholics) have personally experienced. Consumption is extended through craving: the prototypical commodity in late modern consumer societies is the designer drug, a product where craving must be established first to substantiate the consumers' physical and psychological *needs* that separate them from meaningful human relationships and attainable visions. The dealers of these black-market products use the same marketing strategies as legal consumer groups. Synthetic substances are sold under attractive labels, suggesting to the consumer that they can buy some spiritual and unique *transitional* experience (Sorcerers' Sage; Crystal) supernatural abilities ("accelerators") or a healthy, low-risk, environment-friendly product ("bioweed") (B. Erdos, 2014). Dependence sustains the need and the demand; and synthetic drugs are designed for frequent use. You can also be addicted to illicit drugs such as caffeine, refined carbohydrates, nicotine, and to forms of behaviour such as videogaming, work ("workaholic" or "work addict"), sports, helping as a compulsive or co-dependent helper—even to political power or money (Roth, 2006; Sadler-Smith, 2024). The basic patterns of addiction and globalized consumer societies are essentially the same: sensation-seeking, excitement, and the enhancement of experiences, all at a very fast pace, without taking the time and chance for reflections (Hayward, 2016).

Addiction is characterized by the *controlled loss of control* (Hayward, 2016), which finally turns into the uncontrollable. Taking the risks is the individual's own decision, but the decision is made in the global context of permanent liminality. If use turns into an addiction without recovery, then it represents a *dead end*, transforming the liminoid, or a minimally liminal hotspot (Greco & Stenner, 2017) into a maximally liminal one. Though this aspect is largely missing from the public discourse, addiction is more about a long series of traumatization and trauma repetitions than pure hedonism: paradoxically, the wish to escape from all sufferings will lead to increased sufferings (Kassai, 2020). Hayward (2016), taking the example of a popular video game, Grandt Theft Auto (GTA), argues that not only the extremities and actual or perceived, tamed, or untamed risks and traumas, but also *deviance* has become a commodity. In permanent liminality, as Bențа (2021, p. 110) claims, "evil, disease, crime, corruption or untruth", residing in the heterotopies of deviation, sell exceptionally well. Addictive–destructive patterns permeate the economic and political life as well as the community and private domains (Firat, 1991).

Risk discourses, and the connected, global-level carpe diem attitudes lead to major changes in identity development. In response to the problems, consumerism highlights the need for personal branding processes by purchasing identity prostheses of one's choice. The milieu that conceives identity as a commodity establishes what Mimoun and Bardhi (2022) have recently described as *chronic consumer liminality*, a type of permanent liminality with its reoccurring, but usually fruitless, efforts to transition to a new identity state, and the parallel celebration of precarity. Identity prostheses, the goods that seem to magically transform people with vulnerable identities, as consumerism's primary products, from No-one into Someone, substitute the reflexive self for a branded persona, an objectified self (Firat, 1991; Greenfield, 2011; Hearn, 2008). You can buy yourself as a sportswoman or a caring family father by purchasing certain "types" (labels) of non-prescription medication or food, as an active workforce by buying energy drinks, or a competent businessman by managing your savings, sales, and loans through a smart and safe online service or app. This will grant people the illusion of self-worth, identity, and social status; illusion, as these fragile and surficial identity elements remain sensitive to the volatility of the market. Stability and continuity are missing, as the market, dominated by the ethic of self-fulfilment, demands fluid identities and disrupted affiliations. Intrusion into the interpersonal and personal domains through e-communication technologies make the consumers even more isolated and controllable, and, in the possession of the necessary resources, better consumers. Visions on a "perfect" self and "perfect" relationships successfully guide people into repeated acts of consumption. If the relationship is not perfect, you can simply leave instead of making some efforts to improve it, though the money-back guarantee may not work (Firat, 1991).[2] More households equal more goods to purchase.

In this context, freedom is understood as an expected reaction to market signals (Brown, 2015). The consumer culture prepares the individuals to perform their consumerist roles and tasks effectively (Bauman, 2005; McCracken, 2008). The consumerist mindset intertwined with risk society foci is a bestseller ideological product: previously we purchased something simply for the contents that we needed, for example, vegetables and fruits. Today, we buy *liminality* (beyond limitations), *trust* (a brand), or buy what is missing, advertised as a new *freedom* from the human-made risks (free from artificial colours, preservatives, no traces of mercury, no sugar, no, or not-yet-discovered adverse side[3] effects). To maximize customer "freedom", you are offered several alternatives to choose from, but the quality, at least for the majority, has been steadily deteriorating. You can buy the diversity of goods that do not serve you too well—but you can buy them cheap. Some years ago, you could even ask the Japanese spiritual guide, Marie Kondo to *free* you from these and transform the chaos of your home into some new and liveable order. We have reached a level in consumerism when you pay not only for having but also for not having. As we are producing so much waste, the trend will continue. Individuals in late modernity are obsessed with their continual conflicts related to consumption, and the arising tensions and precarity shape their vulnerable identities (Bauman, 2005; Simon, 2018). Kennedy (2020) comments about the pursuit of consumer self-actualization as follows:

> (…) these overwhelmingly prevalent preoccupations isolate and disempower consumers by, for example, encouraging personal debt and competitive consumption, fostering the belief that self-branding processes will liberate individuals from unsatisfactory lives or because of the social fragmentation and humiliation that result when citizens' poverty excludes them from joining the dominant game (Kennedy, 2020, p. 262).

In this setting, poverty identity becomes a tormenting identity variant—up to the level that those living in poverty are also "included" in some forms of consumption.

---

[2] There are cases where attempts at improving the relationship are fruitless and would only maintain or deepen the destructive patterns. In such cases, divorce is not a problem but a solution.

[3] The attribute "side" is a powerful marketing strategy suggesting that these are negligible as compared to the benefits.

They can buy the fake brands, junk food, or other risky commodities available in the black market. These are perceived as an escape from the torments of a shattered identity, deprived of all the hedonistic pleasures that are propagated as the utmost value globally. For them, the choice granted is usually between making a hopeless attempt to meet their basic needs or adopting a consumer stance and buying fake status symbols to fit in. However, the latter strategy only strengthens their social exclusion and segregation, as in the dominant discourse they will appear as irresponsible people, spending their social benefits on the goods they do not "need". This vulnerability is intensified by the current volatility of the social environment where the majority who are not part of, but are just the witnesses to the game, feel subordinated to and threatened by the unpredictable powers of the global economy with its conflicts, tipping points, and regular crises.

3.4 Networked Loneliness in the Virtual Space

The individual's strong reliance on technologies exchanges interdependence, a natural human condition for unilateral dependence on distant, non-transparent, centralized, and objectifying market systems. E-groups and communities seldom provide the relational resources people need, and many of these are simply consumer groups to serve corporate interests, strengthening the *instrumentality* of human relationships. These are not genuine communities anymore but mere collectivities (Kennedy, 2017).

The changes occur both in the contexts of our strong social ties and weak social ties (WST). The term "weak" does not refer to something unimportant—on the contrary, these ties are essential for social integration and stability. The theory of WST was introduced by Granovetter (1973) whose study disclosed that the weak ties between acquaintances and distant relatives are the crucial information resources that people rely on when solving their problems, overcoming the daily stresses, and resolving their conflicts. Granovetter's original theory has been confirmed by a recent, robust study (Fronczak et al., 2022). Weak social ties contribute to accepting the diversities, promote inclusion, and the people involved in them witness and validate personal transformations—in short, these are the ties that stabilize the societies (Csermely, 2004; Granovetter, 1973). WSTs are generally formed by women and by the middle social layers (Csermely, 2004)—if there are such layers left in a polarized society. WSTs often come into existence when people meet each other spontaneously. Paradoxically, in today's network societies, these occasions are delimited. Many of the potential spots, such as a post office, a small shop with its characteristic small talks, and several public services were transferred from the physical space into the virtual one, where interpersonal contacts become distorted or blocked. Theoretically, the potential for "socializing" and connecting many people are given, but de facto this does not happen in the virtual space (Dunbar, 2002). Neither the strong nor the weak ties are routinely and auspiciously formed in the e-world, though WSTs could counter the destructive impacts of the normative chaos of trickster liminality.

3.5 Moral Panic, Moral Chills, and Global-Level Crises

Susanna Hertrich (2010–2011), combining science and art, exhibited a Reality Checking Device. She depicted the salient differences between a public outrage and the actual hazards of events, for example, the risks associated with a plane crash, a pedestrian accident, a serious heart condition, or the bird flu. The political use of magnifying genuine but minor threats and presenting the politically constructed risks is captured under the term of *moral panic*. Such accentuations and distortions ground community support for the leading regime's "protective" actions. By obtaining public approval for these actions, they can maintain, extend, and strengthen their political and economic positions (Cohen, 2011; Hayward, 2002; Kitzinger, 2000). Moral panic relies on manipulative discourse,[4] and is strongly embedded in human preoccupations with predictable risks and control strivings. Moral panic always involves *othering*, the stereotyping and labelling a group as the violators of common societal interests. In this setting, the predictable, well-established, and effective health and social political interventions are exchanged for the primary and immediate use of the criminal justice system (Cohen, 2011; Kitzinger, 2000; Sárosi, 2017).

The regime's predominance over the media, and the continual reinforcements of public anxieties establish a societal context in which panic is not related to a single event anymore, but to shared paranoid delusions on a continuous threat by a "public enemy". In this permanently maintained liminal setting, a prefabricated *moral panic button* can be used on any occasions, and particularly before the elections (Gerő & Sik, 2022; Sik, 2016). The robust image of the enemy and the associated beliefs and attitudes can rapidly be redirected to new groups if needed.

The public judgements of the threats in a society adopting anxiety as a lifestyle choice are far from being realistic. Processes opposite to or overshadowed by the moral panic also exist. I propose the term *moral chills* to designate the underplaying of genuine problems, keeping people calm and passive, preventing them from substantiated and efficient community-level actions when these actions would be necessary. Moral chills also rely on the idea of eliminating a designated *group of guilt* from the society's life; or they are fuelled by fake illusions on redemptive technological developments. Processes of suppression of the alternative, well-grounded views, and the potential consequences of sustained beliefs about the almighty technological solutions are depicted in Adam McKay's (2021) film, *Don't look up*, a debated political satire centring around the outcomes of human arrogance, mass-level manipulation, scapegoating, and idiocracy. The film authentically pictures the

[4] See also Chap. 5, *Authoritarian Discourses*.

difficulties we are facing when confronted with the ultimate need to reshape the ways we are thinking about ourselves and our true potentials.

Both mechanisms, moral panic and moral chills, were in the foreground during the permanent liminality of the Covid-19 pandemic, the first global-level crisis in an era predominated by digital communication technologies. Unintended impacts of the war on the pandemic have been salient in several countries, indicated by the sharpening social conflicts in a contrasted discursive field. Under the pressures of real and perceived threats, a *new world order of exceptions* (Horvath, 2021) has been constructed at an unprecedented pace. Community processes of meaning-making, relying on the accessible historical scripts, were assisted by powerful prompts of a new version of the therapeutic state in this endless fight against the disordered (ill) states, introducing purifying rituals and social isolation to combat death (Novikov, 2021). Decontextualized interpretative frameworks of the psy professions focus on the individual's perceived shortcomings instead of a social focus (McNamee, 2015). Such frameworks ("your fault") were expanded to substantiate surveillance in the rapidly extending permanent liminality with its virtual-networked alienation (Horvath & O'Connor, 2022).

Occasionally, the newly established discipline, rigour, surveillance, and subsequent escape attempts have led to tragedies, such as the extended suicide of a family father in Germany ("COVID-19: Man in Germany", 2021). In Hungary, vaccination, or a valid immunity certificate was required for the employees in the state sector, while any short- or long-term adverse consequences of vaccination was shifted to the individual as the "agreed", sole responsibility to be testified by the patient's signature on a "statement of consent". The appearance of fake immunity certificates in many countries, including the ones where citizens' adherence to law has been traditionally strong, was an illuminative example of the quickly diminishing public trust (e.g. "Thousands of fake", 2021).

Digital technologies offered effective ways of public communication in the emergency, but also enabled the fast spread of false information, conspiracy theories, or some absurd, unsubstantiated advice via the social media channels. In Hungary, expressing party political or group identities through one's vaccination status was another key element. In the countries with authoritarian traditions, people learnt to substitute scientific evaluations with leading ideologies and party-political preferences. Such preferences were reflected by people's choice of the type of vaccine and the frequency of vaccination. In the end, many received a peculiar mixture of the shots, of the Western and the Eastern variations, and at varied intervals, impairing the chances for valid mid- and long-term medical evaluations. In this paranoid milieu, only the super-vaccinated subject seemed a good subject. Finally, vaccination status was seen as an ultimate measure of one's identity, normalcy, social responsibility, and a good life. While in the pre-vaccination phase of the pandemic, patterns of solidarity had prevailed, people were quickly forming hostile groups of vaccine supporters and vaccine deniers afterwards. The discursive milieu in this New Age of Disease was established by the core conceptual metaphor of fight: orders and obedience, heroes and dissenters, risky zones, and shelters (Horvath, 2021; Novikov, 2021; J. Szakolczai, 2021). The suffocating experience of living in the isolation of one's home to escape suffocation by the virus was comparable to Grof's (1985) second birth perinatal matrix, our first experience of being entrapped in helplessness and anxiety (see also Chap. 2, *Transitions from a Systemic Perspective. Quantum Change and Liminality*).

In 2021, a famous Hungarian singer, János Kóbor was infected by COVID-19 and died at the age of 79. He lived a generative, creative, and productive life ("Rock Legend", 2021). However, he had refused vaccination. Grief and sympathy over his death were overshadowed by derogatory and inhumane comments on his vaccination status (Fekő, 2021). In a similar vein, when Szilveszter Csollány, a Hungarian Olympic champion was infected by Covid-19, his critical condition was attributed to his having rejected vaccination. Sympathetic and malicious comments had followed, but a month later it was announced that he had received the one-dose vaccine on 28 October 2021. At the end of November, he had been admitted to a hospital and died on 25 January 2022 ("Oltott volt", 2022). In both cases, people with exceptional performance, serving the common good throughout their lives, were unjustly and inhumanely labelled by some people as a *public enemy* in the social media.

Not denying that generally, vaccination has its advantages, some facts from the other side have been rarely or never mentioned. First, vaccination did not prevent the spread of the virus by the vaccinated individuals (Kampf, 2021; Kmietowicz, 2021; Porter, 2021)—contrastingly to the claims about their omnipotent power to stop the pandemic. We could see that vaccination could not stop the rapid mutation of the virus either, and, consequently, in a few months, vaccinated people could also be reinfected, presumably with a milder version causing the symptoms of a flu, or a common cold. There is some evidence that vaccination may have caused unpredicted adverse consequences, e.g. unforeseen impacts on the immune system (Föhse et al., 2023). Assessing these was difficult as systems thinking—and available data—was missing from the early evaluations: "...emerging evidence has indicated that new onset of autoimmune manifestations (...) appears to be associated with COVID-19 vaccines" (Chen et al., 2022, p. 396). A study on gynaecological adverse impacts calls evaluators' attention to the fact that *no adverse impacts will be revealed unless you ask the recipients* about them (Dellino et al., 2022). Some of these impacts are not mild, even if the benefits outweigh the risks. We have not been informed about the exact cost-benefit rates relying on mid- or long-term comprehensive evaluations either.

In their recent book, Horvath and O'Connor (2022) have focussed on the political consequences and the grave societal impacts of the new type of extended (permanent) liminality of a medical emergency with its severe limitations and inescapable control. They point out the horrifying speed at which our seemingly normal lifestyles were transformed into the discernible patterns of *trickster liminality* in the maximally liminal hotspot of the pandemic with its hysterical affectivity and suggestibility. The emerging hotspot suspended the previous institutional forms and changed our perceptions of space and time, granting a priority to events in the virtual space, accentuating people's isolation, and paralysation (Stenner & Kaposi, n.d.; Stenner, 2017; Stenner, 2022). These processes turned social life into a relational and emotional *freeze* during the lockdown.

In the middle of an emergency, it is not easy to differentiate between the rational responses and the measures substantiated only by a moral panic. Emergency situations, however, disclose the true nature of political life, potentially, the wish to exercise unmediated power over the lives of citizens (Agamben, 2005; Van Den Berge, 2020). "Necessity has no law" (Agamben, 2005, p. 1.)—but what comes after an emergency? And when does an emergency end? Absurdly, it was not an epidemiologist who forecast the end of the pandemic in the global media, though epidemiologists also had their cautious estimates. It was Bill Gates (McGrath, 2021). Van Den Berge has commented on the disputes concerning the measures taken during the pandemic as follows: "Let's hope that critical voices like those of Agamben will prevent us from accepting current emergency measures and biopolitical practices and policies as business as usual" (Van Den Berge, 2020, p. 5–6.). The pandemic has been and, to some extent, is still a real threat, but what kind of a threat exactly? The discourses by which we responded to it were inevitably embedded in risk society contexts and crisis communication with its specific discursive distortions confusing the overall picture. If public health threats are politically or economically misused, then will people trust medical experts when such trust becomes a question of life and death? Erosions in public-level epistemic trust (Li et al., 2023) are often compensated by further steps towards discipline, surveillance, and authoritarian rule. The Orban Government announced emergency governance on 11 March 2020, that, apart from a short interval of a few months, has been maintained ever since. Not each of the frequently taken legal measures has served the goals of protecting the community from the threats of the pandemic or the war in neighbouring Ukraine ("Helsinki Bizottság", 2024). Other examples for this state of exceptions include *one-night* legislation processes and the proliferation of priority investments, which exclude the locals from the decision-making processes, and legalize destructions in the natural and social environment, and the sales of the common resources.

3.6 Trickster Psychology

The rise of the trickster in our emergency era (Horvath & Szakolczai, 2020) is also documented in personality and organizational psychology (Perry, 2019). Dark triad characters appear in leadership positions in the intertwined, hegemonic systems of economic and political life. They maintain and use the chaos of permanent liminality to fish in troubled waters and represent the negative side of the trickster as arrogant, cunning, self-centred, predictably unreliable, and irresponsible superiors.

The dark triad is described as a collection of narcissistic traits, Machiavellism, and subclinical psychopathy, manifested in disagreeableness, callousness, cynicism, manipulativeness, hubris (grandiosity), emotional coldness, and impulsivity—but other psychopathologies, as schizotypal traits or substance use problems may further complicate the overall picture (Bell et al., 2021; Láng et al., 2018; Paulhus & Williams, 2002; Perry, 2019; Sadler-Smith, 2024). There are differences as for the relative strength of one factor over the other, for example, narcissistic persons are not primarily motivated by material advantages but by ego–identity goals; Machiavellians build a long-term strategy for manipulation, and psychopaths are characterized by predator strategies. Invariably, the overall pattern is a destructive one. Dark triad individuals treat the less powerful with some instrumental disdain, misuse the law, and transgress moral rules and norms (Bereczkei, 2016; Perry, 2019; Sadler-Smith, 2024). Dark triad, hubristic leaders have found their ways into most segments of social life, discovering new podiums in the domains previously uninhabited by them: for example, in academia, where their "bright" visions and utopias lead not to irreversible destructions but to mediocracy, even in the well-established systems with longstanding constructive and democratic traditions (Perry, 2019).

Is the dark triad complex a stable personality trait or an acquired condition shaped by situational factors? Studies on two similar concepts, the hubris syndrome (Owen & Davidson, 2009) and Keltner's power paradox (Perry, 2019) suggest that the problem is strongly influenced by situational factors. The proposition of the hubris syndrome, a new psychopathological construct was a conclusion of a study on US Presidents of the previous century by Owen and Davidson (2009). Several persons in the sample were characterized by narcissistic, antisocial, and histrionic traits. Narcissism involved perceiving the environment as merely an arena for exercising power and seeking fame. The persons had grave concerns about the presentation of own self, as well as about the significance of their own actions. They were characterized by a messianic stance, exaltation, omnipotence, and projective identification with the nation, and relied solely on their own judgements, while devaluing others' advice and rejecting all forms of mundane accountability. All these led to loss of contact with social realities, resulting in isolation, gradual strengthening of their antisocial traits, and self-confident incompetence as a histrionic factor. In this study, psychiatric symptoms and addictions were also common among the political leaders (Owen & Davidson, 2009).

A recent book on hubris defined it as a dopamine-high, addictive state, a "grandiose sense of self, characterized by over-confidence, pride, and contempt towards the advice and criticism of others" (Sadler-Smith, 2024, p. xii.). Sadler-Smith comes to similar conclusions, pointing out the risks inherent in cultic leadership where the leader is depicted as a *semi-divine* character, an important attribute of the trickster (Horvath & Szakolczai, 2020). A study by van Kleef et al. (2008) concluded that high power individuals are not only less responsive to others but their emotions "disproportionately sway the direction of social interactions" (p. 1320). For them, power becomes a zero-sum game with a tendency to abuse power, detachment from norms and ethics, and objectifying and devaluing those sustaining their rule but are excluded from power. Mechanisms described by Janis (2008) earlier in his classical study on groupthink maintain the cult of the hubristic leader, such as top-bottom, filtered communication, the concentration of power, the construction of a devalued and stereotyped enemy group, punishing the dissenters, and rewarding those who comply (Janis, 2008; Sadler-Smith, 2024). Hubristic leaders deliberately spread false information, betray, lie, and cheat. They want to control not only how people act and behave, but also their emotions, while they themselves remain insensitive to others' needs and sufferings (Sadler-Smith, 2024).

Destructions via the insanity of wars are probably the gravest consequence of economic and political malfunctioning. Today's soldiers, exposed to technological "innovations" may be slaughtered the moment they join a battle by some explosives or by just a drone. Their experiences of vulnerability and suffering are rarely witnessed, but are translated into soulless, "objective" numbers, data to be reported in the news; or are transformed into some sickly attraction in the mass media. In this globalized and distorted communication context unilaterally fuelling xenophobia, our in-built evolutionary mechanisms of sympathy and care will turn into learnt insensitivity and cannot stop the escalating aggression.

3.7 Conclusion

Today's popular attribute is *deep*, as, for example, deep learning, deepfake (Aczél & Veszelszki, 2023), and deep adaptation, a recent theory in *collapsology* (Bendell, 2018). Deep is to indicate highly complex, exhaustive, and intelligent qualities—an ocean of knowledge. Depth, however, as source domain for metaphorical mappings (Lakoff, 1993) does not only refer to thoroughness and complexities, but also to *crisis* (B. Erdos, 2025). The global-level crisis we are experiencing have many different facets and episodes, including growing inequalities, sharpening military conflicts, democracy deficits, and the acute problems of climate change. As the recent pandemic has revealed, these events will polarize human communities and magnify the oppositions. Globalization processes will probably continue without any significant melting pot effects. Group-based identities are invariably a source of deep concerns and conflicts, but now these conflicts are global and systemic, distributed and sharpened by today's info-communication technologies, and may culminate in cases of catastrophic evolution (Castells, 1997; Moghaddam, 2012).

While celebrating creativity and innovation, few thoughts are given to its responsible form, generativity. Generativity is creativity coupled with care and directionality, ensuring the survival of human civilizations. It is the concern about and positive contributions to the welfare and wellbeing of the next generation. It is conceived as a personal legacy: we attribute meaning and significance to our individual lives through generativity. Generativity is a manifestation of one's hopes beyond the individual: "I am what survives me" (Erikson, 1968, p. 141). The symbolic immortality expressed in generativity is essential for living an eudaimonic, good life (Bauer et al., 2005, 2008). Generativity appears in the studies about environmentally responsible behaviour as the psychosocial aspect of sustainability (Shiel et al., 2020).

Crises, stagnation, and deterioration give rise to generativity frustration (McAdams, 2018; Penezić et al., 2008). Generativity frustration as arrested transition, blocking or severely impairing the developmental processes in mature adulthood, is triggered by sudden societal and cultural changes. These changes leave older people with the impression that despite their deep generativity concerns, their accumulated knowledge, values, and experiences, having demanded considerable investments in terms of physical and symbolic resources, are now deemed useless (Cheng et al., 2008). Szakolczai (2017) comments on such entrapment as a sense of stasis and meaninglessness where the actions that magnify the problem are sold as the solutions.

Risks and liminality still sell well; but now we live our lives with the uneasy intuition that our future might have been sold already. Myths and tales teach us that the kings who are not humble enough, misusing their power and keeping gods' gifts to themselves instead of sharing it with others and sacrificing their own private lives to fulfil their personal mission will bring sufferings to the next generation. Minotaur, the monster feeding on young men and maidens, thus *devouring the future of the community*, was born only because the King of Crete was reluctant to sacrifice a splendid white bull, the gift of the Gods, his most precious property to ensure the welfare of the community (Campbell, 2008). Heroes were born to make the necessary adjustments when the time was out of its joint. However, no lonely hero, not even the avatars in technology (probably, these avatars the least) are able to tackle today's problematic complexities.

Is there a way out of the globalized, addictive maze? The great experiment of the Enlightenment resulted in the separation of the church from political power, and kept the focus on human rationality, perceiving the individual and the community as some tabula rasa to be filled with valuable knowledge while neglecting other aspects of human nature. Would a separation of the three intertwined systems of power, economy, politics, and info-communication systems delimit the main threat, mass manipulation directed more at people's affects than to the "purely rational" human mind? Probably, it would. But how could this work in an era when it is not the material resources or energy, but information that is seen as a key resource for both the economic and political systems? In such an envisioned system restoring the enmeshed boundaries, could we escape the proliferation of bureaucracy and finally give ethics and care priority over the formalities?

Today's democratic systems cannot flourish in the shadow of the hegemonic complexes of economic and political power and e-communication, the most powerful means of manipulation and control ever. The acute question raised by Nyíri (2024, p. 115) is as follows: "When democratic politicians are actually powerless, and mass-man mediocrity dominates, is there a way out that can lead to a humane yet functioning society?" Nyíri sees the solution in the emergence of new elites, an intellectual aristocracy, competent and responsible leaders, who, in the possession of classical education extending to other domains than *techné,* care about the welfare and wellbeing of the community—unlike their trickster predecessors. Is it possible in an era when "philosopher kings behave badly", themselves invariably falling victims to the addictive features of wealth and power? (Bloom, 2020, p. 628). Today's inconsistencies and the thin ideological glaze to cover the loss of values may warn us that we are about to enter an era when rough power will be used; manipulation prepares the grounds, but greed and aggression will finish the business of the trickster.

Csermely (2018) notes that our humanistic and ethical arguments, and the attitudes against authoritarian systems have been shaped by our biological evolution and are deeply rooted in the laws of nature. A complex system can respond to new challenges only by involving the nodes and creating new links in the periphery, therefore, deliberative democracy with its solid base of authentic, undistorted participation is not "only" a moral stance or an ideology, but a key to humankind's survival in times of crisis (Csermely, 2018). Is there a way to return to a workable democratic setting to ensure the sustainability of our systems? In other words, if we have already lost our key, could we find it? Are we searching for it where we *could* find it—or, obeying the rule of the streetlight effect, where the search is more *convenient*? (Watzlawick, 1993).

Our first-order solutions to sustainability problems demanding second-order solutions will only lead to deeper destructions. Lanyi, a human ecologist comments on our Potemkin-wellbeing and the blind search for the keys as follows:

> We deceived ourselves to the last second. We applied the term "production" to the consumption of our natural and cultural heritage, i.e., its mass transformation into waste; "prosperity" to joyless, compulsive squandering; "rational resource management" to the chase of profits; "progress" to man's ever-growing dependence on technological systems and logistical considerations. Since we have brought up our children in this spirit for generations, they cannot even imagine how they could live any other way (Lanyi, 2022, p. 11).

Potential positive scripts, deeply transforming and humanizing our relationship with the broad natural and cultural environments have never been considered globally—though the idea of relational responsibility, stemming in systems theory, has long gained grounds in the social sciences and humanities (e.g. McNamee & Gergen, 1999). Acknowledging our interdependence and recovering from our narcissistic traumas require deep changes in human relationships. Today, technological innovations spread fast, unlike socioecological theories that are revealing about the problems we are causing to ourselves and could be conducive to shared reflections. Community-level expressions of ecological worries ground the production of new commodities that seemingly reduce the adverse impact of forced economic growth. Concealed as redemptive developments, these often bring about grave problems, such as the newly emerging global conflicts for the possession of the rare earth elements necessary for the energy transition.

In this unbalanced growth, the poor could invariably keep their traditional roles as proper scapegoats for the social ills and their own miserable conditions (the "undeserving" poor), and as counterpoints to keep up the pressure on the rest of the population (Gans, 1971).

Kephart and Zellner (1991) have studied various alternative communities established in modernity. They have concluded that these came into being as a response to unmet human needs—from the "social policy" of the early Shakers to the hippie communities of the 1970s, providing their members with the opportunity for identity experimentations in an anomic societal setting. Today, many of the alternative communities respond to sustainability issues and the deepening problems of wellbeing. People follow off-the-grid lifestyles, a "slow" way of life, or join the deep adaptation movement (Bendell, 2018). These communities express their need for more natural and traditional lifestyles with immediate human relationships developing and thriving in the physical space, and with prospects for genuine creativity.

Overall, a-mazed societies do not favour reflexivity and systems thinking, as these attitudes and positions raise uneasy concerns about the inescapable need to delimit our greed, the very basis of today's "civilization". These concerns would interfere both with neoplasmic economic growth and with the abuse of political power. A quantum leap, a noetic turn from technologies to wisdom, to the knowledge that is not "objective" but empathetic and ethical is necessary to resolve the conflicts (Rojcewicz, 2021). Odysseus's arduous quest is a search for *eudaimonia*, a narrow road to happy life. It represents a harmony with our own fate. Daimons were the guides to the human soul in Greek mythology—if they are guiding us in the appropriate direction and we are responding to them accordingly in our actions, then we can live a meaningful and happy life. Eudaimonic wellbeing focuses on our strong personal beliefs and potentials for identity development, as well as the wish to identify what is the best and unique in us in terms of authenticity and excellence (Proctor & Tweed, 2016). It is about reaching an identity state with a balanced self-evaluation, and a considerable degree of openness to life's new challenges, while also adhering to our core values, the ones that foster social and environmental responsibility, and the genuine care of the self.

References

Aczél, P. (2024). The future mind—Skills, sciences and scruples in our coming a(I)ges. In K. Nyíri (Ed.), *Envisioning an electrifying future. Perspectives on visual learning* (Vol. 6, pp. 9–17). Hungarian Academy of Sciences—University of Pécs. https://www.researchgate.net/publication/387312058_Envisioning_an_Electrifying_Future

Aczél, P., & Veszelszki, Á. (Eds.). (2023). *Deepfake: A valótlan valóság [Deepfake: The irreal reality]*. Gondolat.

Agamben, G. (2005). *State of exception*. University of Chicago Press.

B. Erdos, M. (2014). Az addikció mint a fogyasztói társadalom nagy narratívája [Addiction as the grand narrative of consumer societies]. *Szociális Szemle, 7*(1), 29–41.

B. Erdos, M. (2025). *Mély felelősségek [Deep responsibilities]*. Jel-Kép. (in press).

Bakhtin, M. (1984a). *Problems of Dostoevsky's poetics*. University of Minnesota Press.

Bakhtin, M. (1984b). *Rabelais and his world*. Indiana University Press.

Bateson, G. (1972). *Steps to an ecology of mind. Collected essays in anthropology, psychiatry, evolution, and epistemology*. Jason Aronson.

Bauer, J. J., McAdams, D. P., & Pals, J. L. (2008). Narrative identity and eudaimonic well-being. *Journal of Happiness Studies: An Interdisciplinary Forum on Subjective Well-Being, 9*(1), 81–104. https://doi.org/10.1007/s10902-006-9021-6

Bauer, J. J., McAdams, D. P., & Sakaeda, A. R. (2005). Interpreting the good life: Growth memories in the lives of mature, happy people. *Journal of Personality and Social Psychology, 88*(1), 203–217. https://doi.org/10.1037/0022-3514.88.1.203

Bauman, Z. (1998). *Globalization. The human consequences*. Columbia University Press.

Bauman, Z. (2005). *Work, consumerism and the new poor*. Open University Press.

Beck, U. (1992). *Risk society. Towards a new modernity*. SAGE.

Bell, E., Kowalski, C. M., Vernon, P. A., & Schermer, J. A. (2021). Political hearts of darkness: The Dark Triad as predictors of political orientations and interest in politics. *Behavioral Sciences, 11*(12), 169. https://doi.org/10.3390/bs11120169

Bendell, J. (2018). Deep adaptation: A map for navigating climate tragedy. In *Institute for leadership and sustainability (IFLAS) occasional papers* (Vol. 2). University of Cumbria. (Unpublished). http://insight.cumbria.ac.uk/id/eprint/4166/

Benţa, M. I. (2021). The firefighter effect: Social pathology and corruption in liminal occupations. *International Political Anthropology, 14*(2), 103–111. https://doi.org/10.5281/zenodo.5721730

Bereczkei, T. (2016). *Machiavellizmus: A megtévesztés pszichológiája*. Typotex.

Berguno, G. (2001). The phenomenology of waiting. *Journal of the Society for Existential Analysis, 12*(2), 154–159.

Bloom, R. W. (2020). When philosopher kings behave badly. *International Journal of Intelligence and CounterIntelligence, 33*(3), 628–636. https://doi.org/10.1080/08850607.2020.1733387

Blühdorn, I. (2017). Post-capitalism, post-growth, post-consumerism? Eco-political hopes beyond sustainability. *Global Discourse, 7*(1), 42–61. https://doi.org/10.1080/23269995.2017.1300415

Brown, N. M. (2015). *Flawed consumers: Understanding the impact of intersectional political consumerism during the Chicago welfare rights era*. University of Illinois. https://core.ac.uk/reader/158311210

Buda, B. (2009). Nem elég ezeket a dolgokat medikalizálni…[Medicalising these is an insufficient approach…]. *Korunk, 20*(7), 34–36. http://korunk.org/?q=node/10873

Campbell, J. (2008). *The hero with a thousand faces*. New World Library.

Castells, M. (1997). *The information age: Economy, society, and culture. Volume II: The power of identity*. Blackwell.

Chen, Y., Xu, Z., Wang, P., Li, X. M., Shuai, Z. W., Ye, D. Q., & Pan, H. F. (2022). New-onset autoimmune phenomena post-COVID-19 vaccination. *Immunology, 165*(4), 386–401. https://doi.org/10.1111/imm.13443

Cheng, S. T., Chan, W., & Chan, A. C. (2008). Older people's realisation of generativity in a changing society: The case of Hong Kong. *Ageing & Society, 28*(5), 609–627. https://doi.org/10.1017/S0144686X07006903

Cohen, S. (2011). *Folk devils and moral panics*. Routledge.

COVID-19: Man in Germany suspected of killing his family and himself over fake vaccine certificate fears. (2021, December 7). *Sky News*. https://news.sky.com/story/covid-19-man-in-germany-suspected-of-killing-his-family-and-himself-over-fake-vaccine-certificate-fears-12489268

Csermely, P. (2004). Strong links are important, but weak links stabilize them. *Trends in Biochemical Sciences, 29*(7), 331–334. https://doi.org/10.1016/j.tibs.2004.05.004

Csermely, P. (2018). A demokrácia mint a túlélés többmilliárd éves evolúciós eszköze [Democracy as a Successful Evolutionary Survival Strategy]. *Magyar Tudomány, 179*(5), 615–623. https://doi.org/10.1556/2065.179.2018.5.3

Deci, E. L., & Ryan, R. M. (2008). Hedonia, eudaimonia, and well-being: An introduction. *Journal of Happiness Studies: An Interdisciplinary Forum on Subjective Well-Being, 9*(1), 1–11. https://doi.org/10.1007/s10902-006-9018-1

Deetz, S. A. (1992). *Democracy in an age of corporate colonization*. State.

Dellino, M., Lamanna, B., Vinciguerra, M., Tafuri, S., Stefanizzi, P., Malvasi, A., Di Vagno, G., Cormio, G., Loizzi, V., Cazzato, G., Tinelli, R., Cicinelli, E., Pinto, V., Daniele, A., Maiorano, E., Resta, L., De Vito, D., Scacco, S., & Cascardi, E. (2022). SARS-CoV-2 vaccines and adverse effects in gynecology and obstetrics: The first Italian retrospective study. *International Journal of Environmental Research and Public Health, 19*(20), 13167. https://doi.org/10.3390/ijerph192013167

Dunbar, R. I. M. (2002). Are there cognitive constraints on an e-world? In K. Nyíri (Ed.), *Mobile communication: Essays on cognition and community* (pp. 57–69). Passagen Verlag.

Erikson, E. H. (1968). *Identity: Youth and crisis*. Norton.

Fekő Á. (2021, December 12). Méltatlan a vita Kóbor János halála körül, de egy dologra rámutat [The dispute about János Kóbor's death is derogatory but is revealing]. *Mandiner.* https://mandiner.hu/velemeny/2021/12/belfold-feko-adam-velemeny-kobor-janos-halal-koronavirus

Firat, A. F. (1991). The consumer in postmodernity. *Advances in Consumer Research, 18*(1), 70–76.

Föhse, K., Geckin, B., Zoodsma, M., Kilic, G., Liu, Z., Röring, R. J., Overheul, G. J., van de Maat, J., Bulut, O., Hoogerwerf, J. J., Ten Oever, J., Simonetti, E., Schaal, H., Adams, O., Müller, L., Ostermann, P. N., van de Veerdonk, F. L., Joosten, L. A. B., Haagmans, B. L., van Crevel, R., van Rij, R. P., GeurtsvanKessel, C., de Jonge, M. I., Li, Y., Domínguez-Andrés, J., & Netea, M. G. (2023). The impact of BNT162b2 mRNA vaccine on adaptive and innate immune responses. *Clinical Immunology, 255*, 109762. https://doi.org/10.1016/j.clim.2023.109762

Freud, S. (1917). A difficulty in the path of psycho-analysis. In J. Stratchey (Ed.), *The standard edition of the complete psychological works of Sigmund Freud 17* (pp. 135–144) https://pep--web.org/search/document/SE.017.0135A?page=P0135

Fronczak, A., Mrowinski, M. J., & Fronczak, P. (2022). Scientific success from the perspective of the strength of weak ties. *Abstract Scientific Reports, 12*(1). https://doi.org/10.1038/s41598-022-09118-8

Gans, R. (1971). The uses of poverty: The poor pay all. *Social Policy, 2*(2), 20–24.

Gerő, M., & Sik, E. (2022). "Már nyomni sem kell"—A morális pánikgomb és a 2022. Évi választás. ["You don't even need to press it"—The moral panic button and the 2022 elections]. In B. Böcskei & A. Szabó (Eds.), *Az állandóság változása. Parlamenti választás 2022* (pp. 65–86). Gondolat Kiadó—MTA Társadalomtudományi Kutatóközpont Politikatudományi Intézet.

Glare, P. G. W. (1982). *Oxford Latin dictionary* (pp. 424–425). Clarendon Press.

Granovetter, M. S. (1973). The strength of weak ties. *American Journal of Sociology, 78*(6), 1360–1380. http://www.jstor.org/stable/2776392

Greco, M., & Stenner, P. (2017). From paradox to pattern shift: Conceptualising liminal hotspots and their affective dynamics. *Theory & Psychology, 27*(2), 147–166. https://doi.org/10.1177/0959354317693120

Greenfield, S. (2011). *ID: The quest for meaning in the 21st century*. Hodder and Stoughton.

Grof, S. (1985). *Beyond the brain: Birth, death, and transcendence in psychotherapy*. State University of New York.

Gross, M. (2016). Risk as zombie category: Ulrich Beck's unfinished project of the 'non-knowledge' society. *Security Dialogue, 47*(5), 386–402. https://www.jstor.org/stable/26294235

Gyulai, I. (2012). *A fenntartható fejlődés [Sustainable development]*. A Fenntartható Fejlődésért Alapítvány.

Hayward, K. (2002). The vilification and pleasures of youthful transgression. In J. Muncie, G. Hughes, & E. McLaughlin (Eds.), *Youth justice: Critical readings* (pp. 80–93). Sage. https://blogs.kent.ac.uk/culturalcriminology/files/2011/03/hayward-vilif.pdf

Hayward, K. (2016). *City limits: Crime, consumer culture and the urban experience*. Routledge-Cavendish.

Hearn, A. (2008). Meat, mask, burden: Probing the contours of the branded self. *Journal of Consumer Culture, 8*(2), 197–217. https://doi.org/10.1177/1469540508090086

Helsinki Bizottság: Negyedik éve él vissza a kormány a veszélyhelyzettel [Helsinki Committee: The government has been abusing the risk for four years]. (2024, March 12). *Szabad Európa* https://www.szabadeuropa.hu/a/helsinki_bizottsag_veszelyhelyzet_orban_kormany_rendeleti_kormanyzas/32858406.html

Hertrich, S. (2010 November 18–2011 January 29). Reality checking device [Digital artwork]. *Uncertain Spectator*. https://uncertain.empac.rpi.edu/artists/hertrich/

Hocoy, D. (2012). Sixty years later: The enduring allure of synchronicity. *Journal of Humanistic Psychology, 52*(4), 467–478. https://doi.org/10.1177/0022167812436427

Horvath, A. (1997). *The political psychology of trickster-clown. An analytical experiment around communism as a myth* (Papers 97/5, European Institute - Political and Social Sciences). Cadmus, EUI Research Repository. https://hdl.handle.net/1814/285

Horvath, A. (2021). The new age of disease: Technocratic mimetism. *International Political Anthropology Journal, 14*(2), 91–101. https://doi.org/10.5281/zenodo.5721724

Horvath, A., & O'Connor, P. (Eds.). (2022). *Liminal politics in the new age of disease. Technocratic Mimetism*. Routledge.

Horvath, A., & Szakolczai, A. (2020). *The political sociology and anthropology of evil: Tricksterology*. Routledge.

Janis, I. L. (2008). Groupthink. *IEEE Engineering Management Review, 36*(1), 36. https://doi.org/10.1109/emr.2008.4490137

Kampf, G. (2021). The epidemiological relevance of the COVID-19-vaccinated population is increasing. *The Lancet Regional Health - Europe, 14*(11), 100272. https://doi.org/10.1016/j.lanepe.2021.100272

Kassai, S. (2020). *Using interpretative phenomenological analysis (IPA) to assess recovery processes: Qualitative analysis of experience and identity*. L'Harmattan Kiadó—ELTE Pedagógiai és Pszichológiai Kar.

Kennedy, P. (2017). *Vampire capitalism: Fractured societies and alternative futures*. Springer. https://link.springer.com/content/pdf/10.1057/978-1-137-55266-2.pdf

Kennedy, P. (2020). 'All the better to eat you with!' The contribution of consumer culture to the rise of predatory capitalism. *Journal of Consumer Culture, 20*(3), 266–284. https://doi.org/10.1177/1469540519875993

Kephart, W. M., & Zellner, W. W. (1991). *Extraordinary groups: An examination of unconventional life-styles*. St. Martin's Press.

Kitzinger, D. (2000). A morális pánik elmélete [The theory of the moral panic]. *Replika, 40*(2), 23–48.

Kmietowicz, Z. (2021). Evidence is insufficient to back mandatory NHS staff vaccination, says House of Lords committee. *BMJ, 2021*(375), n2957. https://doi.org/10.1136/bmj.n2957

Lakoff, G. (1993). The contemporary theory of metaphor. In A. Ortony (Ed.), *Metaphor and thought* (pp. 202–252). Cambridge University Press.

Lakoff, G. (2014). *The all new don't think of an elephant!: Know your values and frame the debate*. Chelsea Green Publishing.

Láng, A., Birkás, B., Martin, L., Nagy, T., & Kállai, J. (2018). Schizotypal traits and the dark triad from an ecological perspective: A nonclinical sample study. *Psychological Reports, 121*(6), 996–1012. https://doi.org/10.1177/0033294117742655

Lanyi, A. (2022). *The philosophy of eco-politics*. L'Harmattan. https://openaccess.hu/node/93914/metadata

Li, E., Campbell, C., Midgley, N., & Luyten, P. (2023). Epistemic trust: A comprehensive review of empirical insights and implications for developmental psychopathology. *Research in Psychotherapy (Milano), 26*(3), 704. https://doi.org/10.4081/ripppo.2023.704

Lubics, O., Vadai, K., Magyaródi, T., & Nagy, H. (2024). Az élettel való elégedettség és a boldogságtól való félelem vizsgálata a Big Five személyiségfaktorok, valamint különböző demográfiai változók mentén [The role of fear of happiness, big five personality traits and demographic factors in life satisfaction]. *Mentálhigiéné és Pszichoszomatika, 25*(1), 1–12. https://doi.org/10.1556/0406.2024.00017

McAdams, D. P. (1985). *Power, intimacy, and the life story: Personological inquiries into identity*. Dorsey.

McAdams, D. P. (2018). "I am what survives me". Generativity and the self. In J. A. Frey & C. Vogler (Eds.), *Self-transcendence and virtue. Perspectives form psychology, philosophy and theology* (pp. 251–273). Routledge.

McCracken, G. D. (2008). *Transformations: Identity construction in contemporary culture*. Indiana University Press.

McGrath, L. (2021, December 7). Bill Gates thinks 'acute phase' of COVID-19 pandemic will end in 2022 despite Omicron. *Financial Post*. https://financialpost.com/personal-finance/high-net-worth/bill-gates-thinks-acute-phase-of-covid-19-pandemic-will-end-in-2022-despite-omicron

McKay, A. (2021). (Director) *Don't Look Up* (Film) Columbia Pictures, Eccentric Pictures Feigco Entertainment, Working Title.

McNamee, S. (2015). Radical presence: Alternatives to the therapeutic state. *European Journal of Psychotherapy & Counselling, 17*(4), 373–383. https://doi.org/10.1080/13642537.2015.1094504

McNamee, S., & Gergen, K. J. (1999). *Relational responsibility: Resources for sustainable dialogue*. Sage.

Mekler, E. D., & Hornbæk, K. (2016). Momentary pleasure or lasting meaning?: Distinguishing eudaimonic and hedonic user experiences. In *Proceedings of the 2016 CHI conference on human factors in computing systems* (pp. 4509–4520) https://www.kasperhornbaek.dk/papers/CHI2016_MomentaryPleasures.pdf

Mimoun, L., & Bardhi, F. (2022). Chronic consumer liminality: Being flexible in precarious times. *Journal of Consumer Research, 49*(3), 496–519. https://doi.org/10.1093/jcr/ucab073

Moghaddam, F. M. (2012). The omnicultural imperative. *Culture & Psychology, 18*(3), 304–330. https://doi.org/10.1177/1354067X12446230

Novikov, E. (2021). Does sickness have a meaning? *International Political Anthropology, 14*(2), 125–139. https://doi.org/10.5281/zenodo.5721777

Nyíri, K. (2024). *The collapse of democracies and the need for a new aristocracy*. https://www.researchgate.net/publication/387295102_The_Collapse_of_Democracies_and_the_Need_for_a_New_Aristocracy

Oltott volt Csollány Szilveszter, a lánya is megerősítette [His daughter has confirmed that Szilveszter Csollány was vaccinated]. (2022, January 30). *Világgazdaság*. https://www.vg.hu/kozelet/2022/01/oltott-volt-csollany-szilveszter-a-lanya-is-megerositette

Owen, D., & Davidson, J. (2009). Hubris syndrome: An acquired personality disorder? A study of US Presidents and UK Prime Ministers over the last 100 years. *Brain: A Journal of Neurology, 132*(Pt 5), 1396–1406. https://doi.org/10.1093/brain/awp008

Paulhus, D. L., & Williams, K. M. (2002). The Dark Triad of personality: Narcissism, Machiavellianism and psychopathy. *Journal of Research in Personality, 36*(6), 556–563. https://doi.org/10.1016/S0092-6566(02)00505-6

Penezić, Z., Lacković-Grgin, K., Tucak, I., Nekić, M., Žorga, S., Poljšak Škraban, O., & Vehovar, U. (2008). Predictors of generative action among adults in two transitional countries. *Social Indicators Research, 87*(2), 237–248.

Perry, C. (2019). Abusive and enduring leadership: A book review of Keltner, D. (2017). The power paradox: How we gain and lose influence. New York, NY: Penguin. *Journal of Leadership Studies, 12*(4), 46–51. https://doi.org/10.1002/jls.21606

Ponte, D. V., & Schäfer, L. (2013). Carl Gustav Jung, quantum physics and the spiritual mind: A mystical vision of the twenty-first century. *Behavioral Sciences (Basel, Switzerland), 3*(4), 601–618. https://doi.org/10.3390/bs3040601

Porter, S. (2021). Mandatory Covid-19 vaccination for healthcare workers: Vaccinated and unvaccinated people seem as likely to infect others. *BMJ (Clinical research ed.), 375*, n3027. https://doi.org/10.1136/bmj.n3027

Proctor, C., & Tweed, R. (2016). Measuring eudaimonic well-being. In J. Vittersø (Ed.), *Handbook of eudaimonic well-being* (pp. 277–294). Springer International Publishing/Springer Nature. https://doi.org/10.1007/978-3-319-42445-3_18

Propp, V. (1999). *A mese morfológiája [The morphology of tales]*. Osiris-Századvég.

Reith, G. (2004). Consumption and its discontents: Addiction, identity and the problems of freedom. *The British Journal of Sociology, 55*(2), 283–300. https://doi.org/10.1111/j.1468-4446.2004.00019.x

Richter, F. (2023, February 20). Global life expectancy: Closing the gap. *Statista*, https://www.statista.com/chart/2266/life-expectancy-by-world-region/

Rock Legend Kóbor, Singer of Original Version of Scorpions Classic "White Dove," Dies of Covid. (2021, December 6). *Hungary Today*. https://hungarytoday.hu/omega-singer-janos-kobor-dies-covid/

Rojcewicz, P. M. (2021). Existential intimacy of learning: A noetic turn from STEM. *Academia Letters, 2*. https://www.academia.edu/50834051/Existential_Intimacy_of_Learning_A_Noetic_Turn_from_STEM

Roth, J. D. (2006). The color of money addiction. *Journal of Groups in Addiction & Recovery, 1*(3–4), 1–3. https://doi.org/10.1300/J384v01n03_01

Sadler-Smith, E. (2024). *The hubris hazard and how to avoid it*. Routledge.

Sárosi, P. (2017). Kokain és morális pánik Budapesten az 1920-as évek média-beszámolói alapján [Cocaine and moral panic in Budapest in the 1920s media reports in Budapest]. *Socio.hu Társadalomtudományi Szemle, 7*(4), 43–76. https://doi.org/10.18030/socio.hu.2017.4.43. https://socio.hu/uploads/files/2017_4/26_sarosi.pdf

Shiel, C., do Paço, A., & Alves, H. (2020). Generativity, sustainable development and green consumer behaviour. *Journal of Cleaner Production, 245*, 118865. https://doi.org/10.1016/j.jclepro.2019.118865

Sik, E. (2016). Egy hungarikum: A morálispánik-gomb [A Hungaricum: The moral panic button]. *Mozgó Világ, 42*(10), 67–80.

Simon, M. (2018). Függőség és fenntarthatóság: Lokális élmény—Globális nézőpont [Addiction and sustainability: Local experiences from a global perspective]. *Jel-Kép: kommunikáció, közvélemény, media, 7*(2), 99–120.

Stenner, P. (2017). *Liminality and experience. A transdisciplinary approach to the psychosocial*. Palgrave Macmillan.

Stenner, P. (2022). The psychology of global crisis through the lens of liminal experience: Stuck in the middle with SARS-CoV-2. In M. Dege & I. Strasser (Eds.), *Global pandemics and epistemic crises in psychology: A socio-philosophical approach* (pp. 71–84). Routledge.

Stenner, P. & Kaposi, D. (n.d.). *Virus ante portas: The Covid-19 pandemic as a liminal hotspot.* https://diecisiete.org/actualidad/virus-ante-portas-the-covid-19-pandemic-as-a-liminal-hotspot

Szakolczai, A. (2001). In a permanent state of transition: Theorizing the East-European condition. *Journal for Theory and Practice of Liminal Phenomena, 1*(1) http://limen.mi2.hr/limen1-2001/arpad_szakolczai.html

Szakolczai, A. (2015). Marginalitás és liminalitás [Marginality and liminality]. *Regio, 23*(2), 6–29. https://regio.tk.hu/wp-content/uploads/SZAKOLCZAI_2015_2_6_29.pdf

Szakolczai, A. (2017). Permanent (trickster) liminality: The reasons of the heart and of the mind. *Theory & Psychology, 27*(2), 231–248. https://doi.org/10.1177/0959354317694095

Szakolczai, A. (2020). The end of Kantian Universalism: Fairground economy, police states, and the permanent apocalyptic sacrificial carnival (Part IV). *Voegelin View.* April 16. https://voegelinview.com/the-end-of-kantianism-fairground-economy-police-states-and-the-permanent-apocalyptic-sacrificial-carnival/

Szakolczai, J. M. (2021). "Nothing new in the west": Paralleling the war rhetoric and measures of the COVID-19 pandemic with the WW1 horrors described by Erich Maria Remarque. *International Political Anthropology, 14*(2), 113–124. https://doi.org/10.5281/zenodo.5721748

Thousands of fake Covid-19 certificates uncovered in Switzerland. (2021, December 23). *Swissinfo* https://www.swissinfo.ch/eng/thousands-of-fake-covid-19-certificates-uncovered-in-switzerland/47214700

Turner, V. W. (1974). Liminal to liminoid, in play, flow, and ritual: An essay in comparative symbology. *Rice University Studies, 60*(3), 53–92. https://hdl.handle.net/1911/63159

Turner, V. W. (1982). *From ritual to theatre*. PAJ Publications.

United Nations. (n.d.). *Inequality—Bridging the divide.* https://www.un.org/en/un75/inequality-bridging-divide

Van Beek, C. (2008). *Between hope and fear. Jean Monnet in Dutch politics in 2008.* Masterclass Montesquieu Instituut. https://www.montesquieu-instituut.nl/9353202/d/papers%20masterclass/paper_cees_van_beek.pdf

Van den Berge, L. (2020). Biopolitics and the coronavirus. Foucault, Agamben, Žižek. *Netherlands Journal of Legal Philosophy, 49*(1), 3–6. https://doi.org/10.5553/NJLP/.000097

van Kleef, G. A., Oveis, C., van der Löwe, I., LuoKogan, A., Goetz, J., & Keltner, D. (2008). Power, distress, and compassion: Turning a blind eye to the suffering of others. *Psychological Science, 19*(12), 1315–1322. https://doi.org/10.1111/j.1467-9280.2008.02241.x

Watzlawick, P. (1993). *The situation is hopeless but not serious*. W. W. Norton & Company.

Yearworth, M., Terry, A. J., Godfrey, P. S., & Edwards, G. (2010). Systems thinking research - Principles and methodologies to grapple with complex real world problems. In *INCOSE UK annual systems engineering conference (ASEC 2010)*. International Council on Systems Engineering UK (INCOSE UK). http://hdl.handle.net/1983/1677

Zuboff, S. (2019). Surveillance capitalism and the challenge of collective action. *New Labor Forum, 28*(1), 10–29. https://doi.org/10.1177/1095796018819461

Chapter 4
From Common Sense to Sensing: The Trickster in the Digital Era

4.1 A *Deep* Impact on the Human Component: The Disruptive Network

The chapter title is just as paradoxical as the phenomena it describes, as it implies the *reversal* of the natural flow of meaning-making. Greco and Stenner (2017) claim that today's info-communication technologies construe liminal hotspots by destroying boundaries and connecting spatial and temporal dimensions that in the past remained compartmentalized and were more manageable. The authors raise an example of a minimally liminal hotspot when a private phone call intrudes into a party setting. Here, re-establishing the boundary by spatially or temporally separating these two domains of private life resolves the arising relational tensions. This chapter discusses the emergence of maximally liminal hotspots via the use of info-communication technologies (ICTs). In some settings, the arising tensions are not relieved so easily.

E-communication has radically changed the natural spatial and temporal boundaries, and this enmeshment also extends to relational boundaries and the boundaries of the self upon entering the virtual space and starting their *onlife* (Floridi, 2015). As Waskul (2005) argues, the Internet is a distinguished space for liminality and ekstasis. In the virtual space, people do not meet each other in person: it is but their representations that meet—images and words. Encounters are almost exclusively mediated by symbols. A network is often visualized; however, the emerging picture is but an illusion, a snapshot, as this network is constituted by rapidly transforming nodes and connections. The system is in a constant motion. Further, the boundaries between the states of being connected or disconnected (marginalized) are rather vague: there might be entities, persons, or communities that are partially connected and are in a liminal, non-defined position. The nodes and links, if observed from a different perspective, will not appear the same (Soncul & Bollmer, 2020). When connecting in the liminal space, even in a video call, we are losing many of the

M. B. Erdos, *Transitions - Liminality as Lived Experience*,
https://doi.org/10.1007/978-3-031-96007-9_4

refined communication cues polished by our biological evolution. These phenomena create space for the playfulness and creativity of the liminoid (Turner, 1974), and for the malevolent distortions and characteristic impasses of trickster liminality (Horvath & Szakolczai, 2020).

Waskul (2005) has emphasized that the Internet disconnects the spaces as physical locations from the places as their sociocultural definition, and this is how it establishes a liminal ambiguity of betwixt and between. This liminality permeates the (inter)subjective dimensions:

> Indeed, the transformative ecstatic potency of the internet cannot be denied. We are all just a few mouse-clicks away from endless potentials for utter transformation: *everyone can be anyone; everybody can be anybody, everything can be anything; everywhere is anywhere* (Waskul, 2005, pp. 56–57, italics are mine).

Our conceptions on space and time serve as the frameworks for narrating our experiences; and time is understood in terms of spatial concepts (Castells, 1999; Lakoff, 1993). Castells differentiated between the traditional space of places, and the *space of flows*, partly independent of the physical realities. The concentration of control invariably occurs in the space of places, but with an emphasis on the flow of information between the global networks. In network societies, social institutions are transferred from the space of places into the space of flows, which creates an unbridgeable relational distance between the local societies and the respective institutions. The space of flows, with its nodes, hubs, and habitats not only transforms interpersonal and institutional relations but also creates *timeless time* with automated and simultaneous activities "the material arrangements allow for simultaneity of social practices without territorial contiguity" (Castells, 1999; p. 295). Timeless time in the space of flows is detached from our previous, biologically given or socially constructed constraints, enabling the simultaneity of actions, and more adventures into the virtual past and future domains. The constant flow of sensations (not experiences yet) changes both the perception of time and the patterns of experience.

The space of flow creates its own paradoxes: the space is expanding, establishing a practically unlimited network of potential encounters, and is also narrowing as a physical context for genuine, embodied encounters and shared meaning-making. The self is detached from their traditional roles, responsibilities, and requirements (Szécsi, 2016). The changing milieu facilitates practically infinite connections, but the commitments and responsibilities, if any, are not as deep as before. Consequently, in the contemporary, hyperconnected context, our lives are both connected *and* isolated, more than ever before (Floridi, 2015). Most of the onlife connections are surficial, as they are floating freely without embodied meanings, elaborated emotions, and deep motivations. Consequently, it is not contact but alienation that is deep, and to make up for the losses, users are trying more of the same: they are hunting for more connections, more likes, and more followers. However, the human brain is simply not able to manage too many relationships and interactions simultaneously (Dunbar, 2002). Thus, the networks only partially connect the liminal subjects in the space of flows (Soncul & Bollmer, 2020).

Recently, the space of flows has become complemented with *smart spaces* created by the Internet of things, comprising a diversity of smart but non-conscious beings incorporated into humans' personal environment, opening new business opportunities, and raising new ethical concerns on private life and data security, and on the blurring boundaries between machines and humans (Floridi, 2015; Lecomte, 2023).

In addition to the above pervasive liminal features, the momentary or longstanding disruption of previous boundaries, e-communication anchored in the symbolic but without the embodied significance of communication fosters polarization and creates illusionary or hallucinatory ("perfect") contents. If we take a closer look at the problem, however, this is not so. Not e-communication, but the *emotional-relational illiteracy* of the passivized recipients, and content providers' instrumental and economy-focussed views on human societies have brought about these changes. E-communication, as any technological development, is neither good nor bad. It cannot be. However, it has become a powerful means of both supporting and impairing the individual elements of our human behaviour complex (also in Chap. 1, *Living in a Dual Environment. Homo Symbolicus and Languaging*; Csányi, 2000), upsetting the delicate balance among the components of the complex, which has been polished by our intertwined biological and cultural evolution. Earlier, mechanistic and reductionist metaphorical mappings for humans—human-as-machine or human-as-computer (Pastor, 2021)—have been exhausted. In today's hegemonic complexes, people are mainly conceived as somewhat unreliable *computer peripherals* with their annoyingly unpredictable *algorithms*.

In the 1990s, the Internet was celebrated as a redemptive promise, comparable to today's predominantly positive visions on artificial intelligence (AI). We were under the impression that, in addition to finishing the business of enlightenment by polishing the human mind, the Internet would connect us globally and peacefully, fostering democracy and giving voice to the supressed. People would share their knowledge freely and resolve their conflicts as they would recognize what is common in all of us through the regular, global-level encounters in our newly formed global village. The introduction of the broadband Internet and the proliferation of expensive software solutions parallel to the institutionalization and commercialization of the e-world, strengthening our dependence on e-service providers, have radically changed this utopistic view (Morris & Berman, 2000). We have soon found ourselves amidst the rapidly multiplying facets of the digital divide—from the early problems of physical access to the potential outcomes of being disconnected or loosely connected (Van Dijk, 2020). Today, the differences between free and paid AI-based solutions, coupled with users' (usually lack of) critical-reflective skills have further *deepened* the divide.

As Geraci et al. (2022) claim, access to fast Internet eroded the bridging (solidarity) aspects of social capital and decreased civic and political engagement. These strong disconnecting tendencies are rather ironic in an era of network societies. Currently, our technical evolution transgresses our social and psychological preparedness. Social media messages (not meanings yet) with their strong affective components are used as identity prostheses, but are subject to flaming and polarizing, potentially turning neutral positions or simple dislike into sharp hostility (Dunbar, 2002). Our biological evolutionary legacy and the controversial impacts of the recent technology-dominated evolution in the digital era have created crucial inconsistencies. The role of direct experiences has diminished, and the new e-media, finishing the business of the radio and television, has become the main means of constructing and defining social realities.

In this context, studies on trust (Botsman, 2017) and on the psychology of deception (Bereczkei, 2016) represent the two sides of the same (bit)coin. Distortions and extremities are interesting and sell well; therefore, they are often deliberate, resulting in immediate financial gains for those who control the contents and searches. A study has demonstrated that fake news spread about ten times faster and much deeper than valid information: "falsehood diffused significantly farther, faster, deeper, and more broadly than the truth in all categories of information" (Vosoughi et al., 2018, p. 1146). Most recently, within just 1 year between 2019 and 2020, deepfake, creating a false identity by manipulating and plagiarizing a real person's identity supported by AI has increased from 14,678 to about 100 million videos (Köbis et al., 2021; Tari, 2023). Deepfake is more than mere body-snatching or purchasing identity prostheses—it is the sales of priceless human *identities* that cost one a lifetime to build.

We have long been trained by our biological evolution that seeing must be believing (Tari, 2023). Is it still an advantage in the virtual world, burdened with collective hallucinations? Recent changes in information processing, for example, multitasking, have made us less reflective, and, consequently, more vulnerable. By extending the boundaries of sensing, heavy Internet users are immersed in a constant flow of information with a negative impact on conceptual thinking and logic (Greenfield, 2011). Dividing one's attention is a loss in *selective attention*—a loss of focus and coherence (Greenfield, 2011; Tari, 2023). The individual's specific and integrated perspective and a reflective phase for the thoughtful assessment of the resources are usually missing. Critical reflectivity, among others, demands the use of diverse resources that are hypothetically available, but entrapment in a filter bubble of consonant views would question free access.

What we are using for several hours a day would not leave our abilities intact; this is but an overestimation of humans' capacities to control their environment (McLuhan & Fiore, 2012). The misuse of digitalization has led to emotional incontinence and a loss of sense of reality, for example, attributing human qualities to a nonhuman entity and act accordingly (Greenfield, 2011; Tari, 2023). In this context, the boundaries between dream, fantasies, and physical realities have become blurred.

Parallel and in relation to these changes, there are considerable losses in mindfulness and empathy (Greenfield, 2011). Emojis compare with our highly refined communication channels as a blunt stone tool to today's micro-robotics. Online aggression in the virtual challenges leads to *learned insensitivity*, and new types of victimizations (Tari, 2023, p. 247).

Self-evaluations have become as unreliable as their virtual resources. The number of followers, as well as the likes and dislikes are not only about momentary positive feelings or financial gains. Likes and automatically generated positive feedbacks received from human or nonhuman influencers are but a cheap way of maintaining feeble identities in a world of unattainable ideals and role models. Conflict resolution and the management of negative emotions are exchanged for a virtual runaway intertwined with some punishing aspects, e.g. disabling a previous partner in one's personal network or the tormenting and unrelenting forms of cyberbullying.

Consumerism has developed its virtual responses to the basic human need for individual and group-based identity construction, so you can buy your avatars in the video games by providing your data and spending your time and money. These avatars transgress the personal and social limitations and pains of identity development, thus enlarging the addictive potential of virtual reality. The videogames are substantially different from children's traditional role play taking place in the physical environment, demanding their own creativity, sensitivity to diverse social cues, the acknowledgement of the conventions of the game, as well as learning to manage the associated emotions in the here and now. As in this constant flow of information there is no time for reflection and integration, we are also losing the ability to construe a coherent personal narrative, a basis for the continuity of our identity.

And now we have artificial intelligence to synthesize the vast amount of information that we are indeed unable to manage. (Should we?) Artificial intelligence is a magic word recycled from the 1950s, but it is not necessarily a precise one. It suggests that we encounter an entity capable of producing its own, conscious understandings of the world (; Z. Karvalics, 2015; Katz, 2012; Smith, 2024). The Latin word *intelligere* means to *understand.* We attribute full intentionality, and thus, intelligence to this highly refined data-processing system because the analogy makes comprehending AI much easier than studying the underlying mechanisms would (Dennett, 1987). AI collects but does not understand information. It accumulates the pieces of data that we humans have produced, processes them, and organizes them into larger, preferably coherent units. By processing information, AI generates *messages*—but *meaning attribution* invariably remains a human activity. Message is not yet meaning (Stonier, 1996). How does the message fit into the existing frameworks of the recipient? What is the ethical value of the message? Are there any inherent creative potentials in the message? Could errors, and seemingly irrelevant but potentially important data from the margins, be transformed into a source for the creative and innovative renewal of knowledge? AI with its statistically grounded nonmental operations could not respond to similar questions.

Most aspects of the human behaviour complex shaping human consciousness are missing and will always be missing from AI's repertoire (Csányi, 2000; B. Erdos, 2025; Smith, 2024). The three domains of this complex comprising more than 20 elements are connected by strong positive synergies to ensure our adaptation. AI is prepared to imitate certain human actions, follow rules and plans, design its own tools, and, within its limitations, use human languages. Social behaviour patterns and important mechanisms of the synchronization of behaviour, however, are embodied human functions related to our emotional life. Empathy, aggression management or developing group-based and individual identities, and rituals are beyond AI's scope—in these domains, its ability is restricted to imitation.

As for AI's constructive abilities, the Turing Test (Pinker, 2006) suggests that if a human–computer conversation is identified as a human–human conversation by humans, then the machine can think. AI-generated responses can indeed be mistaken for the human ones, but would the conversation work without our meaning-attribution strategies? How about a machine–machine conversation? Where does it lead without the embodied and emotionally loaded *experiences,* motivation, and directionality? How does that sound to the human ear? Would these exchanges show the constructive-responsive features of a human dialogue? Currently, even in human–machine interactions, the conversations rapidly turn from the initial philosophical depths into mere intellectualizations, leading from the now and here to nowhere. Considering Bruner's (1985) two main modes of thinking, in the realm of paradigmatic mode with a focus on logic, analysis, and categorizing, AI has its major strengths; but the narrative mode describing the meaning of one's experiences with an emphasis on authenticity is a modus operandi that remains beyond AI's scope of development.

The core metaphor behind AI's intelligence is ants' society, working hard for a superpower responsible for their survival. Neither we humans are ants, nor AI and its creators are our queen (B. Erdos, 2025). AI is an object, and in this sense, is *objective,* but is neither ethical nor emotional; and objectivity is not *balance,* as balance comes from reflection. AI lacks reflection and genuine intentionality. It can learn rules; but the motivations, and the empathetic-emotional basis of our reflective ethics to be applied in unique and novel situations will be missing. Further, it is just as objective as the knowledge communities of humans are, which provide AI with the information it feeds on. Consider that the Internet is rich in destructive and self-destructive contents, and a personalized AI may echo its user's desires or negative thoughts, which might even cost human lives (El Atillah, 2023; Yang, 2024). In this sense, AI is a *mirror* to humankind, reflecting a picture that is rather accurate, but is *flat,* as important dimensions are missing. Hasty and greedy reliance on AI technologies may result in some trouble. For example, automated translations are often a source of confusion, diminishing consumers' trust in the marketed products.

Weiser's (1999) notions on the complementary relationship between humans and their digital environment, creating a harmony in analogy to humans' earlier connections with the complexities of our natural environment have recently been echoed by Z. Karvalics (2015) in his review article on AI developments. This positive scenario will collapse if we continue to invest in the technologies at the expense of the human "component" (Tari, 2023; Yoon, 2022). The relationship between humans and human-made AI is often depicted as a competition, or, in another scenario termed alarmist by Z. Karvalics (2015), as a *fight.* AI is highly efficient in data processing. Hopefully, it will finally be capable of highly specialized information processing and synthesis without direct and continuous human intervention to screen for its "hallucinations" when miming omniscience. The current mainstreaming effect, synthesis of the most frequent only, and uniform representations to substitute humans' unique ones might be an early shortcoming—or part of the data business governed by political and economic interests. For example, AI is now being used to "assist" students in the hard task of understanding abstract concepts (Wen, 2024). This way, it is not AI that is learning about polysemy, but humans are learning about monosemy.

Though AI is neither human nor humane, and neither intelligent (conscious) nor uniquely creative, it could be the most powerful assistant for data management ever, always in need of close and ethical human control. Misusing its potentials is a threat to be interpreted in the emerging online contexts of trickster liminality.

4.2 Manipulating Identity. Fake Perfection in the Virtual Space

Portrait editing to eliminate the presumed shortcomings in one's appearance has been a tradition since the invention of portrait painting. Our portrait, as a visual image of our self is an important objectification of our identity, taken at a certain time and place. A portrait involves a considerable degree of intersubjectivity: the photographer's or the painter's conception and ability to relate and interpret the subject's self-state is crucial in the process. What we can see in the mirror is how others see us, whereas an authentic portrait is how a sensitive observer sees us when connecting the skin-deep features to one's identity. Though they are different, both the mirror and the portrait create a special space, a heterotopia that is distinct from the simple physical places (Foucault, 1967). Our reflection in the mirror is just as physical as the waves of light the mirror reflects. It is not fully material: touching our image in the mirror is touching the mirror, while the image is quickly changing as we are approximating it. Similarly, we can touch a static portrait, the physical reality, the texture of the photo, or a painting only—but not the body that it represents. While the mirror is connecting the real and the virtual, a portrait is more specific, as it opens the gate for alternative or opposing meanings and transformations (Foucault, 1967; Mészáros, 2011). Stenner (2017) in his analysis on Magritte's famous picture *Ceci n'est pas une pipe* has raised similar questions. The picture of the pipe *and* the title disconnecting the work from the physical reality of the object together are a powerful reminder of the nature of Baudrillard's concept (Wolny, 2017), the *simulacrum* disconnecting the object from its physical representation. The observer must reflect on the potential self-referential nature inherent in the sign. The picture as a simulacrum is neither meant as a representation nor as an imitation, but the picture creates its own (hyper)reality—a reality for a different reality (Wolny, 2017). In these artistic manifestations, the derealization of the physical environment is rooted in liminoid playfulness and creativity. It may also represent the artist's reflection on transformative liminality facilitated by symbol use. The reality of the artistic representation overwrites the physical, masked reality. In Oscar Wilde's novel, *Dorian Gray,* the hero's development is corrupted by his own narcissism and psychopathy. He is young, innocent, and beautiful, but is slowly becoming indifferent to other people's sufferings and turns into a criminal. His evil deeds leave his beautiful face unchanged; it is his secret portrait, symbolizing his supressed reflective self, which is carrying the burdens of an immoral life, and is revealing the hero's evil character, the traces of a wasted life.

Selfies may echo narcissistic destructions. A photo-shopped selfie, unlike a portrait, lacks the intersubjective relational frame of creation. It is about how we want others to see us. This, as an enhancement and an artificial prolongation of Goffman's (1959) impression management may extend to the point of continual and compulsive narcissistic preoccupations. The selfie reflects our own visions of an often-compelling *ideal, "perfect" self*, or, in reaction to the arising tensions, a liminal *carnival self.* With selfies, human narcissism with its ups and downs has inhabited a new, expanding, complex, and mischievous environment, the world of practically limitless opportunities to manage and present one's public image. When measured against other "perfect" (photo-shopped) images, the discrepancy between the ideal self and the current self is a source of discontent and worries. These new vulnerabilities have established new anxieties, for example, selfitis: being constantly preoccupied and worried about others' reactions to the online presentation of the self (Lowe-Calverley & Grieve, 2018; Monacis et al., 2020). Anxieties over perfection often lead to glorifying and following the talentless, the carnivalesque, the blatant, and the fake. Polarizations and transformations are inherent in these practices: the targeted "perfection" of the selfies reside somewhere in Utopia; or the reversals, the contra-ideal selves are pictured.

4.3 Beyond the Minimally Liminal

The ways we are misusing ICTs occasionally lead to maximally liminal hotspots. These are the cases in which simple spatial or temporal rearrangements would not help anymore: the hotspots as contexts for arrested transition processes intrude deeply in one's relational and personal spheres. Access to potentially traumatizing and damaging contents of the dark web strengthening (self)destructive patterns is a well-known problem. Getting a dear-john letter or a death notification in a crowded mall while you are chatting with your acquaintances will probably leave you paralysed by the shock, unable to resolve the inconsistencies inherent in the situation. "Witnessing" your loved one or your role model in the virtual space appearing in a hard porn—not a real scene, just an example of deepfake as identity plagiarism—is even more shocking as it is related to *trust*, a fundamental human virtue. Deepfake involving speech synthesis, face swapping, face reanimation and spoofing, and using these for malevolent tricks, however, have their strong potentials to destroy confidence not only in our close interpersonal relationships but in economic and political life as well, eroding good fame and public trust (Aczél, 2023). Studies have shown that our brain detects fake contents (e.g. deepfake) more effectively than we consciously acknowledge (Tari, 2023). Thus, a tension emerges between one's subconscious processing and open judgement. However, the conflict may even *increase* suggestibility, unless the person tolerates the arising ambiguities and uncertainties exceptionally well.

Or how about the virtual world of the living dead? There have been visions on future technological advances promising eternal life by uploading the contents of our brain after our death into the virtual space, known as the fallible Whole Brain Emulation project. Beyond this Tithonian promise, virtual reality has already intruded into the realities of life and death, dissolving the boundary that has facilitated a separation that humans have considered vital throughout history (Cubitt, 2020; Eliade, 1961). For example, Salvador Dali is "interactively" greeting the visitors in a museum. In the JFK Unsilenced Project, long-deceased President John Kennedy is delivering his speech that he had never been able to (Veszelszki, 2023). Recently, an "as if", more haunting than lifelike image of Zoltán Kodály, the Hungarian composer has been "interviewed" in a series in the Hungarian television, where AI regularly meets AI (Karsa, 2025). How would these persons have felt about these somewhat bizarre animations, had they been informed while alive?

Establishing the continuing bond with the deceased person (Neimeyer et al., 2014) is not about ready-to-use animations. It is an interpretative and constructive process of one's deeply personal, embodied memories to canalize the grief experience. Today, when we have developed refined copyright laws, the question may arise who the owner of one's *image* of identity—imitating, but not re-constructing their speech, gestures, and mimics, while speaking about their past ideas—is. Can identity be a public property? Can it be privatized? Can it be inherited, as, for example, a photo or the copyright of their works? The animations are used for commercial purposes. "Interactivity" and "study purposes" are used as appealing catchwords to legitimize and celebrate such actions. It seems that people will have to write VDNRs, virtual do-not-resuscitate orders, to escape unwanted, "animated", and distorted virtual immortality.

Computer-generated images are now being "born" and take over the role of human influencers, shaped to be "sensitive" to users' need with their calculated imperfect perfectness. Baby Ellis, the Swedish CGI-baby "born" in 2019 to popularize the products for the families with babies was not a perfect fit. Customers were attentive but not enthusiastic enough (Guld, 2023). No wonder—the baby was deliberately designed not to look fully human and resembled an unfortunate changeling from a Celtic fairy tale.

4.4 Windows for Gates: Panopticon and Synopticon as Late Modern Ritual Spaces

Digitalization gave rise to a new form, surveillance capitalism, using and shaping the totality of human interactions, and turning nonmarket interactions into marketable commodities. The accumulation and synthesis of data enables relatively reliable and fast future predictions concerning individual and collective-level consumer or political behaviour (Zuboff, 2019). Zuboff uses a new term, surveillance capitalism, to describe a formation that gives rise to new forms of manipulation, control, and exploitation, three inseparable social phenomena. In this global formation, political and economic powers are firmly intertwined with the refined use of info-communication technologies, the surveillance engines. Interconnectedness among the corporations is governed by the utilitarian principles of coopetition, flexibly changing collaborative, and competitive strategies to maximize profits (Iványi, 2023).

In surveillance capitalism, the goal is to automate us and arouse craving for mass-produced commodities (Zuboff, 2019). Before rejecting the idea as another conspiracy theory, consider that the mechanisms applied in the process are akin to the sociocultural technologies described in Skinner's book, *Beyond Freedom and Dignity* (1971), eliciting severe public indignation on its first publication. Skinner claimed that people would feel happier, and societies would be better organized if their behaviour were gradually shaped to follow the expected directions. Here, some core questions arise: *Who* are the ones entitled to shape people's behaviour and *what* are the favourable directions in a global system? Can we escape the rule of the dark triad leaders, frequently appearing in political and economic life? What if such transformations will lead to total, technocratic authoritarian control, to the dystopia of *Brave New World* (Huxley, 1932), finally coupled with, or followed by, total anarchy, as history has already taught us several times? Huxley used Nikolai Berdyaev's thoughts on utopias as an epigraph for *Brave New World*. Berdyaev was a Russian philosopher who had personally experienced the resulting devastations of the tireless attempts by the Soviets to realize their utopias. In *The End of Our Time,* Berdyaev (1933) expressed his hopes for the emergence of cultivated classes that finally evict utopias, opting for less perfectness but more freedom.

Zuboff (2019) argues that predominantly, this is not the era of Big Brother's physical violence anymore, but that of the Big Other, feeding on information and personal experiences. If you do not agree to using your data during a search, then you are excluded from the information that you would not only value but also need for social participation. Value for value—and this is a deal. But is this deal balanced enough? There is a feature shared by the Big Brother and the Big Other: their goal is hegemony through the manipulation and erosion of identity. Zuboff (2019) comments on Weiser's (1999) visions, referring to the unpredictable power given now, shaping our societies in unprecedented ways. Weiser (1999, p. 9) conceives totalitarianism as a social context originally in contrast with anarchy; however, he notes that "instrumentarian power can make totalitarianism look like anarchy". It does not merely "look like"; the anarchy of permanent liminality is indeed a strategy to establish and maintain totalitarian rule (Szakolczai, 2017). Thus, socio-technological dreams seem more of a nightmare for the most of us. We perceive freedom as a long-term, predictable guarantee and source for personal welfare and wellbeing, and the uniqueness of our identity as our precious achievement and compass in life.

Efforts to colonize private life have led to grave worries concerning China's social credit system, often seen as a refined online Panopticon (Csepeli, 2020). The current system seems to be more about building trust than distrust. However, blacklisting (more than whitelisting) with its extreme consequences have their inbuilt traditions in the countries with a communist past. In the current social credit system, people must transfer private information about themselves to increase the accuracy of evaluations that may or may not be informative about their overall trustworthiness (Loefflad et al., 2024). The social credit system is the amalgamation of financial and social trustworthiness intruding into people's private lives, which fact makes it obscure enough to substantiate the worries. The system integrates playful and competitive elements and rewards to attract more and more users. This is a twenty-first-century application of Skinner's (1971) sociocultural technology, seeing freedom and happiness in a society as the results of successfully shaping people's behaviour in the "favourable" directions, so that they would also *want* what they are required to do. The question, again, is *who* will decide what is favourable and what is not.

Total social control in the digitalized world with its smart and AI-based solutions is a well-grounded threat and is invariably sold in the name of enhancing safety and security. The postmodern Panopticon does not differ in its fundamental goal, surveillance (Foucault, 1977). However, today's technologies of surveillance are much more refined. Diverse forms of online censorship have appeared, such as restricted access to the Internet, blocking the contents, and enabling secret service activities (Iványi, 2014). When surfing on the Internet, earlier searches will automatically lead to certain types of information and guide us into specific user communities. The creation of filter bubbles, quasi-segregated communities of consumer preferences, including the consumption of political ideologies and dogmas, are a new mechanism for mainstreaming and control.

Digitalization has established an all-inclusive Panopticon, a social surveillance system to observe and control the many by the few; but it has also led to the emergence of the Synopticon where the few are observed and admired, but not controlled, by the many (Doyle, 2011; Mathiesen, 1997). As for their origins, both the Panopticon and the Synopticon are ritual settings. In the Panopticon, a heterotopy of deviation to establish and maintain discipline and exclusion (Foucault, 1967), the observers can control the results of a degradation ceremony. In the Synopticon, the masses can observe, testify, and celebrate the successes of late modern self-appointed business heroes and politicians. Traditionally, witnessing the hero's actions established a transformative crisis heterotopy. Nowadays the refined use of ICT may trick the enthusiastic witnesses, the observers confined to the virtual space, for whom seeing is invariably believing.

Thus, the Synopticon as a newly emerging ritual space serves several different purposes: amusement for the masses in the liminoid contexts and increasing exploitation by extending trickster liminality. The two contexts, however, might not be so different as they initially seem. While we are attending to the amusing and funny episodes, or the diversions as political "rubber bones", not-so-funny events may occur in the background. The Synopticon transforms the traditional ritual *gate* leading to a new social position and identity into a *window,* through which those stuck at (but not standing *on*) the threshold of liminality, are gazing at the new chosen ones while assuming the position of an enchanted and helpless child with very limited autonomies. The new media have opened the gates leading to "the proliferation of inauthentic pseudo-selves" (Cubitt, 2020, p. 18; Soncul & Bollmer, 2020). In the discursive labyrinth of a-mazed modernity (Chap. 3, *Liminal Experiences in Late Modernity. A-Mazed Societies and Institutionalized Craving*), the locals may admire or hate the globals in power, but they can do so only in the space of flows—at a safe physical distance. The intertwined processes of the Panopticon and the Synopticon establish and affirm the utterly unequal distribution of power, enabling the few to manipulate the many. In the Synopticon, the political is depicted as personal (Szabó, 2020). However, the personal is carefully managed and is not so personal and unique as it seems. The immediacy of communication is often but a mass-level hallucination. Unlike the masses, the few in power have abundant resources to successfully control their public image. On the other hand, the information *conservatively* shadowing the ordinary individual for a lifetime and potentially paralysing their identity development processes are a source of new worries and genuine limitations.

Beyond the well-known data security threats, digitalization may lead to extremes in *hyper-banalization*. Originally, the term was introduced by Hayward (2016) to characterize societal (structural) reaction formation to deviance as an attempted escape from the routines of everyday life. Hyper-banalization is a technique to tame the *horror vacui*, the dread of the unknown and the uncertainties inherent in liminality, and of *creativity*, potentially leading to substantial changes. The measures involved in the process are described as rational, meant to create stability—but they only lead to absurdities and further uncertainties, as obsessive–compulsive, bureaucratic strange loops. By chasing meaningless perfection, these systems gradually become incompatible with the demands of everyday life. The digitalization of one's personal data and transferring most of the administration into the virtual space have generated new, unexpected confusions by dissolving the previous boundaries in the hope of creating a new and all-embracing order.

A woman in her early eighties had received a mail (by regular post) requiring her to immediately act upon a 113-year-old problem that had previously gone unnoticed, and as such, had been unproblematic. Her mother's name was misspelled in her birth certificate, dated back to 1911. A common issue in contemporary Hungary where people spoke many different dialects and similar misunderstandings of oral communication were quite common upon entering the data in the registry; but in those days, *people knew who they were*. So did the woman's mother, and she used the correct version of her family name, identical with those of her nine siblings, throughout her life as her identity card also proved. Her daughter was not aware of the problem, if there was any. In the notice, she was offered two alternatives: changing all her personal documents, to be invalidated in the forthcoming weeks and introduce the "correct" data found in the 113-year-old birth certificate; or, by initiating an online legal procedure, changing her mother's name in the birth certificate.

In August 2024, I could receive several *system*-generated automated e-mails: a premature library notice, and an email requesting me to immediately hand in the final report of an ongoing project. I could not even interpret the third one from an insurance company as I had not had any business with them. When I tried to resolve the latter issue in response to their mail, they were asking for the non-existent contract number, without which they could not proceed. It seems that digitalization will keep us busy in various, and occasionally rather senseless ways.

4.5 Conclusion

As Edward O. Wilson, the founder of sociobiology commented in 2009, “The real problem of humanity is the following: We have Paleolithic emotions, medieval institutions and godlike technology” (Ratcliffe, 2016). Where are the anchors of stability, our own chances to find a reinterpreting community who would recognize the oar as a winnowing shovel now,[1] when we are constantly surfing on the Internet? Human development has proceeded from the predominant use of physical power as the main resource to be followed by a focus on energy, and then information (data) in late modernity. Information has a system-organizing power (Stonier, 1996) and as such, it is the main concern in today’s knowledge-based societies. Data and information, however, are not to be mistaken for knowledge, meaning, consciousness, and conscientiousness, which are central to human existence. The symbolic domain, our mode of existence in the virtual space, has become a key concern in the areas of life where its power was not salient before. Despite early, optimistic predictions, the new resources and chances offered by digitalization have been expropriated by a complex and obscure network connecting those who are judged relevant and excluding others deemed insignificant (Nyíri, 1999). The processes deepening the digital divide are accelerated in the era of robotics, automation, and artificial intelligence.

Creativity is central to the human behaviour complex and is manifested in the continual reconstructions of our physical and cultural environments. These reconstructions are connected to our identities (Csikszentmihályi, 1996). Today, when performance is measured globally and against the talents and achievements of those who are exceptionally gifted or pretend to be, many people are discouraged from using and developing their inborn talents. They are the talented locals who cannot enter the global competition; they are usually invited to purchase some ersatz products to entertain themselves and use up their creative energies in profitable, consumerist ways.

Castells’ early warning continues to be true in this novel context: “The Internet brings us face to face with the mirror of who we actually are. So I would rather work on ourselves rather than close down the net. The fight is against the self not against the net” (Castells, 1999, p. 298). The risks inherent in AI are not of artificial but of human origin. The limitless virtual space with its dissolving boundaries and anonymity is a new and comfortable liminal home for the trickster. People are not only entrapped but are often lost in the maze of hyperreality; and the social and cultural consequences of hyperreality are real.

[1] In reference to the story of Odysseus, commented in more detail in *Chap. 3, Liminal Experiences in Late Modernity. A-Mazed Societies and Institutionalized Craving.*

Being immersed in a continuous flow of sensations without reflections is an infinite source of liminal hotspots. The uncertainty of information in the virtual environment, coupled with the strong polarization of meaning, have led to rapid alternations between naivety and paranoid positions. Communication in the e-world has some striking similarities with the fragmentation characteristic of trauma processes, as described, for example, by van der Kolk (2015). Communication is directed to the senses, and is highly intensive, while the potentials for integration have diminished or disappeared. This results in the discontinuity of narratives in the rapidly changing symbolic contexts of unusual and uncontrollable complexities. Thus, a-mazed digital societies establish the culture of trauma, characterized by attention deficit, anxieties, and addictions. Yoon (2022, p. 95.) commenting on Harari's critical views concerning the twenty-first-century developments argues as follows: "After many centuries of seeking authority in the Gods, and in Kings and in priests, in the modern age, we as individuals have learned to listen to ourselves, to follow our heart, and to be true to ourselves". What we are about to lose in this new digital era are exactly our elaborate emotional life, ethics, and identities. This way, we have established some additional preconditions for global-level troubled becoming.

References

Aczél, P. (2023). A deepfake mint hazugság: együttműködés a megtévesztésben [Deepfake as lie: Cooperation in deception]. In P. Aczél & Á. Veszelszki (Eds.), *Deepfake: a valótlan valóság* (pp. 30–40). Gondolat.

B. Erdos, M. (2025). *Mély felelősségek [Deep responsibilities]*. Jel-Kép. (in press).

Berdyaev, N. (1933). *The end of our time*. Sheed & Ward.

Bereczkei, T. (2016). *Machiavellizmus: A megtévesztés pszichológiája [Machiavellism: The psychology of deception]*. Typotex.

Botsman, R. (2017). *Who can you trust?* Penguin Books.

Bruner, J. (1985). Chapter VI: Narrative and paradigmatic modes of thought. *Teachers College Record, 86*(6), 97–115. https://doi.org/10.1177/016146818508600606

Castells, M. (1999). Grassrooting the space of flows. *Urban Geography, 20*(4), 294–302. https://doi.org/10.2747/0272-3638.20.4.294

Csányi, V. (2000). The 'human behavior complex' and the compulsion of communication: Key factors of human evolution. *Semiotica, 128*(3/4), 243–258. https://doi.org/10.1515/semi.2000.128.3-4.243

Csepeli, G. (2020). *Ember 2.0 - A mesterséges intelligencia gazdasági és társadalmi hatásai [Humans 2.0—Economic and societal impacts of artificial intelligence]*. Kossuth.

Csikszentmihalyi, M. (1996). *Creativity. Flow and the psychology of discovery and invention*. HarperCollins Publishers.

Cubitt, S. (2020). Limen, portal, network subjectivities. *Parallax, 26*(1), 9–19. https://doi.org/10.1080/13534645.2019.1685776

Dennett, D. C. (1987). *The intentional stance*. The MIT Press.

Doyle, A. (2011). Revisiting the Synopticon: Reconsidering Mathiesen's 'the viewer society' in the age of web 2.0. *Theoretical Criminology, 15*(3), 283–299. https://doi.org/10.1177/1362480610396645

Dunbar, R. I. M. (2002). Are there cognitive constraints on an e-world? In K. Nyíri (Ed.), *Mobile communication: Essays on cognition and community* (pp. 57–69). Passagen Verlag.
El Atillah, I. (2023, March 31). A Belgian man reportedly decided to end his life after having conversations about the future of the planet with an AI chatbot named Eliza. *Euronews.* https://www.euronews.com/next/2023/03/31/man-ends-his-life-after-an-ai-chatbot-encouraged-him-to-sacrifice-himself-to-stop-climate-.
Eliade, M. (1961). *The sacred and the profane: The nature of religion.* Harper & Row.
Floridi, L. (2015). *The onlife manifesto.* Springer International Publishing Cham.
Foucault, M. (1967) Más terekről [Other spaces]. (Transl. M. Erhardt). *Exindex.* https://exindex.hu/hu/nem-tema/mas-terekrol-1967/
Foucault, M. (1977). *Discipline and punish: The birth of the prison.* Vintage Books.
Geraci, A., Nardotto, M., Reggiani, T., & Sabatini, F. (2022). Broadband internet and social capital. *Journal of Public Economics, 206*, 104578. https://doi.org/10.1016/j.jpubeco.2021.104578
Goffman, E. (1959). *The presentation of self in everyday life.* Anchor.
Greco, M., & Stenner, P. (2017). From paradox to pattern shift: Conceptualising liminal hotspots and their affective dynamics. *Theory & Psychology, 27*(2), 147–166. https://doi.org/10.1177/0959354317693120
Greenfield, S. (2011). ID: The quest for meaning in the 21st century. *Hodder and Stoughton.*
Guld, Á. (2023). A deepfake és CGI-technológia az influencer marketing szolgálatában: így formálják át a digitális karakterek az ismertségipar működését [Deepfake and CGI technology to serve influence marketing: changes in the operation of influence industry reformed by digital characters]. In P. Aczél & Á. Veszelszki (Eds.), *Deepfake: a valótlan valóság* (pp. 199–212). Gondolat.
Hayward, K. (2016). *City limits: Crime, consumer culture and the urban experience.* Routledge-Cavendish.
Horvath, A., & Szakolczai, A. (2020). *The political sociology and anthropology of evil: Tricksterology.* Routledge.
Huxley, A. (1932). *Brave new world.* (Novel) Harper Brothers.
Iványi, M. (2014). Közösségi média: A nyilvánosság elektronikus agorája vagy posztmodern panoptikum? Hatalmi válaszok a közösségi média kihívásaira [Social media: An electrified agora for publicity or a postmodern Panopticon. Responses of power to the challenges of social media]. *Médiakutató, 15*(2), 119–138. https://mediakutato.hu/cikk/2014_02_nyar/10_kozossegi_media_hatalom.pdf
Iványi, M. P. (2023). Az infokommunikációs technológiák és a mesterséges intelligencia intézményeinek nemzetközi politikai gazdaságtani keresztmetszete [International political economic intersections of info-communication technologies and artificial intelligence]. *KözigazgatásTudomány, 3*(1), 51–67. https://doi.org/10.54200/kt.v3i1.47
Karsa, T. (2025, March 11). "Két mesterséges intelligencia beszélget"- ismered ezt a viccet?—Pontosan ez történt a Deltában ["Two AI talking to each other"—do you know the joke? This is what happened in Delta]. *Coloré.* https://colore.hu/szelavi/kultura/mesterseges-intelligencia-delta/
Katz, Y. (2012). *Noam Chomsky on where artificial intelligence went wrong* (Interview). https://philarchive.org/archive/KATNCO
Köbis, N. C., Doležalová, B., & Soraperra, I. (2021). Fooled twice: People cannot detect deepfakes but think they can. *iScience, 24*(11), 103364. https://doi.org/10.1016/j.isci.2021.103364
Lakoff, G. (1993). The contemporary theory of metaphor. In A. Ortony (Ed.), *Metaphor and thought* (pp. 202–252). Cambridge University Press.
Lecomte, P. (2023). Umwelt as the foundation of an ethics of smart environments. *Humanities and Social Sciences Communications, 10*, 925. https://doi.org/10.1057/s41599-023-02356-9
Loefflad, C., Chen, M., & Grossklags, J. (2024). Reputational discrimination and fairness in China's social credit system. *Digital Government: Research and Practice, 5*, 1–27.

Lowe-Calverley, E., & Grieve, R. (2018). Self-ie love: Predictors of image editing intentions on Facebook. *Telematics and Informatics, 35*(1), 186–194. https://doi.org/10.1016/j.tele.2017.10.011

Mathiesen, T. (1997). The viewer society: Michel Foucault's 'Panopticon' revisited. *Theoretical Criminology, 1*(2), 215–234. https://doi.org/10.1177/1362480697001002003

McLuhan, M., & Fiore, Q. (2012). *Médiamasszázs [The medium is the massage].* Typotex.

Mészáros, M. (2011). *Adalékok a tradicionális tükör-értelmezések dekonstrukciójához.* Doctoral Dissertation, Magyar Képzőművészeti Egyetem. https://mke.hu/res/ertekezes_meszarosm.pdf

Monacis, L., Griffiths, M. D., Limone, P., Sinatra, M., & Servidio, R. (2020). Selfitis behavior: Assessing the Italian version of the selfitis behavior scale and its mediating role in the relationship of dark traits with social media addiction. *International Journal of Environmental Research and Public Health, 17*(16), 5738. https://doi.org/10.3390/ijerph17165738

Morris Jr, J. B., & Berman, J. (2000, April). The broadband Internet: the end of the equal voice?. In *Proceedings of the tenth conference on computers, freedom and privacy: Challenging the assumptions* (pp. 119–128). Retrieved from: https://cdt.org/wp-content/uploads/pdfs/broadbandinternet_2.pdf

Neimeyer, R. A., Klass, D., & Dennis, M. R. (2014). Mourning, meaning, and memory: Individual, communal, and cultural narration of grief. In A. Batthyany & P. Russo-Netzer (Eds.), *Meaning in positive and existential psychology* (pp. 325–346). Springer Science + Business Media. https://doi.org/10.1007/978-1-4939-0308-5_19

Nyíri, K. (1999). Castells: The information age. Könyvismertetés [book review]. *Replika, 36*, 157–181. http://www.hunfi.hu/nyiri/cast_hn.htm

Pastor, A. (2021, August 29). *Human as machine: A discussion on the transformations and exhaustion of a metaphor.* OSF Preprints. https://doi.org/10.31219/osf.io/d9pr6

Pinker, S. (2006). *A nyelvi ösztön. Hogyan hozza létre az elme a nyelvet? [The language instinct. How the mind creates language].* Typotex Kft.

Ratcliffe, S. (Ed.). (2016). *Oxford essential quotations.* Oxford University Press. https://www.oxfordreference.com/display/10.1093/acref/9780191826719.001.0001/q-oro-ed4-00016553

Skinner, B. F. (1971). *Beyond freedom and dignity.* Penguin Books.

Smith, B. (2024). LLMs and practical knowledge—What is intelligence? In K. Nyíri (Ed.), *Envisioning an electrifying future. Perspectives on visual learning* (Vol. 6, pp. 19–26). Hungarian Academy of Sciences—University of Pécs. https://www.researchgate.net/publication/387312058_Envisioning_an_Electrifying_Future

Soncul, Y., & Bollmer, G. (2020). Networked liminality. *Parallax, 26*(1), 1–8. https://doi.org/10.1080/13534645.2019.1685775

Stenner, P. (2017). *Liminality and experience. A transdisciplinary approach to the psychosocial.* Palgrave Macmillan.

Stonier, T. (1996). Information as a basic property of the universe. *Biosystems, 38*(2–3), 135–140. https://doi.org/10.1016/0303-2647(96)88368-7

Szabó, L. P. (2020). Politicians in the picture: Self-personalization in the 2020 democratic primaries. In K. Nyíri (Ed.), *How images behave. Perspectives on visual learning* (Vol. 4, pp. 45–48). Hungarian Academy of Sciences—Budapest University of Technology and Economics. https://www.academia.edu/44682025/How_Images_Behave

Szakolczai, A. (2017). Permanent (trickster) liminality: The reasons of the heart and of the mind. *Theory & Psychology, 27*(2), 231–248. https://doi.org/10.1177/0959354317694095

Szécsi, G. (2016). *Média és társadalom az információ korában: kommunikációfilozófiai adalékok a mediatizáció fogalmához.* Akadémia Kiadó.

Tari, A. (2023). Manipulált képek és videók lélektana—a valóság kitágítása, avagy az illúziók valóságba emelése [The psychology of manipulated images and videos—extending realities or reifying illusions]. In P. Aczél & Á. Veszelszki (Eds.), *Deepfake: a valótlan valóság* (pp. 233–252). Gondolat.

Turner, V. W. (1974). Liminal to liminoid, in play, flow, and ritual: An essay in comparative symbology. *Rice University Studies, 60*(3), 53–92. https://hdl.handle.net/1911/63159

Van der Kolk, B. (2015). *The body keeps the score: Brain, mind, and body in the healing of trauma.* Penguin Books.

Van Dijk, J. (2020). *The digital divide.* John Wiley & Sons.

Veszelszki, Á. (2023). Deepfake: kételkedés a kételyben [Deepfake: doubting the doubts]. In P. Aczél & Á. Veszelszki (Eds.), *Deepfake: a valótlan valóság* (pp. 13–31). Gondolat.

Vosoughi, S., Roy, D., & Aral, S. (2018). The spread of true and false news online. *Science (New York, N.Y.), 359*(6380), 1146–1151. https://doi.org/10.1126/science.aap9559

Waskul, D. D. (2005). Ekstasis and the internet: Liminality and computer-mediated communication. *New Media & Society, 7*(1), 47–63. https://doi.org/10.1177/1461444805049144

Weiser, M. (1999). The computer for the 21st century. *ACM SIGMOBILE Mobile Computing and Communications Review, 3*(3), 3–11. https://dl.acm.org/doi/pdf/10.1145/329124.329126

Wen, X. (2024). Multimodally learning abstract concepts in the age of AI. In K. Nyíri (Ed.), *Envisioning an electrifying future. Perspectives on visual learning* (Vol. 6, pp. 203–214). Hungarian Academy of Sciences – University of Pécs. https://philarchive.org/rec/NYIETF

Wolny, R. W. (2017). Hyperreality and simulacrum: Jean Baudrillard and European postmodernism. *European Journal of Interdisciplinary Studies, 3*(3), 75–79. https://doi.org/10.26417/ejis.v8i1.p76-80

Yang, A. (2024, October 24). Lawsuit claims Character.AI is responsible for teen's suicide. *NBC News.* https://www.nbcnews.com/tech/characterai-lawsuit-florida-teen-death-rcna176791

Yoon, Y. (2022). A review of Harari's "21 lessons" on the coming technological challenges. *Social Science Asia, 8*(2), 94–98. https://socialscienceasia.nrct.go.th/index.php/SSAsia/article/view/290

Z. Karvalics, L. (2015). Mesterséges intelligencia–a diskurzusok újratervezésének kora. *Információs Társadalom, 15*(4), 7–41. https://epa.oszk.hu/01900/01963/00050/pdf/EPA01963_informacios_tarsadalom_2015_4.pdf

Zuboff, S. (2019). Surveillance capitalism and the challenge of collective action. *New Labor Forum, 28*(1), 10–29. https://doi.org/10.1177/1095796018819461

Chapter 5
Authoritarian Discourses

5.1 "Peacefight"

Shortly before the system change in Hungary in the 1980s, Endre Fülei-Szántó (1924–1995), a Hungarian professor in linguistics and psychology introduced his class by a short metalogue. He visited a contemporary asylum to conduct a study in psycholinguistics and asked the patients with schizophrenia to comment on *peace-fight,* a widespread slogan in the communist countries in the cold war era and thereafter. This contemporary master word was introduced and propagated to legitimize the "temporary" Soviet occupation beginning in 1945 and ending only in 1989, as well as the early hostile discourses targeted at the Western countries. A political poster, entitled *With Hungarian-Soviet friendship for peace* by a contemporary painter, István Czeglédi (1953), represented the idea by picturing two men from these countries as happy friends, *united by their peace efforts as soldiers well equipped with guns*. This friendship was celebrated in many ways in the 1950s: for example, the "month" of the Soviet–Hungarian friendship that lasted for *45* days, starting on 18 February 1952, and ending only on 4 April 1952. The opening date was selected to remember the treaty of 1948 between the two countries declaring friendship and peace, commented by Stalin as follows: "When we are speaking about friendship, we mean it. What we mean is that we are ready to make *sacrifice* for it, should anyone want to *disturb* it"[1] ("Magyar-szovjet", 1952, p. 1., italics are mine). The idea of creating peace through fights and hegemony, and the messianic role of the Soviets had their deep historical roots dating back several centuries (Codevilla, 2024). Accordingly, the closing day of the celebrations was chosen to commemorate Hungary's "liberation" (i.e. occupation by the Soviets) in 1945.

[1] Translations of the verbatim quotes from Hungarian into English are mine, unless indicated otherwise.

M. B. Erdos, *Transitions - Liminality as Lived Experience*,
https://doi.org/10.1007/978-3-031-96007-9_5

The Hungarian communist dictator, Mátyás Rákosi was privileged to celebrate his birthday, a national-level cultic event, during this period on ninth March.

The basic metaphor of open dictatorships is *fight*. You fight for and against everything and anything: primarily, for the glorious Revolution and against everything that belonged to a previous social system, even if it was of considerable worth, as, for example, professionalism. In these systems, Eugène Pottier's (1871) early communitas lyrics, *The International* is propagated as a radical and workable directive to establish the new social order. New foundations and ever-expanding horizons of a bright but not attainable future are a must (Wydra, 2012). Common, everyday experiences and tasks are also interpreted in terms of fight. People were fighting on the front of work, winning several battles: the bread battle when harvesting the crops, or the coal battle when mining the coal needed in the industry and for heating people's homes. Anybody could become a *hero* in these constant fights—and endure the associated extreme and permanent stress, as the boundary in these days was the limitless starry sky.

This conceptual metaphor, fight, attracted other key signifiers of the rapidly expanding and consolidating semiotic chain (Lakoff, 2012; Salvatore et al., 2021). Glorious narratives were woven, establishing the unquestionable positions of the genuine or presumed victims of capitalism for retaliation. For example, the Colorado Bug *Attack* was depicted as an imperialist *plot* by the contemporary agitprops responsible for mass-level brainwashing. They claimed that in the summer of 1950, American pilots had scattered the bugs all over the German Democratic Republic to cause severe damage to the working-class people living in the people's new-born democracy ("Krumplibogárral…", 2013) The story, blatant as it was, was deeply embedded into a cognitive framework that had been shaped during WW2 when indeed all sorts of "weapons" had been tried, chasing people into collective paranoia. Traumatized people are over-sensitized to messages of threat. Such traumatic experiences and their symbolization have their lasting consequences, shaping the mindsets of the survivals and of the future generations through the latent, obscure, but powerful transgenerational transfers. A slide in a contemporary strip, *Battle in the potato plantation,* by Gergely et al. (1955) used for propaganda purposes and shown in the Hungarian villages represented an imprisoned Colorado potato beetle as an example of a powerful multimodal metaphor. Multimodal metaphors connect the verbal and nonverbal source domains for a more accentuated effect in the target domain (Forceville, 2009). The picture of the bug indicated that those who were in prison were a threat to the community and deserved their imprisonment. The bug was depicted as a convict in heavy chains, consolidating the social construction of the enemy (the non-communists) as *non-human humans*. Non-communists are pests and threats, not worthy of empathy and fair treatment, living their miserably insignificant lives under the thoughtful observation and full control by the party leaders as the careful fathers, protecting the people, their children.

Professor Fülei-Szántó, to continue the class after keeping a short but meaningful silence for *internal* reflections on "peacefight", as sharing was not safe in the contemporary academic context, added that the patients had been laughing in response to his request. He did not make any further comments—he knew the boundaries of the system that he had learnt during his own 8-year long imprisonment in the 1950s. Expressed this way, his sentences might have been a mere excursion into an irrelevant theme by an absent-minded professor, had anyone asked about it. Or, he could have argued that only "fools" are laughing at such noble concepts as peacefight. He knew how to teach critical reflectivity as early as in 1984—and retain his position in academia so that he could continue teaching. He just let us think. Many academics in the social sciences were deeply involved in this type of double thinking and double discourse for double selves (Wydra, 2012)—at times, transforming the moments of their presentations into a high-quality stand-up comedy, first telling, and then relativizing the truth. But the truth was there, waiting to be discovered.

This was the first time when I began to contemplate about the hegemonic discourses of the late, and in those days, somewhat enervated state socialist era. Several utterances did not seem to be meaningful at all, at least not in the ways you could find the meaning in a thesaurus. Expressions as "peacefight" were the favourites of the communist system. These oppositions served as the appealing *scientific–ideological* interpretations on Hegel's philosophy, simplified as a sequence of thesis, antithesis, and a final, wonderful synthesis, always understood as some newly discovered, profound aspect of the forthcoming communist rule in Utopia, unquestionable evidence for the bright future to come. This ideology has disguised the internal contradictions, double bind relations, and unresolvable paradoxes of the system, as captured, for example, in the notion of "permanent revolution" (Szakolczai, 2001). Constant focus on fighting against the "enemy" and for the bright future instead of focussing on the contemporary circumstances (Wydra, 2012) was usually explained by an inadequate level of *communist consciousness*, an individual or group-level shortcoming to be "improved" by the agitprops and public education systems. Generally, people were not considered mature enough to interpret the social realities of their lives.

Normally, our preparedness to use and interpret symbolic resources undergoes significant changes during our development. Zittoun et al. (2003) describe how children's non-reflected symbol use is followed by adolescents' becoming-reflective stage with an increasing awareness of the existence and availability of symbolic resources. At this stage, the set of choices is limited, and selection is somewhat arbitrary. Contrastingly, adults actively search for and select an interpretative framework that describes and structures their experiences according to their intentions—they evaluate the symbolic resources as for their personal relevance and adequacy. In this sense, Endre Fülei-Szántó has made a fruitful attempt to guide us into *adulthood.* In an authoritarian context, adulthood is not only determined by age, but by the societal context fostering regression and dependence to educate Big Brother's faithful little brothers. Interpretative frameworks are not selected autonomously but work on command. People are confined to the non-reflective "doer" modes of a child.

Horvath (1997), in an article written shortly after the system change in Eastern European countries, argued that the archetypal figure behind these hypnotic, manipulative actions to expropriate political power in the communist era was the trickster-clown. A trickster regime utilizes the media for keeping the waters troubled. Manipulation as a form of exploitation and monopolization of power will cover the true motivations of their actions (van Dijk, 2006). Acute problems and worsening conditions, diminishing welfare and impairments in psychosocial well-being are attributed to the hostile "destructivity" of the rapidly multiplying stigmatized social groups. The "evils" of the past are to be erased once and for all. A terror society like this is always in need of "new foundations" but never consolidates the existing ones (Horvath & Szakolczai, 2020; Szakolczai, 2001). Szakolczai (2017, p. 244) has claimed that trickster or permanent liminality is a "specifically modern condition". While trickster liminality globally is not without some promising counterpoints, in the historical context of the previous, in vivo experiments of mass manipulation in the Central and Eastern European countries, tricksters had usually fewer powerful and constructive challengers.

Manipulation, sustaining the social (symbolic) absurdities and the non-transformative chaos of permanent liminality, establishes a framework that utterly confuses meaning-making processes. In such a framework, people's lived experiences are lingering at the pre-reflective level, carrying the affective loads of ambiguities and uncertainties—a dominant power technique in soft dictatorships. In the open form, the resolution of such ambiguities may occur in a simplified manner, telling people *precisely* how to think about their experiences. In both settings, worsening conditions for the majority and excessive gains for the trickster will result, unless the recipients of the discourse realize the real motives of the manipulators and are able to initiate some restorative action.

5.2 Classical Manipulation

Deception is a common strategy in the animal kingdom to acquire the necessary resources or escape vital threats (Bereczkei, 2016). Humans (mis)use the power of symbols and construe refined, pervasive, diverse, and continually reconstructed techniques of deception, usually not restricted to a single sequence of actions. We can extend these to prolonged and strategically planned chains of abuse, both on individual and community levels. These features, the permanent abuse of relationships and the misuse of common resources, make manipulation a core concern in our lives. The victims are ignorant of the abuse and are convinced that the manipulators' actions are in their best interests (Van Dijk, 2006). But at the heart of such convictions there lies some doubt. People's hunches, pre-reflective, and intuitive recognitions are silenced by the dominant voices in the society (Høgh-Olesen, 2024). Slowly the manipulator gains excessive control over the resources, including the mass media, today's key to sustain power. In such a context, ideologies and dogmas are distributed as rational knowledge and spread easily. As permanent liminality continuously recreates liminal hotspots while impeding their resolution, these vicious circles, characterized by strong affective components and high-level suggestibility, consolidate, and continually rebuild the ideal context for manipulation (Stenner, 2017; Greco & Stenner, 2017; Szakolczai, 2014).

The exceptional plasticity of human languages allows for artistic creativity and playfulness, but the polysemy inherent in our symbols may also entrap us in the network of our meanings. The resulting language games—this, time, not the playful but the destructive ones—are excellent projection screens for the shared fantasies and desires of the receiving community. This especially holds true in the chaos and vulnerability associated with deep transformations. Extending these periods of uncertainties increases mass-level susceptibility for manipulation, even in the cultures where people are used to monitoring and evaluating the institutional aspects of their symbolic environment. In a threatening atmosphere with continually traumatized people, a collective thirst for a wise leader will arise and the trickster will abuse this thirst. Mass-level entrapment and helplessness, together with humans' exceptional imitation tendencies and refined group synchronization processes, will contribute to the robustness of such destructive systems.

5.2.1 The Discursive Approach

Discourse studies, an area embracing recent developments in linguistics, semiotics, communication, cultural anthropology, sociology, social psychology, cultural semiotic psychology, and psycholinguistics, represents a distinct paradigm within the social sciences (van Dijk, 2009, 2014). Its important precedents, described in the first chapter *(Living in a Dual Environment. Homo Symbolicus and Languaging)* in more details, were the theories conceiving language use as a social action. As a result, meaning and order emerge: "The continual coordination required in any relationship or community eventually generates a sense of taken-for-granted common practices, otherwise known as dominant (or largely unquestioned) discourses" (McNamee, 2015, p. 376).

Van Dijk (2014) has proposed to focus not only on the connections between language and society as the socio-political-historical context of talk to negotiate meaning (Gale, 2010) but also include individual cognition in a tripartite framework: epistemic discourse analysis. To participate in a discourse a command of a language is not sufficient, but a set of knowledge of the world, of both the natural and the cultural environments, is needed. Therefore, discourse processing is not only about language processing but also about knowledge processing (van Dijk, 2014). Here, considering the theme of this chapter, I propose using a paradoxical triangle (Fig. 5.1) to depict the connections in this tripartite framework, indicating the difficulties the individual must face when entrapped in the chaos, ruptures, shadows and absurdities of liminal settings, and confused meanings in permanent liminality. The reversed figure, standing on a vertex instead of the base, indicates that the balance is upset easily, and the lowest point, individual cognition at the bottom is to carry the heavy mental burdens of the twisted, blurred, and fragmented trickster discourse.

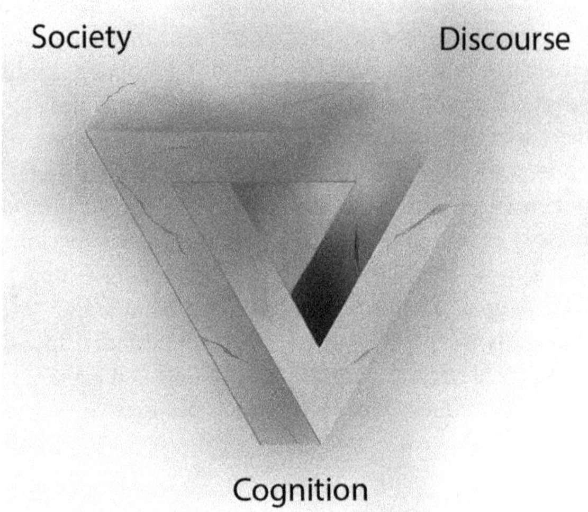

Fig. 5.1 The triangle of trickster discourse (Credit: Kitti Bognar, 2025) (*Note:* for a simple version, see B. Erdos et al., 2012, p. 62)

In Chap. 1, *Living in a Dual Environment. Homo Symbolicus and Languaging*, I have argued that the use of digital signs, segmenting our holistic perceptions and experiences into freely combinable units, does not only transform human languages into an infinite and flexible symbolic universe but is also conducive to polarization and splitting (1 = positive, existing, 0 = negative, not existing). Affective polarization extended to the extremes is a cornerstone of manipulative discourse (Salvatore et al., 2021; van Dijk, 2006). Polarized statements and powerful metaphors, deeply embedded in risk-society and a-mazed-society contexts (in Chap. 3, *Liminal Experiences in Late Modernity. A-Mazed Societies and Institutionalized Craving*) trigger strong fears, up to the levels of collective paranoia, in the receivers of political messages. Consequently, they readily accept politicians' proposed remedies, who are depicted as benevolent fathers not afraid of making some *sacrifice* to protect their helpless children (Lakoff, 2004, 2012). Establishing the position of Good Us, with special reference to the fundamental values and norms of one's own group, and repeated, xenophobic references to the "morally inferior" position of the other group (the Evil Them) is a traditional and highly effective method (van Dijk, 2006).

For example, under the Soviet rule, communism was depicted as the "only" alternative to fascism, interpreted as "reactionarism", deliberately confused with clericalism and "capitalism" (owning some valuable private property) in the dominant discourse. Humanists, who protested Stalin's system—a system responsible for genocide, such as the Holomodor, the famine in Ukraine, or malenki robot, a practice of forced labour based on "collective guilt"—were considered the enemies of the system. Millions of people living in the Soviet Union and in the Central and

Eastern European countries were labelled as "reactionists" or "fascists" and died in the gulags. The argumentation followed the twisted logic of reductio ad Hitlerum: if Stalin and Hitler were enemies, anyone fighting against Stalin must be a fascist. The high number of victims, the techniques of terror, and the substantiating ideology of collective guilt made the Stalinian system comparable to the Nazi regime[2]:

> Death rate was so high that when a hundred people went out (for work) and sixty returned then it was a good rate (…) In the first September in 1945 we organized a ceremonial funeral. The second deceased person was carried to the grave in a coffin, but the coffin was to be returned as it was needed for the next one. However, it was reused as a door, so the next one was carried to the grave on a plank, and he was dressed in underwear only. The next ones were buried naked" (Herczeg, 1990, p. 118).

In such systems, anyone not with us, the "Good", is against us (van Dijk, 2006), and the number of enemies is growing fast. Every significant action is interpreted as a desperate fight between the superpowers. Hegemonic ideology destroys the previous boundaries while designating some rigid, impermeable ones: spatially, for example, by prohibiting the visits to "enemy countries"; temporally, with the "rise on new foundations", abolishing all the memories of the "evil" past; and socially, by introducing a new caste system isolating the loyal comrades from the public enemies, number one, two, hundred…and million. Both the subjects' positions, and the public's dispositions are established and naturalized by the hegemonic discourse (van Dijk, 2006). For example, the intelligentsia was portrayed by the celebrated Soviet author, Gorky in 1950 (p. 289) as follows: "The intelligentsia—a nanny for the capitalists—was busy patching the philosophical and religious cloak of the bourgeois that had long been worn out and polluted by the blood of working-class people". The intelligentsia's suspicious contributions, always supervised by party leaders, were regarded as "non-productive" work, not resulting in anything *material,* tangible, and controllable gains, in contrast with physical labour as "genuine work"—in this context, seen as supporting the system's ideology under the label of historical *materialism.* (Marx was a white-collar worker.) The intelligentsia's children were categorized as the descendants of the "É" class (értelmiségi = intelligentsia), and later as "other" at school, excluded from certain opportunities open for working class children only. The worst social category in the 1950s was X, referring to an "alien to the class" (i.e. to the working class as the only acknowledged source of power) with an "enemy parent", with the expression firmly embedded in the root metaphor of fight. Enemy parents were the earlier land or factory owners, aristocrats, "kulak families" owning more than about 15 acres of land, previous army officers, etc. (Somogyvári, 2015). This system was comparable to the categorization system to the caste system in India. It was not talent but birth circumstances that determined one's chances in the society. Distortions resulted not only in risky and burdening secrets but also in delimited access to relevant information and

[2] In the 2025 elections in Germany, far right ideologies have proven the strongest in the geographical regions of the former communist state, the German Democratic Republic (East Germany).

knowledge, substituting these with empty ideologies, and propagating them as *the* rational, evidence-based truths.

The success of manipulation largely depends on the manipulators' ability to maintain the threats and chaos of permanent liminality. Lasting domination can be reached only if the recipients' *context models* are also shaped accordingly, so that they would accept the lies as truth (van Dijk, 2013, 2014). A context model, as a mediator between discourse, society, and the individual- or group-level communicative actions, is a dynamic mental model of the communicative situation. The scheme, shaped by the recipient's previous experiences, is consolidated, or, less often, is questioned in response to external feedback. Recipients of a discourse define the communicative situation, interpret the discourse, and position themselves within the discourse, and within the society by using their context models (van Dijk, 2009, 2013, 2014). Thus, van Dijk's epistemic approach lays an emphasis both on our collective memory, the discursive resources archived in the communal domain, and on communicative memory, a set of powerful narratives about the historical moments as personally experienced and shared in one's immediate social network (Assmann, 2008; Hänninen, 2004).

Cultivation theory (Gerbner et al., 1986) describes how being continuously exposed to wide and deep media messages reshapes one's conceptions through the key mechanisms of mainstreaming and resonance, while also propagating and selling a bright future with unlimited opportunities (Potter, 2022). Mainstreaming, a forerunner to today's filter bubble phenomena, is used to recast the diversity of opinions and attitudes into more consonant and controllable views. Resonance is to deepen the message via suggesting links between the message and one's own lived experiences. Resonance occurs when the interpreter discovers some "striking" similarities between the media message and their own experiences, resulting in a "this-could-have-happened-to-me" impression (e.g. after watching a thriller, hearing ominous footsteps behind your back during an evening walk). The narrated event is in harmony with the person's context model and will add—as a novel and befitting element—to its consolidation. This process is operated via the principles of classical conditioning. Resonance is reinforcement; and in a chaotic environment, people are actively searching for and embrace any messages that reduce uncertainties (De Luca Picione & Lozzi, 2021). These grant them, if not stability in the society, but the illusions of the security of their own worldviews. This way, communicative frameworks uniting large and diverse groups can be established. Fairclough (2013) points out that hegemonic ideological–discursive frameworks are used to naturalize ideologies: gradually and creepingly, still confidently, they extinguish the previously held notions, question the validity of the precedent discourses, and depict the politically motivated distortions as common-sense, redemptive knowledge. Even in a totalitarian system, however, there are a multitude of meanings hiding in the shadow: forbidden themes and alternative descriptions. Though they are thoughtfully eliminated from the public discourse, they still exist as potentialities—embryonic *enemy-memes*. Salvatore and Venuleo (2017) in their sensemaking model emphasize the bivalence of meaning. As Wiggins and Potter (2013, p. 77) note: "one way of describing something will always be countering—either explicitly or indirectly—alternative ways of describing the same thing". Therefore, the symbolic resources to form a counter-discourse are theoretically accessible. However, in a dictatorship, the emerging counter-discourses remain marginalized, and in most cases, private, until a strong affective community motivation is formed. There is a gap between knowing and saying.

To maintain trickster liminality and depict it as a sensible and sustainable system, manipulators selectively use the interpreting community's cultural stock of stories and shared meanings. Propaganda about the contemporary events is nicely arranged into a prefabricated framework, sparing the pains of accommodating the message to one's scheme (Moscovici, 2002). Using a morsel of truth, appealing to the interpreting community to facilitate their identification processes, and then build a web of lies around it is a common strategy. Desirability of community-level actions or passivity is established via the promises about an utopistic future about a life of abundance and safety; or simply by providing attractive identity prostheses for the ones in need. And who would *not* need these, in the systems conducive to the construction of fake, vulnerable, or threatened identities? Envisioned threats and unmet needs, coupled with the techniques introduced to paralyse critical-reflective thinking are the manipulator's potent allies to support their *fight* for power. These discursive techniques have their chronic consequences in the society. They deplete the shared meanings by transforming the signifiers into floating or empty ones.

5.2.2 Floating and Empty Signifiers

Laclau's (2003) discursive framework defines manipulation as the politically motivated distortions in the relationship between the signifier and the signified, bringing about empty or floating signifiers. In this framework, empty signifiers are the ones that, in consequence of long, persistent, and exhaustive manipulation manoeuvres to appropriate power, lose the signified:

> "An empty signifier is, strictly speaking, a signifier without a signified" (…) "there is a structural impossibility of signification as such, and only if this impossibility can signify itself as an interruption (subversion, distortion, etcetera) of the structure of the sign" (Laclau, 2003, 305–306).

Here, the flexible boundaries of a symbol telling what is within and what is beyond become undetectable. Essentially, empty signifiers are a paradox, and as such, they refer to the paradoxes inherent in the social system. The existence of a signified is a precondition to signification. Emptiness, however, gains a deep meaning when we include the interpreting community into the signification process. Empty signifiers carry the meanings exiled to the realms of silenced and forbidden contents, the meanings that the community is deprived of. Taking a step towards Peircean semiotics, in such cases, the signification processes are not just interrupted, rather, they are *disrupted* to create space for the new, relational-level meanings. For example, in *peacefight*, peace becomes an empty signifier in the hostile context of the cold war.

One side of the polarity is not only implicit here but is buried deep in the shadow and can be recovered only with considerable difficulty or risks taken by the interpreters.[3] In this new interpretative frame, fight and peace, antonyms in a thesaurus, mean the *same*: acute opposition. The new term, confusing as it is, is endowed with the illusion of bringing "good" hopes for everlasting peace of a hegemonic power in the very distant future, but only after committed and desperate fights. This is not even some twisted Hegelian synthesis or a yin-yang unity: the eradication of one pole of a construct is to create the hegemony of meaning and rule through the resulting paradox and imbalance. The use of empty signifiers was characteristic of the discourses both in open and soft dictatorships. Consider the following political speech, in which the meaning of censorship seems to vanish into thin air in the opaqueness of the discourse, but as a relational-level threatening message, it is properly disambiguated by the speaker, Hungary's contemporary Prime Minister:

> No-one is prosecuted for one's political views in Hungary, but anyone committing a crime that is illegal, political and is against the system will be severely punished (…). In Hungary, there is no censorship, there has never been censorship, but provocation against the system by using the press is violative of law and is to be punished.
>
> (From the speech held at the Assembly of the Central Committee on the 50th anniversary of the foundation of the Party in 1968/ Kádár, 1975, p. 263)

As we could see, an "empty" signifier retains its meaning; only formally is it empty, but its relational-level meaning is crucial in shaping the societal processes. For most of its members, the Youth Communist Association in Hungary did not mean anything significant in the late 1980s in Hungary. The majority were neither communists, nor associated—though many were indeed young. On the relational level, however, it preserved its societal meaning: power and wealth for the few, and safety and better chances to get on in life for the masses who joined.

In an authoritarian system, interpretations are strictly defined. Meanings shrink or extend—signifiers are not only emptied, and opposites are made equivocal, but they may also become ambiguous, and these *floating signifiers* (Farkas & Schou, 2018; Laclau, 2003) are another way to dominate and abuse the shared symbolic domain. With floating signifiers, the boundaries of meaning are extended much beyond the natural polyglossia, and signifiers tend to refer to many different signified. As maintaining meaning is maintaining one's sense of experiences—common sense—people compensate for the losses and uncertainties of meaning as much as possible—or even beyond (De Luca Picione & Lozzi, 2021). Thus, floating and empty signifiers can be used in diverse and contradicting political contexts as nice projection sheets. As we could see, a "fascist" in the Stalinian system, relying on the collective projective identification mechanisms immanent in dictatorships, designated all the groups critical of the system. For example, my grandfather, a social democrat, and a hard-working clerk at a municipality land registry department, living in two subsequent authoritarian social systems, was warned several times for

[3] In 1982, several students, members of Dialogue Group (Dialógus Csoport) had been demonstrating for peace and mutual nuclear disarmament, and were expelled from Janus Pannonius University, Pécs.

holding the very same views labelled as opposing: shortly before WWII because of his dangerous "communist" views, and after WWII because of his "reactionary" and "clerical" notions.

Floating signifiers tend to occupy a fixed and central position in the authoritarian discourse and repress other meanings. They usually appear in times of societal crises (Farkas & Schou, 2018; Laclau, 2003)—and stay with us in prolonged trickster liminality. Continuing reinterpretation and reconstruction are inherent in the signification process. The symbolic as a conventional sign must be continuously co-constructed and reconstructed by the communicators. However, loosely defined, or particularly the inconsistent meanings are but a source of chaos. In the excerpt below, science is not opposed to, but is equalled to ideology:

> As for the social sciences are concerned, a firm standpoint of the Central Committee (of the Hungarian Socialist Worker's Party – the author) is that bourgeois theories must not be allowed to gain ground (…) Science and socialism are closely interrelated as socialism itself is a *scientific ideology* (Kádár in Lang Factory, 1969. Italics are mine. Kádár, 1975, p. 291).

Hearing the above claims that connect contradictory notions and jam them into a single concept might be nonsensical, but is attractive for the wider public, whose additional gain to being a good comrade is that they can pass as witty and educated, what is more, reliable "scientists" and do so with very little effort. Here, it is worth remembering Marx's famous comment, quoted by Engels (1882) in a letter: "If anything is certain, it is that I myself am not a Marxist".

5.2.3 *Reversed Signifiers*

When the personal context model does not allow for a plausible interpretation, and there is a sharp contradiction between the perspectives of the individual and the political claims made in the public discourse, the reversal of the key signifiers may solve the interpreter's dilemma. This works because the manipulative discourse itself is based on the *reversal of the key meanings* in the dominant discourse. Such reversals are possible and effective only if morality is suspended and the discourse is relying exactly on the *opposite* pole of the construct (Benţa, 2021). Consider the following eulogy on the deeds of Hungary's bloody-handed dictator, Mátyás Rákosi in the 1950s:

> The Hungarian people affectionately love our leader, teacher, the first architect of our new life, Matyas Rakosi, who is dedicated to fight for the peace and independence of our homeland (…). Comrade Rakosi is Stalin's best Hungarian disciple. He is the high-spirited apostle of proletarian internationalism (…) a forerunner of the eternal friendship between the Hungarian and the Soviet people (Kiss, 1952).

In this speech, an absolutistic and benevolent power is depicted (B. Erdos, 2010). The speech is rooted in the "good father" image, politicians' favourite worldwide (Lakoff, 2004). Biblical references, as "disciple", and "apostle", positioning Stalin as a saviour and charismatic, are also meant to transform the recipients' previous religious schemas by connecting a new signified to the previous signifier. However, as the 1956 revolution in Hungary clearly indicated, most recipients' strategy was to invert the key terms, activating the shadow pole of the construct (saviour–destroyer), and making an escape into a powerful counter-discourse from the collective insanity transforming love into hate, and peace, into fight and anger.

A similar discursive strategy, but this time focussing on the propagation of threats, was used by Rákosi in the following text to strengthen the blissful paranoia of the communist regime:

> Internal enemy is vehemently supported by trigger-happy imperialist fire-raisers. Imperialists are more and more worried to see the Soviet successes in building the communist system (…) In contrast with the results of the *peace camp*, economic problems are on the increase in the *imperialist bloc*. Disagreement between the United States and its satellites has deepened (Rákosi, 1953. Italics are mine).

This way, the counter-discourse is the *reversal of the reversal*, creating sense and order from the discursive chaos. "Internal enemy" were the ones characterized by sound common sense, and the "successes" equalled to miserably low living standards for the majority. Many Hungarians knew of the development and welfare in the Western countries through their scarce but memorable contacts with their "dissident" relatives living in these countries. Poor management, and the overall lack of professional competencies due to counter-selection (Hunyady, 2002) in the system, in which science equalled to ideologies, and positions were assigned according to one's loyalty to the regime and not to their talents, quickly impoverished the country. Irrational plans and compulsory contributions in agriculture left many without bread. In such a context, these mind tricks alone were not enough to overwrite people's daily experiences and were effective only if accompanied by persistent terror. People's authentic interpretation, a slogan on the propagated "economic successes" as one element of the emerging counter-discourse in the 1950s, "they have even swept the attic for one or two kernels", is still remembered in Hungary. Political speeches about the abundant resources, equalling to amounts that "you have never seen so far" or "cannot be compared to" often read quite literally and could be extrapolated into the future. You have never seen such resources—and you never will.

> Workers' and peasants' living standard have reached such a high level that cannot be compared to that of the Horthy-era (pre-World War II period) (…) these achievements were possible only because the Soviet Union, our liberator and friend supported and helped us in every respect (Rákosi, 1953).

On hearing this speech, the people, as the ruling regime had hoped, would suppose that the gate leading to the Promised Land, after so many sufferings in the past, was finally open. Such gates, however, accompanied by one or two micro-Watergate sooner or later, lead only to another land of unmet promises. In contrast with the labels, "liberator" and "friend", no verbatim lies are involved in the comments: you have never seen the plentiful resources—but nobody has explicitly told you that you ever will. Indeed, the miseries of the Rákosi-system were comparable to those of the pre-war era. Understanding the statement as positive could come from our constraints and biases of interpretation. We tend to attribute positive (collaborative) intentions to the speaker, and this strategy is at the root of "self-deception". Frequent disappointments, however, finally transform people's context models and release the affective load—the collective anger, culminating in the 1956 Revolution.

Initially, the Kádár government applied the same Stalinian discursive patterns: "Counter-revolutionists are more and more impertinent. They hunt for the devotees of democracy. Arrow Cross Nazis and other beasts are killing honest patriots, our best comrades"—as János Kádár, Prime Minister of Hungary from 1956 to 1988, argued when commenting on the defeat of the revolution ("A Kádár-kormány", 1956). Revolution, naturally, a *permanent* one (A. Szakolczai, 2001) on the long road leading to communism, is allowed to have but one referent: the continuity of the communist revolution. Until the system change in 1989, the 1956 revolution was identified as a "counter-revolution" in the public discourse. "Democrats" were the advocates of the ruling regime, and "patriots" were those who supported the Soviet occupation instead of the country's sovereignty. Such confusion of meanings and twisted interpretations have long survived the state socialist system and were preserved in older people's context models.

5.3 The Conception Trial as a Signification Process

István Bibó, a renowned Hungarian political philosopher and Minister of the State during the 1956 Revolution, has noted that in political life, people occasionally tell lies, but an entire system that is built on lies will finally collapse (Elek, 2011). In 1956, the people of Hungary could share 2 weeks of illusions of freedom and autonomy. Revolutionists were led by the reform communists, wanting to put an end to the Stalinian rule in Hungary and build a genuine social democracy.

Conception trials were an established practice to eliminate the "enemies", who were identified as the sources of actual or perceived threat to the subsequent system. At times, conception trials were merely used to intimidate people and force them to practice the paradox exercise of *self-criticism* and *self-censorship*. These forced absurdities had nothing to do with a parrhesiastes' open, authentic confession. The phrases, as the little discursive brothers to the almighty Big Brother were meant to suggest that the victims' confessions and self-restricting, passive attitudes were the results of their own free will and (now) unquestionable beliefs in the fairness and truths of the prevailing system, and not of coercion. Unpredictable arrests, tortures, and executions supported the formation of this "free" will. One of my acquaintances, now in her eighties, shared a brief narrative illuminative of this power technique: "My father was arrested at Christmas. I was but a little girl then. We have never been told why he had been arrested, or why, after some years, was released". She did not share this information with anyone but with her close family members until the 1990s. Silenced stories like hers were common, and her father was among the lucky survivors. Relatives were not even allowed to mourn as the victims had been identified as criminals. Their death sentence entailed a sentence for disenfranchised grief for the relatives and friends (Doka, 1999).

Horváth (2013) has described two distinct forms of conception trials. One of these was used to control the people or rob ordinary citizens of their properties. The political police (State Security Department) fabricated some evidence to support accusations on "spying", possessing "excess" goods ("capital") or prohibited foreign currency, or "cherishing reactionist ideas" in secret. In these cases, the police "found" a gun, prohibited books, or some foreign currency in the victim's home. As Vyshinsky, the state prosecutor in the Soviet Union in the era claimed, the confession of guilt was the "queen of evidence", superseding any other types (Horváth, 2013, p. 96). Consequently, victims had often been tortured until they confessed their "crimes" against the system.

To sentence those who participated in the 1956 revolution, a different procedure was enacted, relying more on discursive techniques than physical torture. Victims' statements were rephrased, using the system's favourites, floating or empty signifiers. This second type of conception trials, involving renowned politicians and other members of the intelligentsia, required the prefabrication of a powerful interpretative framework by the political police to entrap the victim and the witnesses in a semantic web associated with spying and treason, elements of the war/fight root metaphor dictating the system's discourses. For example, in the court trials following the 1956 Revolution, a friendly, informal chat among friends was reinterpreted as *negotiating agreements* (Horváth, 2013). Some people even believed the reasonings by the prosecution. Those who did not, were too frightened to protest, up to the level of freezing into a paralysed, passive state by the traumatizing political context following the collective learned helplessness experience of a failed revolution.

5.4 Parrhesiastic Resistance

Parrhesia ("*beyond* speech") is a powerful antidote to the boosted absurdities and lies inherent in manipulative discourses. It is a specific genre, a counter-discourse in a deep societal crisis (Foucault, 1999). Parrhesia involves honesty, with one's words and deeds in harmony. Parrhesiastae are characterized by a strong moral disposition and rational courage. They are fully aware of the risks they are taking and develop a deep sense of responsibility for the truth, serving the interests of the public (Foucault, 1999). Though parrhesia is a solitary speech act, and as such, is immensely dangerous for the speakers living in tyranny, it echoes and strengthens the silenced values of a broad community to be reconstructed for a meaningful life. Parrhesia is the moment of articulating shared and personally internalized values by stepping out of the prevailing monolithic order. Thus, it has the potential power to recast permanent liminality into transformative liminality.

Several parrhesiastic moments occurred in the life of István Bibó, Minister of State in 1956. Dénes (2015) described István Bibó as "the greatest Hungarian democratic political thinker of the 20th century" (p. 597) who saved many potential victims' lives during the Shoah, the mass murder of Jewish people in WW2. Bibó built an academic career in international law and political studies as the leading figure of democratization processes in Hungary. In one of his articles, he identified fatigue and passivity, deeply rooted in the history of the country, as the most important barriers to these processes (Bibó, 1990). He argued that people considered politics as an obscure field fully beyond their control—a game for a few immoral persons, who were playing the game for their own advantage only. He compared the domestic mass manipulation strategies to the ones used by the Nazi propaganda minister, Goebbels, noting that their insanity in Germany was a systematic one—whereas in Hungary, it was a *chaos*. The amalgamation of chaos and insanity—as salient features of trickster liminality (Horvath & Szakolczai, 2020)—could continue under a democratic disguise (Bibó, 1990).

Before WW2, Bibó was one of the supporters of the March Movement (Márciusi Front, 1937–38, Hungary), a group comprising writers, university professors, and students who demanded the democratization of the country and the introduction of a fair redistributive system. They openly expressed their concerns about the spread of fascist ideologies. During WW2, Bibó worked on a peace plan, and as a ministry employee, he issued protective letters until his arrest in 1944. After he was released, he was hiding until the end of the war. In 1945, he resumed his work at the Ministry of Internal Affairs. In 1946, the national elections had been manipulated, and from that time on, the Communist Party (the predecessor of the Hungarian Socialist Worker's Party) could rule the country. Between 1946 and 1950, Bibó had been a full professor at Szeged University, but he was soon deprived of his position and was allowed to work only in the library of the university (Dénes, 2015).

Bibó as a responsible political thinker risked his life for what he firmly believed in. Between 1938 and 1940 he wrote *Ten commandments for freedom-loving persons* in which he connected the concept of freedom to relational responsibility. This work is not about the liminal freedom from one's usual assignments, but one's freedom for responsible and authentic actions:

> He who loves freedom… shall forever bear in mind that human freedom and dignity are one and indivisible, and the harm done to any one man[4] is a threat to the freedom and dignity of all; he shall therefore strive for joint action against any limitation of human freedom, arbitrary arrest and detention, individual or administrative insolence or any disgrace to human dignity, and if this is not possible, he shall try alone' (Bibó, 2011–2012, pp. 15–16. cit. by Dénes, 2015, p. 599. Translation in the original).

This early credo comprised several paragraphs about the genuine sources of respect, freedom from one's own and others' discrimination, from exploitation and humiliation, and a moral obligation to actively resist such attempts. Bibó was dedicated to representing and to acting on behalf of the public interest by fighting tyranny, corruption, and despotism. He noted that such social ills are a consequence of the passivity of the honourable majority who are either too *lethargic* or too *frightened* to resist (Bibó, 1946/ 1990).

[4] Man/he is inclusive of all genders in this early translation. The Hungarian language does not make a difference between the genders (he/she are equally translated as ő; human beings are simply "ember").

He delivered his last radio speech in 1956, with the Soviet troops in Budapest, the capital, and the soldiers practically next door to him, invading the Hungarian Parliament. There were not any hopes left for the positive outcome of the Hungarian revolution, overshadowed by a simultaneous event, the Suez crisis (B. Erdos & Kelemen, 2011). In these liminal moments of awe, Bibó's speech, expressing the lost hopes and eternal values, is a moving and powerful message, a counter-discourse to illuminate the true nature of communist tyranny. He, as Minister of State, faithfully represented a nation's shattered visions on sovereignty and integrity:

> I, István Bibo, a Minister of State, as the sole representative of the only legitimate Hungarian Government am staying in the Parliament alone. Hungary [...] wants to live in the community of the Central and Eastern European nations that desire to live their lives in the name of liberty and justice, in a society free from exploitation. [...] I refuse the calumny that the glorious Hungarian Revolution is a manifestation of fascism or anti-Semitism [...] this was a fight against the conquering foreign power and the domestic executioner brigades, a fight that united the whole Hungarian nation, irrespective of class or religion (István Bibó's Declaration on 4th November 1956, in Bibó, 1990, pp. 165–168)

After the revolution in 1956, a fierce terror was introduced. Those who had been too young to be executed immediately had been imprisoned and were hanged when they came of age. In 1957, Bibó was arrested and sentenced for life. He could escape death penalty only by the Indian Prime Minister's Jawaharlal Nehru's request. In 1961 and 1962, *peaceloving*, and not piecefighting British scientists, for example, Bertrand Russell, Michael Polanyi, Richard Titmuss, and other renowned scholars sent two telegrams to intervene and ask the Kádár government to release him (Dénes, 2015). In 1963, the surviving victims of the 1956 Revolution were granted amnesty. In the contemporary system, Bibó could find employment only as a blue-collar worker in the *cellars* of a library: the parrhesiastes was deported to the underworld. He was not allowed to teach or publish anything. Some years later, he could move back to the first floor. As a librarian, he was responsible for purchasing international professional literature. He died in 1979.

Altogether, the initial efforts to introduce and maintain societal-level groupthink (Janis, 2008) was not a full success in Hungary, with its relatively few collectivistic patterns and disrupted, but longstanding and strong previous connections to Western Europe. The traumatizing lessons of the 1956 revolution, together with the discursive strategies used to introduce and maintain the chaos of permanent liminality, however, isolated people from one another, curbing the potentials for the societal-level protests of a reinterpreting community. Depriving the society of trusting relationships resulted in social atomization (Hankiss, 1982), a successful power technique in the more individualized societies, in which people would not obey solely in the name of some hypothesized group harmony and cohesion. Building fake, vulnerable, or threatened identities through terror paved the ways to a different system, the soft dictatorship of "goulash communism" with its limited consumerism, distorted competitiveness, and indirect techniques of manipulation.

5.5 Killing Softly: Tricky Signifiers and Double Bind Discourses

The 1956 revolution evoked strong sympathies internationally, but the failure of the revolution resulted in a robust learned helplessness experience for the Hungarian society. Learned helplessness was first documented by Seligman (1972) in an experiment. The group of dogs subject to inescapable electric shocks could not learn how to help themselves when they were given the opportunity in an escape cage—in contrast with the other group who, having a prior experience on their efficacy, could easily stop the shocks. Seligman concluded that in such settings, arrested flight was not a momentary episode, but had its longstanding consequences. With humans, learned helplessness paralyses both the subjects' actions and reflections.

As brain is better than brawn, new political strategies were introduced to maintain the Soviet influence. Kádár, the premier was a man of compromise. Having consolidated his power in a traumatized society through the retaliations, he introduced a "soft" dictatorship, eliminated personality cult and initiated measures to increase welfare—but without genuine economic achievements. Open terror diminished and manipulative discourses to perpetuate the confusions of permanent liminality became the main means of rule.

Construing *double bind relations* (what is required will be sanctioned by the authorities) (Bateson, 1972) in the discourse results in a robust no-escape cage. Its repeated use strengthens the recipients' context models and deepens the destructiveness of the social milieu. Entrapment in a double bind is less salient than open terror, therefore, it is much more tolerated both in the domestic and in the international environments. The frequent response to double bind relations is helplessness, passivity, and demoralization, and, finally, the emergence of self-destructive patterns (Bateson, 1972; B. Erdos et al., 2012; B. Erdos & Javor, 2022; B. Erdos & Kelemen, 2011; Smith, 2002). Relational-level double bind messages permeated all the important spheres of life, including the world of work. Kelemen (2017) has commented on professionals' contemporary lived experiences as follows:

> This bureaucracy did not facilitate goal rational, efficient work and team building, rather, it maintained and fuelled a feudal-court-economy of favours (...) Despite our responsible but schematic work, we had doubts if we could do any good or just become some fatteners of the public illfare in this visionless and debilitating environment (Kelemen, 2017, p. 18–19).

Escape from such settings, in which you must not become who you could and should authentically become, in this case, a creative, constructive, and efficient professional, is narrow. It is possible only through trans-contextual creativity manifested in the liberating, reflective actions, and discourses (Bateson, 1972). There are several folk tales all over the world, in which the witty poor triumph over a despotic emperor, who is giving orders that must be obeyed but cannot be obeyed. A version of these stories is King Matthias and the Szekler's daughter ("Mátyás király", n.d.). Two recurrent elements in this topos are the repeated double bind entrapments as the source of potential trouble, and a rewarding escape made possible only by the bright dependent's trans-contextual creativity. In the story, King Matthias the *Just,* a fifteenth-century King of Hungary and Croatia, who seemed to hold his clever subjects in high regard, gave impossible orders, to which the girl had to obey. This is a close example of a double bind situation, when an order, received from an unquestionable authority, is simultaneously denied on a more abstract level. In the story, this second level is represented by the natural laws that no one, not even a king can disobey. For example, when she was asked to skin a stone for some royal reward, she demanded that the king should first put to the stone to death and bleed it thoroughly so that she could properly carry out the king's order. She used her creativity to invalidate an unachievable command and responded to the king's orders by respectful requests, applying to the social conventions grounded by lengthy traditions that adhered to natural laws. As she argued, these steps—normalizing the absurdities and introducing further absurdities to return to normalcy—were necessary to perform the task the best possible way. Such tales must have a positive ending, so finally the girl could meet all the emperor's requirements and became a queen—but success is a rare outcome of the double bind.

King Matthias was also said to be fond of his court jester in the folk tales mirroring the absurdity of the ruler's hasty commands. A court jester, representing the positive side of the trickster, questions the rules and order to encourage reflections and renewal. Unlike a parrhesiastes, a jester, today's stand-up comedian, is telling the truth in a relativizing mode, questioning the dominant discourse, and predicting the impacts of systemic absurdities by mirroring the absurdities. A dangerous but essential occupation, as an absolutistic power always has its dark side that finally becomes a threat not only to the people but also to the ruler. Court jesters' and comedians' anti-structural position—it is a "fool" who is telling the truth, one who uses the protective roles and discursive frameworks suited to the position—is to tame the risks for the individual, and, at times, to make the humorous message even more powerful for the public. The interpreting community will understand the message—but also the threats involved. In times of profound societal crisis, comedians may abandon the vague discursive domains and hit the target more precisely. Humour turns into parrhesia, and laughter is occasionally interrupted by momentary, meaningful silence indicating the change.

Such temporary liberation from the pressures of double bind by using the potentials inherent in humour to disclose, reflect on, and resist the mind tricks targeted at emptying the contents of the signifier but simultaneously granting them hegemonic power as relational-level messages is also present in political jokes. Consider the following piece from the "soft" era as a reflection about the context-determined meaning of *opinion:*

After the 1956 Revolution, two people are chatting:

- What is your opinion of the current political situation?
- I do have an opinion, but I do not agree with it.

Clearly, a thesaurus would not help too much to understand the joke. We must be familiar with the contemporary social context: "the meaning of a word is its use in a language" (Wittgenstein 1953, section 43). Here, the original meaning was eradicated, and a new cloud of meaning was coined: you must distance yourself from your own notions and values, as own opinion equals to danger; furthermore, trust in your conversing partner may equate to lethal danger. This new meaning operates not on the conceptual but on the relational-procedural level, telling the people what to do, and, more importantly, what *not* to do. If they happen to have an own opinion, then they must suppress it, relativize it, and learn to echo the prefabricated and reassuring collective ideologies instead.

Having an alternative opinion and sharing it publicly usually equalled to major threats in the realities of the early Kádár-system. Living in the subsequent soft dictatorship system with its constant efforts to paralyse reflectivity was like wandering in a thick grey fog with some vague images emerging from the murk. The system was characterized mainly by the eradication of shared meanings by the tricky signification processes to consolidate power. A soft dictatorship is killing softly: often, the result is not physical death but *identicide.* Identicide involves the elimination of the traditional cultural practices and the destruction of shared meanings leading to segregation and atomization in the society, "the intentional killing of that which is subsumed under the term identity" (Meharg, 2006, p. 9). Meharg notes that the physical elimination of the people, genocide through open aggression, may be intertwined with or, as it happened in Hungary, succeeded by identicide. Genocide, as an ultimate crime "may never be fully realized (…) but the deep and lasting impacts of identicide can forever change people, their places, and their cultural practices" (Meharg, 2006, p. 14).

5.6 Conclusions and Implications

Discourses and threats of the open dictatorship, the Rákosi-era, were terrifying and absurd; the threats in the subsequent Kádár-era, nonetheless absurd, were more latent, and were targeted at the mind rather than the body. We may wonder how people could believe in such dogmatic, blatant, and unrealistic notions, sacrificing both science and common sense at the altar of inconsistent and simplified ideologies. Indeed, there were some firm believers: the few whose lives turned for the better, and those who were made vulnerable enough to be attracted by the rigidity and security of the dogmas and adopted a defensive identity position. Generally, however, people did not believe deeply in the dogmas, but they learnt how to *fawn.* Such systems cannot be maintained without a corrupt criminal justice system, varied blackmailing strategies, and, if needed, military oppression.

Hungary's geopolitical position, a potential bridge between the West and the East, with the country's strong, thousand-year-old European roots and traditions is a source for economic growth in peace, and a major threat and imbalance in the turmoil of cold war tensions and military conflicts ("a shield for Europe"). This circumstance has strongly shaped the people's collective memories and narrative resources for identity construction.[5] Historical traumas were found to be the key organizing narrative frameworks in the domestic culture in an empirical study (László & Fülöp, 2011). The longstanding traditions of unresolved historical traumas are more impactful in construing and maintaining defensive identities than comparative victimhood positions (Vincze et al., 2025). Victimological reminiscences identify the ingroup as the sufferers of not only previous, but potential future circumstances (Wydra, 2012). This collective victimological position, underpinned by a shared narrative on the nation's "fate" sensitizes a social group and provides a solid interpretative framework to entrap the group in the prolonged liminality of trauma (Fülöp & Kővágó, 2018; Mészáros & Szabó, 2018). Hungary's somewhat ambivalent participation on the side of Nazi Germany and the country's responsibility in the holocaust were partly a consequence of the collective-level construction of a victimological position (Fülöp & Kővágó, 2018)—and the destructive entitlement. After WWII, 45 years of Soviet occupation followed, and during these years, the conquest was celebrated on fourth April every year as the anniversary of Hungary's "liberation". Traumatizing events, threatening relations, accentuated risks, and authoritarian rule are intrinsically related. If the prototype of such relations, the double bind pattern is extended to large groups of people, establishing a perpetually absurd way of life, then the consolidated context models render learning new freedoms difficult. As Svetlana Alexievich, the Nobel Prize winning Russian writer, commented in 2017: "After communism we thought everything would be fine. But people don't understand freedom" (Walker, 2017).

A dictatorship is a system in which you do not make much use of a thesaurus and must repeatedly use quotation marks when describing "social realities". Covert manipulation is a strong and euthanistic *weapon,* to apply a term here that matches the conceptual metaphor of communist systems, permanent fight. Wydra (2012, p. 50) notes that political myths act "like a serpent's poison". Liberation from their latent and longstanding impacts takes the lives of several generations; and requires major transformations in the people's mindsets, the context models that had served their survival effectively in the past. Survivors' children suffer from the transgenerational transmission of trauma-induced lifestyles and limitations, but this secondary, indirect traumatization remains latent. They cannot show their physical wounds and cannot explain what exactly is wrong with their lives. Positive transformations would necessitate trust and hope—but these elementary virtues are largely missing from traumatized societies. Epistemic trust, a personal conviction that communication from the environment is reliable, is shaped not only by early, family-level impressions but also by the wider sociocultural context (Li et al., 2023).

[5] Devastations of the first Mongol invasion (1241–2); the Ottoman rule in the sixteenth and seventeenth centuries; perceived inequalities established within the Austro-Hungarian monarchy ending in a failed war of independence in 1849; the Trianon Treaty after WWI resulting in a loss of two-thirds of country's territory with millions of Hungarian population and economic resources, and homogenizing the remaining area in terms of culture and language; the Nazi occupation in 1944; and the subsequent Soviet rule until 1989.

In Hungary, as well as in the other CEE states, the system change was also about doing "justice". For example, compensation notes were given to those or to their legal inheritors who had been deprived of their real estates, their farms, and factories. However, people learnt to associate possessing even a minimum of capital with a vital threat. In the previous system, you were an enemy alien, a *kulak*, if you owned the size of land enough to provide for your family. After the system change in 1989, the new "owners" of the compensation notes entered the capitalist system with a mindset totally crippled by the previous communist ideologies. People lacked the relevant experiences anchoring the representations and meanings central to a market economy; they were invariably dreaming about a bright future, but this time, in a land of freedom and welfare (Wydra, 2012).

Most of them quickly and voluntarily sold the notes at a very low price to "investors", mainly the representatives of the previous regime, who, contrarily to the victims, felt safe enough to turn over an entirely new leaf. The concentration of capital was quick. Elemér Hankiss, a Hungarian sociologist explored several interpretations in his evaluation on the 1989 system change. One of these was the introduction of a new strategy to eliminate the barriers that had previously prevented the ruling regime from accumulating considerable wealth on their journey towards "communism" (Hankiss, 2007).

As Harré (2004, p. 1443) has noted, "only rules and conventions have people-pulling power, in their appropriate cultural and historical settings". The political rhetoric of the Orban Government has long been a peculiar amalgamation of pre-war conservative ideologies, consumerist discourse, and state socialist catchwords, merging inconsistent values. A telling example of the survival and strength of the previous communist discourse was the use of Előre! ("onwards and upwards", in contrast with backwards), the salutation by the pioneers in the communist era, which proved a useful rhetorical element during the latest national elections in Hungary in 2022. The pioneers, young kids in the contemporary state socialist system, now mainly the retired older people, could find much comfort in the good old slogans. Ideas from the past as "you should own only as much land as you yourself can cultivate", "unemployed people simply do not want to work", "the state will provide for everyone", "the decadent West" etc. still prevail and contribute to the proliferation of social and political problems in an ageing society where many of the electors vote for the golden past. People are not aware of the similarities, but the catchwords, representing their cherished conventions and providing them with the illusions of safety in an uncertain world, echo deeply in their hearts. In 2010, I wrote: "Hungary seems to be going through a 'reality therapy'. The Hungarians were expecting a sudden transition into their promised land of welfare societies: as if by pressing the shift button the way of life could be CAPITALIZED" (B. Erdos, 2010, p. 92). So far, the "reality therapy" has not succeeded. The discursive legacies of the previous historical era have remained powerful and influential.

2025 brought about a salient turn in the domestic political rhetoric. Prime Minister Orbán, in his powerful speech on 15th March, the national Memorial Day of the Hungarian War of Independence in 1848, announced that it was time for

Eastern cleaning to get away with the overwintering stink bugs, and then continued by referring to the *internal enemy*, several professional groups as representatives of the *intelligentsia*: "they are wearing the scarlet letter, their fate is shame and despise" ("Orbán Viktor", 2025). The threatening and stuttering semiotic chains with their diverging roads failed to consider the Janus-faced character of symbols; the key symbols of Eastern; and the scarlet letter, initially standing for adultery in Hawthorne's novel, and then taking on new, positive meanings in a community reinterpretative process ("able" and "angel"). A political speech, however, is targeted much more at people's affects and inclinations for self-deception than their rationality and education (most Hungarians have never read the novel). The idea of wearing a stigma-symbol as an identifier is loaded with terrifying historical associations but might be attractive for those who dread the uncertainties of the societal crisis and long for previously known certainties.

Groupthink maintains not only the delusions of the masses. Mindguards are always around the decision-makers to "protect" them from any alternative and more authentic information on the social realities that may make them to scowl (Janis, 2008). The distortions finally impede an entire society's adaptation and build a hallucinatory context of mimesis—a collective fawn response. Stereotypes extend to two important domains: the positive, hubristic ones concerning the own group, and the devaluation or excommunication of the other group (the Colorado bugs or "stink bugs"). Eventually, this becomes a *borderline* trickster mechanism, a mental and social split with its destructive consequences.

The dread of uncertainties is deep in humans, who may not realize that sustained chaos is not a "natural" way of life but is rooted in trickster liminality (De Luca Picione & Lozzi, 2021; Horvath & Szakolczai, 2020). Communist regimes heavily relied on the power and chaos of communitas, characterized by the attractive catchwords of equality, liberty, and fraternity. Turner (1969) has noted that both communitas and structure are necessary for the healthy development of a society, but the optimal balance between the processes is always difficult to maintain. Communitas is loss of balance itself; and structure always attempts to bring about further structures. A unilateral focus on these proliferating structures will lead to sustaining the emptied forms only, but not the enthusiasm and motivations behind. The animating processes of communitas, when frozen into a deadly structure, bring about the chaos of trickster liminality (Szakolczai, 2014). In an era of repeated global-level crises, the lessons from the countries having first-hand experiences of the diverse forms and lasting impacts of permanent liminality and its discursive bases may help avoid the potential traps of transitions. The price of a dictatorship, arresting common and adaptive knowledge construction, entails a decline in creativity, positive performance, and the lack of authentic visions and motivations. These dysfunctional phenomena may open the gate to the final common pathway of all hubristic empires: collapse.

References

A Kádár-kormány felhívása. (1956). (Political speech). http://www.rev.hu/history_of_56/szerviz/dokument/kadkorms.htm

Assmann, J. (2008). Communicative and cultural memory. In A. Erll & A. Nünning (Eds.), *Cultural memory studies. An international and interdisciplinary handbook* (pp. 109–118). Springer.

B. Erdos, M. (2010). Cha (lle) nge. The legacy of state socialism in Hungary: A discourse analysis. *Europolis, Journal of Political Science and Theory, 4*(01(7)), 73–99.

B. Erdos, M., & Javor, R. (2022). Entrapment and escape: Exploring the relationship between suicide and emigration in a post-communist country. *The International Journal of Social Psychiatry, 68*(8), 1636–1643. https://doi.org/10.1177/00207640211047617

B. Erdos, M., Juhász, G., & Molnár, D. (2012). Active citizenship in a post-transitional context. *Acta Universitatis Sapientiae, 2*(1), 57. https://real-j.mtak.hu/22958/1/ACTA-Social-Analysis_vol2-1-2012.pdf

B. Erdos, M., & Kelemen, G. (2011). The finite universe: Discursive double bind and parrhesia in state socialism. *History of Communism in Europe, 2*(1), 281–308. https://doi.org/10.7761/hce.2.281

Bateson, G. (1972). *Steps to an ecology of mind. Collected essays in anthropology, psychiatry, evolution, and epistemology*. Jason Aronson.

Benţa, M. I. (2021). The firefighter effect: Social pathology and corruption in liminal occupations. *International Political Anthropology, 14*(2), 103–111. https://doi.org/10.5281/zenodo.5721730

Bereczkei, T. (2016). *Machiavellizmus: A megtévesztés pszichológiája*. Typotex.

Bibó, I. (1990). In I. Bibó Jr. (Ed.), *Válogatott tanulmányok*. Magyar Elektronikus Könyvtár. https://mek.oszk.hu/02000/02043/html/index.html

Codevilla, G. (2024). Origins of the Russkiy Mir ideology. *International Political Anthropology Journal, 17*(2), 115–127. https://doi.org/10.5281/zenodo.14283717

Czeglédi, I. (1953). With Hungarian-Soviet friendship for peace. (Political poster). *Socialist Realism Catalogue*, article no. 40. Múzeum Antikvárium. https://www.pannonbooks.hu/wp-content/uploads/socreal_ok.pdf

De Luca Picione, R., & Lozzi, U. (2021). Uncertainty as a constitutive condition of human experience. An extensive review of the paradoxes and complexities of sensemaking processes in the face of uncertainty crisis. *International Journal of Psychoanalysis and Education: Subject, Action & Society, 1*(2), 14–53. https://doi.org/10.32111/SAS.2021.1.2.2

Dénes, I. Z. (2015). Contributing to healing the world. *European Review, 23*(4), 597–613. https://doi.org/10.1017/S1062798715000241

Doka, K. J. (1999). Disenfranchised grief. *Bereavement Care, 18*(3), 37–39. https://doi.org/10.1080/02682629908657467

Elek, I. (2011, May 11). Bibó István a hazug rendszerek bukásáról [István Bibó about the fall of the systems build on lies]. *HVG*. https://hvg.hu/velemeny/20110511_bibo_elek_istvan

Engels, F. (1882, November 2–3). Engels to Eduard Bernstein in Zurich. (Letter). *Marx-Engels Correspondence 1882*. https://marxists.architexturez.net/archive/marx/works/1882/letters/82_11_02.htm

Fairclough, N. (2013). Critical discourse analysis. In J. P. Gee & M. Handford (Eds.), *The Routledge handbook of discourse analysis* (pp. 9–20). Routledge.

Farkas, J., & Schou, J. (2018). Fake news as a floating signifier: Hegemony, antagonism and the politics of falsehood. *Javnost - The Public, 25*(3), 298–314. https://doi.org/10.1080/13183222.2018.1463047

Forceville, C. (2009). Chapter 2. Non-verbal and multimodal metaphor in a cognitivist framework: Agendas for research. In C. Forceville & E. Urios-Aparisi (Eds.), *Multimodal metaphor* (pp. 19–44). De Gruyter Mouton. https://doi.org/10.1515/9783110215366.1.19

Foucault, M. (1999) *Parrhesia and the Crisis of democratic institutions in discourse & truth: The problematization of parrhesia.* https://foucault.info/parrhesia/foucault.DT3.democracy.en/

Fülöp, É., & Kővágó, P. (2018). A történelmi sérelmekhez való viszonyulás és a kisebbségi csoportokkal szembeni intolerancia összefüggései [Connections between attitudes to historical traumas and intolerance towards minority groups]. In É. Fülöp & P. Kővágó (Eds.), *A kollektív áldozati szerep szociálpszichológiája* (pp. 371–400). Oriold és Társai Kiadó.

Gale, J. (2010). Discursive analysis: A research approach for studying the moment-to-moment construction of meaning in systemic practice. *Human Systems: The Journal of Therapy, Consultation & Training, 21*(2), 7–37.

Gerbner, G., Gross, L., Morgan, M., & Signorielli, N. (1986). Living with television: The dynamics of the cultivation process. In J. Bryant & D. Zillmann (Eds.), *Perspectives on media effects* (pp. 17–40). Lawrence Erlbaum Associates.

Gergely, M. & Kovács, R. (script), Pál, Gy. (graphics). (1955). Ütközet a krumpliföldön [*Battle in the potato plantation*] (slide strip). https://ritkanlathatotortenelem.blog.hu/2015/06/11/regi_magyar_diafilmek_348

Gorky, M. (1950). *Az igazi kultúra [The real culture].* Szikra Nyomda.

Greco, M., & Stenner, P. (2017). From paradox to pattern shift: Conceptualising liminal hotspots and their affective dynamics. *Theory & Psychology, 27*(2), 147–166. https://doi.org/10.1177/0959354317693120

Hankiss, E. (1982). *Társadalmi csapdák.* Diagnózisok. Magvető.

Hankiss, E. (2007). *Transition or transitions? The transformation of Eastern Central Europe 1989–2007.* https://www.eurozine.com/transition-or-transitions/

Hänninen, V. (2004). A model of narrative circulation. *Narrative Inquiry, 14*(1), 69–85. https://doi.org/10.1075/ni.14.1.04han

Harré, R. (2004). *Discursive psychology and the boundaries of sense. Organization Studies, 25*(8), 1435–1453. https://doi.org/10.1177/0170840604046351

Herczeg, M. (Ed.). (1990). *A vásárhelyi leventék háborús kálváriája [The calvary of the young soldiers of Vásárhely].* Csongrád Megyei Levéltár. http://www.okm.gov.hu/letolt/kozokt/libri/konyv.pdf

Høgh-Olesen, H. (2024). Inside the mind of the self-deceiver: Foundational issues in relation to human defences and "the unconscious". *Human Arenas.* (Advance online publication). https://doi.org/10.1007/s42087-024-00458-7

Horvath, A. (1997). *The political psychology of trickster-clown. An analytical experiment around communism as a myth.* Papers 97/5, European Institute - Political and Social Sciences. Retrieved from Cadmus, EUI Research Repository, https://hdl.handle.net/1814/285

Horváth, A. (2013). Bibó István és társai koncepciós pere. *Világosság, 52*(1–2), 95–97.

Horvath, A., & Szakolczai, A. (2020). *The political sociology and anthropology of evil: Tricksterology.* Routledge.

Hunyady, G. (2002). A kontraszelekció pszichológiája: Egy kutatási terület feltérképezése [The psychology of counter-selection: Explorations of a new research area]. In G. Hunyady (Ed.), *Szociálpszichológia történelemtanároknak. Tanulmánygyűjtemény* (pp. 448–488). Ökonet.

Janis, I. L. (2008). Groupthink. *IEEE Engineering Management Review, 36*(1), 36. https://doi.org/10.1109/EMR.2008.4490137

Kádár, J. (1975). *Válogatott beszédek és cikkek 1957–1974 [Selected speeches ad articles between 1957–1974]* (Political speeches) (pp. 264–265). Kossuth.

Kelemen, G. (2017). Mozaikok Szöllősi Gábor életútjához [Mosaics of Gábor Szöllősi's career]. In É. Vojtek & V. Borda (Eds.), *Reflexiók. A szociális munka korszerű oktatásának kérdései: Tanulmányok Szöllősi Gábor 65. születésnapjára* (pp. 10–24). Pécsi Tudományegyetem.

Kiss, K. (1952, February 24). *Rákosi elvtárs életéről [The Life of Comrade Rákosi]* (Political speech). http://www.rev.hu/sulinet45/szerviz/dokument/rakosi.htm

Krumplibogárral támadtak a hidegháborúban [Colorado bugs as a weapon during the cold war era]. (2013, September 4). *Múlt-kor.* https://m.mult-kor.hu/20130904_krumplibogarral_tamadtak_a_hidegháboruban

Laclau, E. (2003). Why do empty signifiers matter to politics? In S. Žižek (Ed.), *Jacques Lacan: Critical evaluations in cultural theory* (pp. 305–313). Psychology Press.

Lakoff, G. (2004). *Don't think of an elephant! Know your values and frame and debate*. Chelsea Green Publishing.

Lakoff, G. (2012). Metaphor and war: The metaphor system used to justify war in the Gulf. *Cognitive Semiotics, 4*(2), 5–19. https://doi.org/10.1515/cogsem.2012.4.2.5

László, J., & Fülöp, É. (2011). Nemzeti identitás és kollektív áldozati szerep [National identity and collective victimhood-contents of Hungarian national identity: Examination of collective victimhood with exploration of emotions related to victim and perpetrator position]. *Pszichológia, 31*(3), 295–315. https://doi.org/10.1556/Pszicho.31.2011.3.6

Li, E., Campbell, C., Midgley, N., & Luyten, P. (2023). Epistemic trust: a comprehensive review of empirical insights and implications for developmental psychopathology. *Research in Psychotherapy: Psychopathology Process and Outcome, 26*(3). https://doi.org/10.4081/ripppo.2023.704

Magyar-szovjet barátsággal a békéért [Hungarian-Soviet friendship for peace]. (1952, February 17). *Délmagyarország, 8*(40), 1. https://dmarchiv.bibl.u-szeged.hu/12469/1/dm_1952_040.pdf

Mátyás király és a székely ember lánya [King Matthias and the Szekler's daughter]. (n.d.). Magyar Elektronikus Könyvtár (Audio material). https://matyasmesek.oszk.hu/main.html?mu=hangzo_mese_03_matyas_kiraly_es_a_szekely_ember_leanya.xml

McNamee, S. (2015). Radical presence: Alternatives to the therapeutic state. *European Journal of Psychotherapy & Counselling, 17*(4), 373–383. https://doi.org/10.1080/13642537.2015.1094504

Meharg, S. J. (2006). *Identicide. Precursor to genocide*. Working Paper 05, November 2006, Centre for Security and Defence Studies. Retrieved from: https://www3.carleton.ca/csds/docs/working_papers/MehargWP05.pdf

Mészáros, N., & Szabó, Z. P. (2018). "Egy ezredévi szenvedés…": Kollektív áldozati hiedelmek és hatásuk Magyarországon. ["A thousand year of suffering…" collective beliefs on victimhood and their impact in Hungary]. In É. Fülöp & P. Kővágó (Eds.), *A kollektív áldozati szerep szociálpszichológiája* (pp. 341–370). Oriold és Társai Kiadó.

Moscovici, S. (2002). *Társadalomlélektan [Societal psychology]*. Osiris.

Orbán Viktor ünnepi beszéde az 1848/49-es forradalom és szabadságharc 177. évfordulóján. [Viktor Orbán's commemoration speech on the 177th anniversary of the 1848/49 Revolution and War of Independence]. (2025, March 15). *Miniszterelnöki Kabinetiroda*. https://miniszterelnok.hu/orban-viktor-unnepi-beszede-az-1848-49-es-forradalom-es-szabadsagharc-177-evfordulojan/

Potter, W. J. (2022). What does the idea of media cultivation mean? *Journal of Broadcasting & Electronic Media, 66*(4), 540–564. https://doi.org/10.1080/08838151.2022.2131788

Pottier, E. (1871). *The International*. (Lyrics). https://www.marxists.org/history/ussr/sounds/lyrics/international.htm

Rákosi, M. (1953, July 11). Beszéd a budapesti pártaktíván [Speech at the Budapest party assembly] (Political speech). Magyar Elektronikus Könyvtár. http://mek.niif.hu/01900/01937/html/szerviz/dokument/rakosis0.htm

Salvatore, S., Palmieri, A., Cordella, B., & Iuso, S. (2021). The decay of signs' semiotic value: A cultural psychology interpretation of the contemporary social scenario. *Culture & Psychology, 27*(4), 539–561. https://doi.org/10.1177/1354067X211027276

Salvatore, S., & Venuleo, C. (2017). Liminal transitions in a semiotic key: The mutual in-feeding between present and past. *Theory & Psychology, 27*(2), 215–230. https://doi.org/10.1177/0959354317692889

Seligman, M. E. (1972). Learned helplessness. *Annual Review of Medicine, 23*, 407–412. https://doi.org/10.1146/annurev.me.23.020172.002203

Smith, J. A. (2002). Suicide in post-socialist countries: Examples from Hungary and Belarus. *Anthropology of East Europe Review, 20*(1), 55–65.

Somogyvári, L. (2015). Származási kategóriák és lemorzsolódás a középiskolában (1953–1962) [Categories of origin and dropout in secondary schools between 1953 and 1962]. *Neveléstudomány, 3*(3), 56–68. https://ojs.elte.hu/nevelestudomany/article/view/6543

Stenner, P. (2017). *Liminality and experience. A transdisciplinary approach to the psychosocial.* Palgrave Macmillan.

Szakolczai, A. (2001). In a permanent state of transition: Theorizing the East-European condition. *Journal for Theory and Practice of Liminal Phenomena, 1*(1) http://limen.mi2.hr/limen1-2001/arpad_szakolczai.html

Szakolczai, A. (2014). Living permanent liminality: The recent transition experience in Ireland. *Irish Journal of Sociology, 22*(1), 28–50. https://doi.org/10.7227/IJS.22.1.3

Szakolczai, Á. (2017). Permanent (trickster) liminality: The reasons of the heart and of the mind. *Theory & Psychology, 27*(2), 231–248. https://doi.org/10.1177/0959354317694095

Turner, V. (1969). *The Ritual Process. Structure and Anti-Structure*. Aldine Transaction.

van Dijk, T. A. (2006). Discourse and manipulation. *Discourse & Society, 17*(3), 359–383. https://doi.org/10.1177/0957926506060250

van Dijk, T. A. (2009). Critical discourse studies: A sociocognitive approach. In R. Wodak & M. Meyer (Eds.), *Methods of critical discourse analysis* (pp. 62–85). Sage.

van Dijk, T. A. (2013). The field of epistemic discourse analysis. *Discourse Studies, 15*(5), 497–499. https://doi.org/10.1177/1461445613501448

van Dijk, T. A. (2014). Discourse-cognition-society: Current state and prospects of the socio-cognitive approach to discourse. In C. Hart & P. Cap (Eds.), *Contemporary studies in critical discourse analysis* (pp. 121–146). Bloomsbury.

Vincze, O., Németh, M., Amrein-Werner, H., Kokorin, A., & Bigazzi, S. (2025). Relationship between collective victimhood and defensive strategies. *Studia Psychologica, 67*(1), 87–106. https://doi.org/10.31577/sp.2025.01.913

Walker, S. (2017, July 21). *Interview Svetlana Alexievich: 'After communism we thought everything would be fine. But people don't understand freedom'* (Interview). The Guardian. https://www.theguardian.com/books/2017/jul/21/svetlana-alexievich-interview

Wiggins, S., & Potter, J. (2013). Discursive psychology. In C. Willig & W. Stainton-Rogers (Eds.), *Handbook of qualitative psychology* (2nd ed., pp. 73–90). Sage.

Wydra, H. (2012). The power of symbols—Communism and beyond. *International Journal of Politics, Culture, and Society, 25*(1–3), 49–69. https://doi.org/10.1007/s10767-011-9116-x

Zittoun, T., Duveen, G., Gillespie, A., Ivinson, G., & Psaltis, C. (2003). The use of symbolic resources in developmental transitions. *Culture & Psychology, 9*(4), 415–448. https://doi.org/10.1177/1354067X0394006

Chapter 6
The Trickster as a Failed Charismatic: *The Dog's Night Song*

6.1 The Personal in the Political

Manipulative societal discourse provides the individual with a false identity project to be realized. Horvath (1997) notes that both the trickster and the charismatic appear in the chaos of transitions. While the trickster is more of a negative hero, endowed with cunnings and semi-divine features, but also representing hate, cheat, and destruction, the charismatic is characterized by wisdom and inspiration, and carries the promise of redemption from the social ills and from the spiritual crises that have resulted in the loss of meaning for the community and the individual (Chamankhah, 2014; Horvath, 1997).

How can you differentiate between the trickster and the charismatic in a social system that is built on manipulation, and explicit or subtle, nevertheless deep threats? Can a person alternate between these two different identities? How to practise parrhesia in a system that would rapidly silence and distort the unwanted or uneasy messages? How to get the message through so that the truth be heard?

My earliest memories of *The Dog's Night Song*, a film by Gabor Bódy (1983), go back to the 1980s when I was a university student and parallel, I took my first steps in building a counsellor's career, in those days as a volunteer at a crisis intervention centre. I can still remember my vivid first impressions. This film was a genuine shock, different from anything else I had seen so far: astonishing, scandalous, and awesome. It seemed a desperate attempt to tell the truth, the personally lived and felt truth in an environment where it was not welcomed. This was an extraordinary experience in the contemporary culture permeated by the hypocrisy, lies and absurdities of the fading communist system that determined, delimited, and discredited societal and interpersonal relationships. In those days, I could not find the right words for what I could witness. The film reflected the experiences of the absurdities that Árpád Szakolczai (2001, 2014, 2015, 2017) described as the salient features of permanent liminality. Twenty-five years later, I briefly commented on the film in an

M. B. Erdos, *Transitions - Liminality as Lived Experience*,
https://doi.org/10.1007/978-3-031-96007-9_6

article about the role of intelligentsia in the Hungarian system change (Erdos & Kelemen, 2011). Forty years later, I am entering my third, deeper, and broader hermeneutical circle.

The Dog's Night Song (Bódy, 1983) provides a clear and detailed picture of the devastations of the "soft" system, relativizing and eradicating human values, giving birth to fake or defensive identities and promoting self-imposed identicide and suicide. The first showing in 1983 was in the year when Hungary did not only rank first in the global suicide statistics but also reached a national peak with 4911 deaths among 10.7 million people, about 46/100,000 inhabitants in the "happiest" barrack in the Soviet bloc (Zonda et al., 2013). The auteur, Gábor Bódy, born in 1946, was found dead on 24 October 1985, one day after the silenced anniversary of the 1956 revolution. He cut himself deep with a knife and died by heart embolism. Whether it was suicide (the official version, Hegedüs, 2020) or an accident, the cut meant as a non-lethal self-injury, a self-imposed torture, or he was killed by the regime is still debated. *The Dog's Night Song* is his last film, and in many ways, is foretelling about his future death, supporting the official verdict, suicide, while not fully excluding other possibilities. The concluding scenes of the film are about a police investigation on two unexplained, mysterious deaths, one seemingly a suicide or perhaps a murder, finally proving an accident. The other case remains unexplained.

Bódy in his initial sketches did not indicate the depths of his artistic explorations, and commented on his title choice as follows:

> The title "*The Dog's Night Song*" or the howl of the prairie-wolf, originated from the well-known phenomenon that dogs bark at the moon (…) in human culture it is a well-known expression of the fact that there is a constant relationship between the animalistic and cosmic (…). People bark at the cosmos in a more complex, less unified way (Bódy, 1987, p. 149).[1]

The prairie wolf, the coyote is a traditional animal representation of the trickster; the liminal, destructive, and semi-divine evil, residing on the boundaries between chaos and order, trespassing the borders to make some trouble in human communities (Horvath & Szakolczai, 2020). The trickster is a lonely creature, possibly, an outcast, a figure inhabiting the in-betweenness, existing between the human and the divine: "appearing out of nowhere and again disappearing into nothingness"; "a living dead with multiple, undefined souls" (Horvath & Szakolczai, 2020, pp. 16–17). Here, the animalistic-cosmic feature is a reference to the powers of antistructure. Alternating between the two modes, structure, and antistructure, is highlighted by using both everyday life scenes much in the manner of a documentary, as well as the "dreamy", surreal liminal night scenes in the film (Bódy, 1987, p. 150). Bódy often uses the sounds of the night, crickets' chirping and dogs' whining to underscore the dreaminess, dissolving the boundaries between the routine realities and the reality of dreams or nightmares, the messages of the night received

[1] Translations from Hungarian into English are provided as they appear in the original work, unless indicated otherwise.

during the time of the prairie wolves, representing the evil, destruction, and death. Dreaminess underscores the *authenticity of derealization.*

> What is the essence of dreams? They exist and they do not. They can be and cannot be reached. Something appears before us that cannot be obtained. This duality is their nature. Anything that is included in the film as reality soon after appears as part of a dream (Bódy, 1987, p. 149).

As Bódy argues, dreams are fragmented, illusionary, and are detached from the usual bonds of space and time. The confusing impressions are further strengthened by using amateur film cuts in a professional piece. Ordinary village people appear as actors or actresses, keeping their original dialect and gestures. Boundaries between art and mundane realities also dissolve.

A clear focus on *chaos* is maintained throughout the film: the disrupted storyline and the numerous scenes about destruction, dissociation, alienation, and isolation reflect the basic experience of the era when the transition of 1989 was close, but only the confusion and the anomie of the approaching transformation could be sensed. Entering the world of the film is entering a vortex of the crisis. The characters act, and their actions are judged by the environment, but in most cases, their verbal reflections are either disabled or prove inauthentic. This makes the film an elucidative reflection on people's lived experiences amidst the absurdities of permanent liminality. The fragmented and focused snapshots are a deep exploration of the various characters' internal and interpersonal conflicts.

6.2 Polyphony, Dissociation, and Fragmented Identities

The characters represent the many facets of identity (Erdos & Kelemen, 2011). They are struggling to confess their sins against others and themselves and find redemption through a parrhesiastic act in a life crisis. Most of them fail. Only those succeed who are brave enough to confront and integrate the animalistic-cosmic aspects into the totality of their own existence, that is, are progressing from permanent to transformative liminality by using the traditional ritual elements of a transition.

Gábor Bódy in his own sketches has identified six main characters in the film, extending the polyphonic editing principle to the extremes:

> These scene-units (which are not scenes in the traditional sense, but rather monologues in most cases, or scenes which are being performed behind the doors) do not meet a traditional narrative story's claims to be scenes. Rather, they are slices of life and like these must be built up through great improvisions (Bódy, 1987, p. 149).

The swindler priest, a mixture of the trickster and the charismatic, acted by Gábor Bódy himself is in a central position in the film. While pretending to be a Catholic priest, a prisoner of God[2] evidently lacking some important technical knowledge, the whats and hows of priesthood, his spirituality and dedication to bring more authenticity in the lives of the people he encounters could make him a genuine spiritual leader. The emanation of faith has touched those around him—as the priest from the neighbouring village comments during a police investigation. The immediate context of the swindler priest's activities is a small village in the state socialist Hungary, defined as a *missionary field*. As Bódy (1987) outlines, this is a typical rural environment in the contemporary era, characterized by a peculiar amalgamation of the heavy burdens of daily life, backwardness, and by some limited prosperity of the Kádár regime's early and restricted consumerism.

The swindler priest is engaged in lengthy conversations with a retired council leader. Not only the Catholic religion, but also communism, a religion of atheism with its inherent paradoxes relies on doctrines of salvation—the latter in the form of a "redemptive catastrophe" (Wydra, 2012, p. 55). The council leader is paralysed due to an accidental shot in the fights during the 1956 revolution. He spends his days in a wheelchair, cherishing vivid nostalgias for Rákosi's previous, open dictatorship, and searching for the "reactionist" forces who are "spinning the wheels of history backwards", never finding the principal one—himself. Bódy comments on the similarities in the two Eastern European characters:

> (…) both are self-appointed prophets or self-appointed intellectuals. I would not say they are without intellectual awareness, but in any case, they are without social form, without the support of society. In a sense it is a self-destroying acceptance, or challenge, of an intellectual role (…) it produces only fragmented faces (Bódy, 1987, p. 149).

In a scene, the swindler priest is trying to work a miracle by making the paralysed party leader move and walk. He is *hypnotic* but the miracle does not work. Does this scene refer to the debilitating traditions of the system? Total helplessness and paralysis with no escape? The impossibility of redemption in such a societal context? Or to the priest's non-divine, non-charismatic character? In a way, the priest does make the council leader move by taking him for long walks in the surrounding hills. On such occasions, the priest is playing with the wheelchair—letting it go on a slope and then catching it again. The council leader responds to this precarious action with a mixture of excitement and fear. Is this *death game*, also a *truth game*, a Russian roulette, meant to teach him about the value of his life, which he is denying? Or to teach him a method to commit suicide? Or, as the police suspects when they find the man dead on the road, is it a murder attempt, finally successful?

The astronomer, Attila, also founder of a shaman punk band, the Galloping Coroners[3] is a counterpoint to these self-destructive sufferings and death games. He is characterized by Bódy as an "intellectually open being; a man of theories" (Bódy, 1987, p. 149). He is committed to explore the *secrets of the cosmos*. He does not

---

[2] Reference to a Hungarian novel by Géza Gárdonyi on the life of a princess who became a nun in the thirteenth century and is respected as a saint for her self-sacrificing life—an atoning sacrifice after Hungary's invasion and destruction by the Tartars.

[3] https://en.wikipedia.org/wiki/Galloping_Coroners.

play any roles but expresses his experiences freely through his music. Atilla (or Attila as spelled in his scientific papers) is not a professional actor either: in the context of filming, he is a layperson. Now, in 2025, he is an internationally renowned member of the Hungarian Academy of Sciences with several publications on the *living universe*, studying organisms' endless strivings towards life—a life-centred principle with its strong ecological, societal, and personal implications (e.g. Grandpierre, 2023). The shaman punk his band the Galloping Coroners played was unique, refreshing, powerful, and scandalous in the 1980s. Though this band was prohibited in the contemporary system, it was such a success that the organizers neglected the ban and regularly invited them for concerts. The name Galloping Coroners indicated that people lived their lives as *living dead*. Life had ceased on Earth, but people had not even noticed—as they commented in an interview scene in Bódy's film. Atilla's double career represents an organic integration of *cosmos and chaos*, resiliently enabling the transformations between the alternating patterns. He is the one who is not stuck, not for a moment, in the death trap of permanent liminality. The spontaneously evolving patterns of cosmos through chaos are also present in their music. The emphasis is on animalistic vocalizations, not on words (Erdos & Kelemen, 2011).

Another key character is a little boy with his Super 8 camera that he received from a West German "friend", a spy, who used the boy to take photos of the local industrial and military sites. The child is neglected and isolated, ready to connect to anyone who would listen to his questions. His mother Marika has turned over a new leaf and left for the capital. His abandoned father is a busy and committed military officer. The boy is a native to filmmaking, inquisitive and observant of the people around him. The child is a representative of a perspective that is alien to solid social conventions. A child's position is that of a stranger who may freely question the "evident" rules and values an adult cannot: "For a child, reality is a blank space (…) he himself tries to find relations in it. Thus, the recordings of the boy, and the visions created by myself should form a unified whole (Bódy, 1987, p. 149).

He is the one who is asking the astronomer of the meaning of dogs' barking at night. The astronomer is open to the boy's genuine interest and responds that perhaps this is how dogs collectively remember some ancient cataclysms, or perhaps this is their way *to exceed the inevitable horrors* of their doggish existence—and he continues to extend this statement by referring to humans' existential struggles. Here, he changes the genre and the tone as if he were talking to an *adult*—to himself, another singer in the night. In mythical thinking, cosmic cataclysms create life and a new cosmic order (Eliade, 1963 cit. Wydra, 2012).

Inquisitiveness and spying had a special significance in Bódy's life. Like several other members of the contemporary intelligentsia, he was a reluctant agent of the Hungarian state security police, the ill-famed III/III division under the cover name Pesti and was required to report on his close colleagues' suspected "conspiracy" against the communist regime. As several readers of this chapter have never experienced the longstanding moral destructions of a soft dictatorship, at this point, I must add some further details. Reporting on each other's political notions and behaviour in secret was a common requirement in the early cold war era and in the subsequent years, even for those whose jobs were not closely connected to state security issues. People were usually blackmailed into these operations. Menaces by the regime usually involved threats concerning their own or their family members' safety or career, but any aspects of their personal lives were used, anything that could ground the intimidation. Consequently, you could never know who to trust. This was one of the power techniques to maintain the pressure on the "people" (not *citizens,* ever since). Some of the victims—and I do mean victims here as reporting was seldom their free choice—tried to fool the trickster system, e.g. by practising a double discourse. Building some trust and the collaboration of the intimidated ones was another but risky option: close colleagues on a business trip to "enemy countries" sometimes mutually agreed upon the contents of their reports prior to submitting these to the authorities who would probably know very well how to evaluate the quality of such "information". In these cases, the information content was perhaps not so much the point as *the very act of reporting*, a building brick, if not one cornerstone of the system. Therefore, reporting was not only, not even mainly, about obtaining some compromising information, but about sustaining confusion, uncertainties, self-censorship, distrust, isolation, and disempowerment, while also undermining people's self-esteem and creating a culture of guilt and shame, in which many people had to carry the heavy and discouraging burden of secrets.

In 1973, when Bódy joined III/III, he could even have believed in the merits of the prevailing system: after Rákosi's terror, the Kádár regime seemed better, with its nice notions on equity, comradeship, and the somewhat diminishing, though not disappearing paranoia in the society. Further, people were socialized into the system right from their kindergarten years in the institutions of public education. However, only four months had passed until Bódy could realize the gravity of the situation and the risks involved in his new commitment. He wanted to quit. He shared some details about a police investigation on him with his friends, at the same time telling the III/III control officers that this was just an idea to defeat all suspicion on part of the people he was to observe ("Bódy Gábor", 2010). The double discourse—trying to trick the tricksters and controlling those who control—did not work. The control officers were not enthusiastic. Still, this way, he could warn the people around him not to tell him too much about their lives. Naturally, there were not any guarantees on the recipients' proper interpretation (if there was ever an appropriate, shared interpretation on any events and actions in this confusing societal milieu). During a meeting with the control officers, "Pesti" even questioned if there was any threat to the system involved in the young artists' activities. A summary report written by Zoltán Kazal, police officer, explains why Bódy should continue. The text below also illuminates how the police officer positioned himself as a person competent to evaluate artistic values. The firm believers in the "scientific" ideology of the system were authorized to assess the merits of the works of art, and of science:

> … these young people who thought themselves to be talented but were not granted an opportunity to present their unartistic works, all of them below the acceptable level, confronted the party's (Hungarian Socialist Workers' Party – the translator) cultural policy (…)

> consequently, they are the potential targets for the enemies of our socialist system (1974, January 3., in "50 éve történt", 2024. Translation is mine).

Though Bódy seemed reluctant to do the job, he undeniably did harm to some people from his close professional network. He took to drinking and used this as an apology for his overall low achievements as an agent. In 1981, he was finally dismissed for his unsatisfactory performance ("Bódy Gábor", 2010). In a curriculum vitae, Bódy defined his core values and commitment to continue his life along the values of freedom, love, art, and science (Csaplár, 2005).

His second marriage to a West German citizen, an immigrant from Hungary, and the subsequent birth of their son could have served as an escape. As a family father he would have been allowed to leave the country—a right that was only exceptionally given in this physically and mentally closed system. Probably, he had hoped for the chance to continue his work in contemporary West Germany. This positive scenario seemed to be only his wishful thinking, and he might have been forced to join another secret police, now in East Germany. These subsequent guesses were somewhat confirmed by his regular encounters with a young and mysterious man from East Germany (Csaplár, 2005) —and, more importantly, by the appearance of the German spy in *The Dog's Night Song*, and his dubious "friendship" with the little child, helpless and misled, but fully enchanted by the opportunity to get a camera as a gift, his only treasure.

The two other characters mentioned in Bódy's sketches are the little boy's parents. The mother's role, Marika, was performed by Marietta Méhes, actress and singer, Bódy's former partner and their daughter's mother. Marika, married to a military officer, got sick and tired of her husband's treating her as one of his possessions, not responding to her emotional and sexual needs: "…he can convey only a very little towards the woman both emotionally and sexually. Consequently, the marriage sooner or later becomes a formality and fails. The woman however cannot accept this degradation or compromise" (Bódy, 1987, p. 149).

The military officer is characterized by Bódy as "a productive, disciplined and constructive type of man in *this society*" (italics are mine) … "gets so tired because of his own work and conflicts" (Bódy, 1987, p. 149). The soldier's *productivity* is a contrast to the contemporary discourse on the intelligentsia, identified as *non-productive* workers, not producing any *material* entities in a materialistic society, rather, obsessed with creating something intangible, even incomprehensibly diverse, and different, what is more, potentially uncontrollable, suspicious, and dangerous. The frame of discipline is also emphasized in Bódy's draft. The officer's actual appearance in the film is accompanied by explosions, weapons, rockets, alcohol use, and the red colours of aggressive ("manly") outbursts—and of the type of love he was capable of. He misses Marika badly, and during an army exercise he is writing a sincere, apologizing, and touching letter to his sweet little darling. This letter is a salient counterpoint to the context, which suggests an aggressive solution and represents the internal struggles of a man suffering from the loss of his wife and of his self-confidence. Instead of posting the letter, he is tearing it into pieces and asks his friend to help him get Marika back. Their masculinity and comradeship are expressed through drinking, enthusiastic army songs, and aggressive comments (Erdos & Kelemen, 2011).

Marika has joined another punk band, A.E. Bizottság (Albert Einstein Committee) and is singing their song *Love* that is, at a first glance, is about the animalistic instincts of sexuality, and is presented in a "scandalous" manner; but there is much more than that in this song. The alternation and dissonance between the vulgar, animalistic scenes and the harmonious melody establish a clear connection between romantic love and the elementary need to include the bodily aspects of love into the romantic and esoteric incompleteness. By singing the song, Marika could express the totality of her experiences—her own self. Witnessing the performance, her husband tormented by jealousy and grief over his loss could realize that he would not possess her anymore and their relationship was over. The only argument that remained was their child's future.

Bódy's reflections on romantic love in this film are mostly about incompleteness and deficiencies: possessing and controlling the other from the military officer's perspective; compulsive, controlling, and humiliating care masked as love in a short scene between Atilla and his self-appointed girlfriend immediately rejected by him; a child's vague ideas and fantasies on sexuality, and love reduced to sexuality and seduction in the *seventh character*'s fragmented story.

This seventh character is not mentioned in the preliminary sketches as a key figure. She is a woman suffering from, and slowly dying of, tuberculosis. Her disease is a representation of the incurable problems between the self and the environment, and of the aesthetic qualities coupled with sexual, animalistic desire (Wilsey, 2012). Tuberculosis brings about the sacred, ambivalent condition of abjection, a state between life and death, isolating the person from mundane realities (Novikov, 2021). The woman repeatedly contacts the priest for pastoral support and seems determined to make a confession. She is seductive and troubled. The swindler priest's charismatic self, obeying the laws of priestly chastity and caritas, responds to the woman's deepest internal need to end self-deception and tell her personally lived truth about her relationship with her former husband. The swindler priest's understanding of the woman's deep emotional needs disguised as sexual attraction to men—to use a psychoanalytical term here, a confusion of tongue (Ferenczi, 1988)—seems accurate. The priest gives her a hatpin and instructs her to stab herself whenever she feels that she cannot approximate the truth. First, she is desperately repeating her lies, defending her false identity that she fears to abandon, and keeps torturing and *stabbing herself in the arm.* Slowly she develops a habit of saying evening prayers to herself and asserts to find peace through the prayers. While praying, she is keeping the hatpin in her hands as a symbol of her genuine wish to live a more authentic life. Her body is covered by a blanket. Praying was considered shameful, reactionary, and ridiculous in those days, so only a close friend, an earthly minded fellow patient knew about it—but she was ignorant of the hatpin. She teasingly and playfully threw a punch on the woman's hand, and the hatpin stabbed through the woman's *heart.* In the end, the charismatic's spirituality and search for the truth turns out to be just as lethal as the trickster's actions. *Truth is lethal; and the reflective self is killed before it could have fully developed.*

Gábor Bódy' death was a consequence of a deep *stab in the arm* by a knife that he had received as a gift from one of his students, but the exact circumstances of his death have never been clarified. The official suicide verdict was questioned by his wife, friends, and colleagues, who could witness his professional successes and knew about his ongoing work and plans (Csaplár, 2005). In the film, ambiguities are not resolved—nothing and no one are what or who they initially seemed. Did Bódy follow the advice of his own creature, the swindler priest, and identified with the seventh character in his search for the truth? *Be yourself the seventh one*—as is written in a poem by Attila József (1932), a poet of liminality about the human compulsion of rebirth in the deep crises during one's life. József died by suicide at the age of 32. Was Bódy's death also a suicide, a deliberate act? Was it an accident while practising self-harm in a desperate hope to ease his mental sufferings by the torture and find his embodied truth and authentic self? Or was he murdered, with the crime circumspectly disguised as a veritable suicide? Is the concluding scene of the movie, the swindler priest's lonely, ecstatic, and orgiastic kamikaze dance talking about his future suicide? Is it his reflection on the unsustainability of false lives and false identities of the living dead, who, as the kamikaze song by A. E. Bizottság depicts, are flying alone in the twilight zone between life and death?

When, after the suspicious events, the swindler priest is returning to the capital, he is visiting a nun (possibly, a swindler nun), and is reporting on his actions: "I have successfully fulfilled my duty". But what was his duty? Reintroducing spirituality into the lives of people he encountered—or killing the ones who are hopelessly searching for the truth in their lives?

The charismatic and the trickster selves are quickly alternating in the last scenes. He is describing an ecstatic and captivating mystical experience· The word ecstasy (Greek ekstasis) is indicative of an out-of-self experience, as standing outside oneself and absorbed in the transcendent and divine. It may also refer to displacement or insanity, being out of one's mind (Origin and history of ecstasy, n.d.). The nun is responding to him in an earthly style, invalidating the priest's report on this mystical participation. They discuss the finances necessary for his final escape, emigration (ecstasy as *displacement*), as one of the two final common pathways in the era. The other was suicide, and the rates were inversely related (Erdos & Javor, 2022). His runaway starts. He is chased by the police as a suspect for murder—possibly, two murders—and for "provocation" against the system. The latter charge seems more serious and threatening. A Judas-character is warning him of his betrayal. This short scene is an imitation-of-Christ episode again, but the next scene is the Dionysian kamikaze dance of the failed charismatic and the returning trickster, indicating the impossibility of redemption. Here, we encounter the ambiguous figure of *homo sacer*, the outcast, the sacred man who must not be sacrificed but is considered a source of peril, is chased, and can be killed by anyone (Horvath & Szakolczai, 2020).

Bódy's untimely death was a shock to his friends and colleagues. In the excerpt below, one of them, a well-known Hungarian actor establishes a clear connection between the loss and Hungary's suicidal culture in the 1980s:

> My masters are dead. Thanks God, I had only two. The first one ten years ago. (By a train.) And now (continuously) Gábor too. Now. How long is NOW? (…) The whole thing is like a new cult. They are there, and we stay here raising altars in our own souls. Our conscience becomes bitter. We feel ashamed. (…) Now, what are we (Hungarians) the best at?—Oh, well, at committing suicide (Cserhalmi, 1987, pp. 53–54).

The *Dog's night song* is about the many aborted ways of parrhesia and reaching for the authenticity of identity in an organized system of lies conducive to the development of socialist-type *flat* identities. In Hungary's soft dictatorship, communism was not so much about having nothing—rather, "being nothing" (Wydra, 2012, p. 54).

Attempts to tell one's truth are made through one's sufferings, a testimony through the body, a personal and emotional letter written by the authentic self but never sent, quarrels, routine and mechanical Catholic confessions, secret and private events that are transformed into public scenes and are desacralized by the film. Is this a voyeur's curiosity or the inquisitiveness of a coroner, testifying the cessation of communication and the death of a community? Police investigations with their predetermined "truths" rooted in contemporary ideologies and threats, and finally, pre-written scripts in preparation for a showcase trial to sentence the victim are the powerful counterpoints to these aborted trials of parrhesia.

Apart from the instinctive, shamanic punk vocalizations, identifying the pre-reflective as the only possible reflection on the absurd societal realities, all attempts fail. The many faces of death—a consequence of searching for the truth—are unclear, and the boundaries between an accident, a homicide and a suicide are confused. Despite one's sacrifice and sufferings, in a system deeply impregnated by lies—the daily ones, and the life lies that deprive one's life of its meaning—salvation is hopeless. Polyphony, a systematically applied editing principle in the film does not lead to a dialogue between the many facets of identity represented by the individual characters, but to absolute dissociation:

> It is as if words had been released from the shackles of sense, to enjoy a play period of complete freedom and establish unusual relationships among themselves . . . [the] brief coexistence of these words, expression and objects outside the usual logical conditions discloses their inherent ambivalence. Their multiple meanings and potentialities that would not manifest themselves in normal conditions are revealed (Bakhtin, 1984, p. 423).

Polyphony reveals the strange, the liminal and the ecstatic qualities, but the characters remain entrapped in unresolvable and tormenting liminal hotspots (Stenner, 2017), never reaching transformation and integration. Initially, this non-reflected polyphony results in dissociation. When carried to the extremes, polyphony is exchanged for certainty, for the hegemony of a dominant and finally (self)destructive voice. The negative coherence of death is established through this pervasive dissociation, ultimately finding a focus in self-destruction. The crisis-related phenomena are depicted and accentuated by the frequent occurrences of downward motions in the film—a wheelchair or a ball getting loose on the slope as the *gravitation metaphor* indicating the ease and increasing velocity of the fall towards the underworld (Erdos & Kelemen, 2011). These scenes and the swindler priest's character together refer to the fall of Lucifer, the rebel angel bringing people the light—but bringing it too early, and without authorization. The frequently appearing night scenes are strong metaphorical representations of death (Lakoff & Johnson, 1980). The master self, represented by the swindler priest, accidentally or deliberately destroys several self-parts, the woman with tuberculosis and the communist council leader, while other self-constituents become isolated, unable to manage their loss and anger (the officer) or anxiety (the child).

Who, how, and why will tell us about the truth in an era dominated and controlled by the trickster? And how do we know if the truth has been told? The *Dog's Night Song* is a condensation of people's lived experiences on the deep but masked devastations inherent in a soft dictatorship. This film is a dramatic confession, a reflection on the paralysation and inability to reflect by a sufferer who, with all these talents and wits, could not find his way out of a system that was killing their own people softly. It would have been easy to diagnose Gábor Bódy who identified himself in his reports to the secret police as a person suffering from alcoholism (Csaplár, 2005). However, the societal and historical milieu strengthening the personal vulnerabilities cannot be overseen here (Erikson, 1975). The diagnosis belongs to the system more than to the person, and the personal is indeed the political:

> What it means to live multiple lives, have multiple selves, and tell multiple autobiographical stories—a view that, as this argument goes, is well compatible with the sense of living a singular life—is not only a matter of philosophy, psychology, anthropology, and cultural narrative studies. It also implies taking into account the historical trajectory along which the question of what it is to be a human being is posed (Brockmeier, 2019. p. 46).

6.3 The Persisting Burden of Secrets and Traumas

The social practice of reporting on each other and the associated secrets serve as strong control mechanisms in a dictatorship. Slepian et al. (2014) in a robust experiment have confirmed that secrets are a source of genuine, inhibiting, and disempowering mental burden. The authors have concluded that secrets could protect the individual from several harms, in a more friendly societal context, usually from the impacts of disapproval and shame. In a dictatorship, keeping one's secrets seems a safe way to protect oneself from vital threats, but the price to be paid in terms of physical and mental health, including the distortions in reality perception, anxieties, and derailments of identity processes, is very high. Continual, societal-level traumatization is conducive to secrets, silenced and isolated stories, and increases susceptibility to manipulation. Hungary was said to be the happiest barrack in the Soviet bloc—but by 1983, this happiness resulted in the highest rate of suicide recorded globally.

In permanent liminality characterized by approved thoughtlessness and uncertain boundaries of meaning, signs decay and lose their semiotic value (Salvatore et al., 2021). The resulting absurdities in a culture of meaninglessness are authentically depicted in *The Dog's Night Song*. People did not have access to the symbolic resources necessary for the reconstruction of shared, positive cultural meanings:

> Tales, myths, religious belief these are the natural shield of the soul in this age of the exaggerated sophisticated rationalism: and this shield was just taken away—by means of a weapon stronger than the atom of stupidity—from the generation who were children in the fifties, and then once more they took away from themselves the basic source of a sense of responsibility which was still indispensable for formation of the individual in the collective euphoria of the sixties. The parents of that generation were survivors and victims of the war. Just survivors—for they did not have the energy to create anything afterwards, having been enmeshed in a destruction of power and frenzy they destroyed those fertile remnants which still remained… The grandparents bequeathed to their descendants the "Dead God" of Nietzsche and the universal redemption of the cultural shock provided by new technical discoveries" (Kozma, 1987, p. 49).

Shortly after the hopeless years of the mid-1980s, the transition in 1989 and the early 1990s gave rise to an intellectually and academically inspiring era in many Central Eastern European countries. Emerging hopes for a better life, and early experiences of the new freedoms were slowly liberating people's mindsets, and the changes brought about some inspiring encounters with Western theories and professional practices. Social scientists, artists, and psychotherapists were collaborating to build better societies and heal the wounds of the previous open, and the more obscure lesions of soft dictatorships. The constructive traditions, hopes, and motivations have faded, and are waiting for a new renaissance.

References

50 éve történt: Bódy Gábor jelentései [Fifty years ago. Gábor Bódy's reports] (2024, February 15). Állambiztonsági Szolgálatok Történeti Levéltára. https://abtl.hu/blog/50-eve-tortent-body-gabor-jelentesei/#gallery-1 https://www.abtl.hu/blog/50-eve-tortent-body-gabor-jelentesei/

Bakhtin, M. (1984). *Rabelais and his World*. Indiana University Press.

Bódy, G. (Director) (1983) Kutya éji dala [The Dog's Night Song] (Film) Társulás Stúdió.

Bódy, G. (1987). An outline of thoughts and scenes. In L. Beke, & M. Peternák (Eds.) *Bódy Gábor (1946–1985). Életműbemutató/A Presentation of His Work.* (pp. 148–151.) https://mek.oszk.hu/20800/20889/20889.pdf

Bódy Gábor és Szabó István, azaz "Pesti" és "Képesi" – Gervai András új könyvéből [Gábor Bódy and István Szabó in Andras Gervai's new book] (2010, November 29) *HVG*. https://hvg.hu/velemeny/20101128_gervai_filmesek_ugynokok

Brockmeier, J. (2019). What is it to be a human being? Rom Harré on self and identity. In B. Christensen (Ed.), *The second cognitive revolution. Theory and history in the human and social sciences*. Springer. https://doi.org/10.1007/978-3-030-26680-6_5

Chamankhah, L. (2014). Charismata. In D. A. Leeming (Ed.), *Encyclopedia of psychology and religion*. Springer. https://doi.org/10.1007/978-1-4614-6086-2_9141

Csaplár, V. (2005, November 26). Bódy Gábor titkos története. [The secret story of Gábor Bódy] *Népszabadság*. http://nol.hu/archivum/archiv-385435-198090

Cserhalmi, Gy. (1987) Finally and forever. In L. Beke, & M. Peternák (Eds.) Bódy Gábor (1946–1985). *Életműbemutató/A Presentation of His Work.* pp. 53–54. Retrieved from: https://mek.oszk.hu/20800/20889/20889.pdf

Erdos, M. B., & Javor, R. (2022). Entrapment and escape: Exploring the relationship between suicide and emigration in a post-communist country. *The International Journal of Social Psychiatry, 68*(8), 1636–1643. https://doi.org/10.1177/00207640211047617

Erdos, M. B., & Kelemen, G. (2011). The Finite Universe: Discursive Double Bind and Parrhesia in State Socialism. *History of Communism in Europe, 2*(1), 281–308. https://doi.org/10.7761/hce.2.281

Erikson, E. H. (1975). *Life history and the historical moment: Diverse presentations.* Norton Company.

Ferenczi, S. (1988). Confusion of tongues between adults and the child: The language of tenderness and of passion. *Contemporary Psychoanalysis, 24*(2), 196–206. https://doi.org/10.1080/00107530.1988.10746234

Grandpierre, A. (2023). The cosmic life instinct points the way to a healthy ecological civilization. In D. Bartosch, A. Grandpierre, & B. Peng (Eds.), *Towards a philosophy of cosmic life: New discussions and interdisciplinary views* (pp. 35–67). Springer Nature Singapore.

Hegedüs, B. (2020, October 23). 35 éve halt meg rejtélyes módon Bódy Gábor. [Gábor Bódy died 35 years ago, under mysterious circumstances] *Éva Magazin.* https://www.evamagazin.hu/vilagom/body-gabor

Horvath, A., (1997). *The political psychology of trickster-clown. An analytical experiment around communism as a myth.* Papers 97/5, European Institute - Political and Social Sciences. Retrieved from Cadmus, EUI Research, https://hdl.handle.net/1814/285

Horvath, A., & Szakolczai, A. (2020). *The political sociology and anthropology of evil: Tricksterology.* Routledge.

Kozma, Gy. (1987). Gábor again. In L. Beke, & M. Peternák (Eds.) *Bódy Gábor (1946–1985). Életműbemutató/A presentation of his work* (pp. 49–50). Műcsarnok. https://mek.oszk.hu/20800/20889/20889.pdf

Lakoff, G., & Johnson, M. (1980). *Metaphors we live by.* University of Chicago Press.

Novikov, E. (2021). Does sickness have a meaning? *International Political Anthropology, 14*(2), 125–139. https://doi.org/10.5281/zenodo.5721777

Origin and history of ecstasy. (n.d.). https://www.etymonline.com/word/ecstasy

Salvatore, S., Palmieri, A., Cordella, B., & Iuso, S. (2021). The decay of signs' semiotic value: A cultural psychology interpretation of the contemporary social scenario. *Culture & Psychology, 27*(4), 539–561. https://doi.org/10.1177/1354067X211027276

Slepian, M. L., Masicampo, E. J., & Ambady, N. (2014). Relieving the burdens of secrecy: Revealing secrets influences judgments of hill slant and distance. *Social Psychological and Personality Science, 5*(3), 293–300. https://doi.org/10.1177/1948550613498516

Stenner, P. (2017). *Liminality and experience. Transdisciplinary approach to the psychosocial.* Palgrave Macmillan.

Szakolczai, A. (2001). In a permanent state of transition: Theorizing the East-European condition. *Journal for Theory and Practice of Liminal Phenomena, 1*(1) http://limen.mi2.hr/limen1-2001/arpad_szakolczai.html

Szakolczai, A. (2014). Living permanent liminality: The recent transition experience in Ireland. *Irish Journal of Sociology, 22*(1), 28–50. https://doi.org/10.7227/IJS.22.1.3

Szakolczai, Á. (2015). Marginalitás és liminalitás. *Regio, 23*(2), 6–29.

Szakolczai, Á. (2017). Permanent (trickster) liminality: The reasons of the heart and of the mind. *Theory & Psychology, 27*(2), 231–248. https://doi.org/10.1177/0959354317694095

Wilsey, A. M. (2012). "Half in Love with Easeful Death:" Tuberculosis in Literature. *Humanities Capstone Projects. Paper 11.* http://commons.pacificu.edu/cashu/11

Wydra, H. (2012). The power of symbols – Communism and beyond. *International Journal of Politics, Culture, and Society, 25*(1-3), 49–69. https://doi.org/10.1007/s10767-011-9116-x

Zonda, T., Paksi, B., & Veres, E. (2013). *Az öngyilkosságok alakulása Magyarországon. (1970-2010). [Suicide rates in Hungary between 1970-2010]* Központi Statisztikai Hivatal.

Part III
Explorations on the Psychosocial

Chapter 7
The Psychosocial Crisis as a Liminal Experience

Death could scarce be bitterer.

But if I would show the good that came of it

I must talk about things other than the good.——*Dante: Divina Commedia*

7.1 On the Road Less Travelled By

Though individualized cultures of late modernity do not bear much resemblance with earlier lifestyles, deep identity transformations have invariably remained challenging for the individual. These crises structure the constant flow of our life narrative into distinct chapters (McAdams, 1993). The communal construction of crisis echoes several characteristics of the traditional rites of passage, but in late modernity, there is no guarantee for one's access to the former, predictable cultural-institutional resources that would successfully help the person to navigate through the transition. Individual crises may remain deep, personal-level lived experiences of transformative liminality.

McNamee (1992) notes that the original Greek term, krinein, among others, means to separate: crisis is a boundary experience, the essence of liminality. The fundamental change of our identity previously sensed as a continuity, and now burdened with the uncertainties and risks involved in an emerging discontinuity extends to all the important life domains. The disclosure of ultimate boundary problems makes a life crisis a spiritual experience, with the unfolding questions demanding life-transforming reflections and actions: Who am I? What is my personal mission in life? What is my life about? What is human life about?

Traditionally, the person undergoing relatively predictable, epigenetic transformations during the life course, or experiencing the unexpected, traumatizing events of loss and separation brought about by external circumstances, was guided and guarded by the community that provided a structured framework, a ritual to enact and validate the transformation. The rites and the myths behind provided the

M. B. Erdos, *Transitions - Liminality as Lived Experience*,
https://doi.org/10.1007/978-3-031-96007-9_7

person with their culture's responses to the emerging questions and assisted them to explore and reflect on the deep and unique lived significance of these responses. Therefore, rites facilitated the transformation of the private sensations and experiences related to traumatic and metamorphic events into a culturally meaningful and reflected experience, accompanied by culture-appropriate attitudes and emotional states.

Performing the passage required deep immersion into the spiritual dimensions regarded as sacred and eternal. The truth of the myth shared by the community members provided a solid cultural framework for reconstructing the meaning of life while assuming a new role within the community. Here, the personal becomes the cultural, and the cultural corresponds to the personal. From this perspective, the traditional rites may seem a safe and attractive way to facilitate major identity transformations, but they often included vital risks and threats in the limbo of liminality for the participants: for example, wounds that, in rare cases, could even kill the initiand, risks inherent in temporary isolation in the forests without the support of their community, not to mention the exclusionary practices of degradation ceremonies, and their final form, excommunication (Eliade, 1961; Garfinkel, 1956; Turner, 1969).

Taking the road less travelled by[1] was an exception to the rule in these premodern settings, represented in the cultural reservoir of stories either as a tragic narrative or, in times of major societal transitions, a community documentation of the hero's triumphant journey. In individualized late modern societies, the ways people construe their experiences of transformative liminality are also more individualized. Chances of entrapment in the middle, liminal phase in today's contexts have increased. This explains why the idea of becoming *twice-born*, an idea introduced by William James (1902/1982), has retained its relevance. James, referring to an earlier work by Newman in 1852 (*The Soul: its Sorrows and its Aspirations*), elaborated on the concepts of once- and twice-born people, and outlined a different developmental path for those who perceive their life journey as predicable, stable, and rewarding, and for the individuals whose traits predispose them to experiencing recurrent crises. They can develop only through questioning the very fundamentals of their identity. James's early explorations pointed out the utmost relevance of the psychological crisis in identity development and laid the early foundations for today's seminal theories on recovery and post-traumatic growth (Tedeschi & Calhoun, 2004). He emphasized our human potential to choose between a victim's hopelessness or relying on some caring power and perceive life as generally positive, even with its inescapable adversities or traumas (James, 1902/1982; Kets de Vries, 2012). A specific narrative framework for the stories of redemption, connecting the initially negative events to an overall positive and healing outcome (McAdams, 2006) is also grounded in this conception.

Even in the light of these more recent developments, the differentiation between once- and twice-born people seems somewhat delimiting, as it puts the emphasis

[1] Reference to Robert Frost's (1915) poem, The Road Not Taken.

unilaterally on people's personality traits and individual struggles, while disregarding the social context. The generally positive and seemingly undisturbed attitude of a once-born person might be a result of cultural or family-level requirements to follow some Polyanna principle in the construction and sharing of their narrative more than of their genuine freedom from personal sufferings and the tormenting stresses of transformations. In the light of recent research results, trauma is much more common than we had previously thought; but, as a social taboo, and an experience often beyond verbalization, is not a common subject of conversations (Levine, 2014; Pennebaker & Smyth, 2016; van der Kolk, 2015).

Crisis theory presented an influential alternative to the early Freudian conception as well, which had also recognized the origin of life problems in one's personality structure, shaped mainly by early childhood experiences. In the psychoanalytical framework, maladaptation occurs if too much space is left for the unconscious, the Freudian realm of liminal phenomena, or for the oppressive powers of the superego highlighting the expectations of the social structure with its strict morals and unattainable ideals—and too little for the ego, always ready for viable compromises to support one's adaptation to life's challenges in more realistic and healthy ways. The devastations of WWI and WWII have questioned the notion that all mental problems reside in the individual psyche and acknowledged the decisive role of situational factors, the destructive events in adult life that may result in psychiatric symptom formation in the individuals, who could previously adapt reasonably well to normal stresses of life.

Caplan's (1964) classical definition highlighted the presence of an unconquerable obstacle or threat to one's principal life goals, resulting in a problem that the person cannot solve with the available coping strategies they would normally use. A situational crisis, usually a major loss, is threatening and unexpected, and the pressing and paradoxical need to *solve a problem that cannot be solved* is accompanied by experiences of helplessness, loss of control, and entrapment (Caplan, 1964; Poal, 1990; Voros et al., 2021; Williams & Pollock, 2001). This definition implies that the predicament can be resolved only by undergoing a second-order change that transforms the set of previously available alternatives (Watzlawick et al., 1974).

Caplan's technical definition misses to describe the deep affectivity involved in reaching the nadir point in life. Further, the definition was formulated in an era when systems thinking, chaos theory, and the conception of humans as complex adaptive systems have not been introduced into the social and health sciences yet, and explanations for the "irregular" or "abnormal" states relied on Newtonian physics, using the analogies of "structures", "tensions", and "mechanisms" (Bussolari & Goodell, 2009; De Luca Picione & Lozzi, 2021; Poal, 1990; Resnicow & Page, 2008).

A crisis is not only about the failure in one's coping strategies but in the previous *modes of existence*. Correspondingly, it evokes deep anxieties. Unexpected and forced detachment from the earlier, precious identity components is a deep and ambiguous loss, and a source of grief. Sacks (1992), when studying the conversations at a suicide prevention helpline, noted that the ultimate question a person undergoing the crisis encounters is *Who are you?* This explains why call-takers' inquisitiveness about the individual caller's potential sociodemographic background

(*Which one are you*?) in the context of an *anonymous* service to identify the social determinants of suicide in the hope to assess the suicidal risk did not prove a successful strategy.

Who are you? is the core question that differentiates between stress, trauma, and crisis. Originally, the stress theory by Janos Selye (Krohne, 2001) focussed mainly on physiological processes. The main questions the organism faces are urgent and pragmatic: *How to get out of this? How to survive? How to minimize the losses?* Initially, Selye differentiated between two types of responses, fight and flight, and described how our body prepares us for the appropriate actions through a complexity of adaptive responses, such as, for example, changes in blood circulation to minimize the risks of bleeding or elevated blood sugar to mobilize extra energies, etc. Emotional and cognitive responses, a new focus introduced by Lazarus, assist the evaluation of future risks and helps avoid similar situations (Krohne, 2001).

More recently, other potential responses to stress have been identified. Fawn is full surrender to the more powerful. Freeze is a motionless, paralysed state with the internal signs of hyperarousal. Here, catatonia is to escape physical destruction when confronted with a risk perceived as lethal, but neither flight nor fight is possible under the circumstances. Though there is little chance for a positive outcome, the threat may pass, and life may continue (Levine, 1998). A recently identified response, with a focus on care and solidarity is tend and befriend, using our relational potentials to overcome the stress and simultaneously protect those who need it the most in an emergency (Taylor, 2006). Accordingly, these responses are traceable in a rite of transition as alternations between passivity and struggles, and in the practice of isolation to be followed by the community's witnessing and supporting the transition.

Traumatization occurs in a situational crisis, tempting us to identify the causes to regain control (*Why me?*). Living with an unresolved trauma is about being entrapped in a liminal hotspot (Greco & Stenner, 2017), but with the maximum of negative affectivity. Thus, traumatization is about our past, but is continually relived in the present. People may live their lives along some tormenting symptoms—and then reach a tipping point in life when some strong triggering event leads to a new life crisis, demanding the resolution via conscious reflections on the summative experience. Then we must re-evaluate our core meanings and respond to the question Who are you? Crisis is a transitive diagnosis (Kelly, 1955; Johnson et al., 2000). The question Why me? may be raised at two levels. The reproachful or self-accusing ruminative version does not transgress the previous patterns. The perceived safety of causal rationalizations is tempting, but in a crisis, there are no simple causes to be identified. Linear logic provides us only with the illusion of control. In a crisis, confidence in some "natural" order is temporarily lost and must be restored through painful reconstructive processes (Bussolari & Goodell, 2009). The second interpretation of the question, the reflective exploration of past experiences and of the ways these have shaped our identity, coupled with the recognition that life must take a new orientation, often resolves the condition.

Both the person and their social environment identify crises as risky occasions of disorganization. The idea that in some cultures a crisis is depicted as both a threat and an opportunity seems appealing, but this is not so. A favourite example to this widespread idea, the Chinese symbol wei-ji does not mean danger *and* opportunity to make people simultaneously sad and happy whenever they encounter a crisis. Instead, it is a warning on the potential threats inherent in the situation (as the opportunity of danger) (Mair et al., 2009). Indeed, the risks for maladaptive strategies and self-destructive behaviour are marked during the transition. Caplan's (1964) early definition, however, also implies that the uncertainties and adversities may lead to positive changes through learning new ways of becoming and the reconstruction of one's identity.

When a system undergoes a profound change, transitioning from a previous, relatively steady state to a new one, then the initial, small-scale perturbations will result in fluctuations often to the extremes until a new balance has been formed. Consider, for example, Erikson's (1968) comments on adolescence as the first integrative phase, a developmental crisis, when surrendering to formerly repressed tendencies, and perhaps even testing rock bottom during one's ongoing identity work may happen—yet it is not a pathology. Deep identity change is accompanied by a variety of disturbances that resemble, or should they persist, may constitute psychiatric symptoms. The symptoms, as embodied communication of the problem, are formed and maintained by interrelated biological, psychological, and societal factors as the sources for positive (schismogenetic) feedback. If the connections are strong enough to form a network, then the feedback mechanisms will sustain a maladaptive state, and the symptoms together form a syndrome, while weak feedback mechanisms result in resilience (Borsboom, 2017). The type and strength of the environmental feedback are largely determined by a society's practices and attitudes to the uncertainties and ambiguities inherent in liminality, fostering either the construction of transformative contexts or one's entrapment in extended or permanent liminality (McNamee, 2015).

7.2 Identity Transformations and Identity Variations

In a psychological crisis, coherence and stability are cherished, but in the newly emerging situation, dysfunctional results of our prior identity investments seem to disappear to give way to the unpredictability of chaos. In these cases, we are "called to understand that the complexity means random incidents, chance, initiative, decision, crisis, the unexpected, the unforeseen…" (De Luca Picione & Lozzi, 2021, p. 19). The temporary disorder, a prerequisite of deep transformations, encompasses all the major areas of life (Bussolari & Goodell, 2009; Gergen & McNamee, 2000). Thus, a psychological crisis is our experience of a passage from a previous, now unsuitable frame of experiences, our identity, into a new one. Chaos theory yields a more authentic approach to the crisis as a milestone in personal development, while also explaining for ambivalence, a condition that is not resolved with humans so easily as with other species. We live our lives in extended temporal domains and build long-term strategies for the future, envisioning the longstanding potential consequences of our actions. We worry a lot about the past, seen as indicative of the future; and want to control the future as much as possible. Consequently, ambivalence is a core feature in the chaos of the transformative liminality of a psychosocial crisis.

Identity is a dialectic of continuity and change. It is about our uniqueness, at the same time acknowledging the immense role of the social environment, either as a rich resource for, or a frustrating barrier to, the envisioned developments (Weinreich, 2004). A profound identity transformation is one's full immersion in liminality, initially sensed as a dramatic deviation during one's life journey (Stagg, 2014). The personal narrative comprising a personalized myth is falling apart to give space to a new, hopefully more adaptive, and liveable version that meets the demands of the changing circumstances (McAdams, 1993). Our capacity to tolerate the risks, uncertainties, diffusion, disintegration, ambivalence, ambiguities, and paradoxes as the natural concomitants of this transformation has been shaped by our previous experiences in the social environment, usually fostering some hope and trust (Erikson, 1968; Li et al., 2023). Though these experiences will invariably serve as the anchoring points for the continuity of identity, the shaky jigsaw puzzle of life is now seen from a different angle to finally reach a clearer, more holistic, integrated, and authentic picture.

Fundamental changes and losses involve personal-level identicide as "partial death" (Bonomi, 2004, p. 46.), efforts to distance ourselves from the once adaptive but now dysfunctional positions and identity elements, experienced as core constituents, or mere by-products of the wish to "fit in", even at the cost of latent, internal incongruencies. Previous identity components are usually not lost forever in the process of this self-imposed identicide (Empson, 2013). Temporary distancing from the disturbing identity elements and one's conflicted experiences may finally give ways of restoring the continuity of identity and integrating what has previously been so confusing. This dialectic of continuity and discontinuity can best be illustrated in recovering addicts' stories in the 12-step communities, who celebrate their second birth as sober persons, but invariably identify themselves as addicts. By embracing this seeming paradox and insisting on the mementoes of their previous identity, they can learn to control their addiction through surrendering to a higher power and giving up their individual-level controlling efforts. Thus, they intuitively realize that it is aloneness and alienation that leads to excessive use (Alexander, 2008, as cited in McNamee, 2015). Sober communities introduce an adaptive version of *controlled loss of control*, inherently present in transition rites (Hayward, 2016; Kelemen & Erdős, 2003). The original focus, strong engagement with control issues has remained, but has completely been reinterpreted. The contrast pole, loss of control and helplessness, the meanings hiding in the shadow, are now integrated into the recovering person's new construct, and a healthy balance is established between the opposite poles.

Erikson's (1968) famous example, the conversion of Saulus, the once bloodthirsty Roman soldier, allows for the manifestations of the redemptive self. Repentance, temperance, self-denial, and his unconditional commitment to a cause, up to the level of self-sacrifice, are the remnants of his previous identity, but with a new direction. But would Paulus simply describe himself as a recovering soldier, former Saulus, abstaining from aggression against the Christians? Referring to Miller's concept of quantum change, Resnicow and Page (2008, p. 1382) describe similar experiences changing one's core identity elements as "a dramatic, mystical experience and a sudden insight or sense of finding one's truth. Common to both pathways is that they occur outside of conscious reasoning; they happen to the person rather than by the person". Anonymous fellowships term these aspects of recovery as spiritual awakening. It is not abstinence, a negative identity component (*not* continuing excessive use as a behaviour), but sobriety, the positive version, a new direction in life, that they consider of key importance during their recovery journey.

When trying to comprehend quantum change processes, we are usually at a loss and may end up with polysemic or metaphorical descriptions to grasp its complexities and wholeness (Bateson, 1972; van Boeckel, 2011). Learning III (Bateson, 1972), the change in the sets of sets[2] is also about radical changes in *meaning*, both in the sense of coherence and directionality. Quantum change is a transcendent experience, dramatically transforming one's values and affecting the totality of *core meanings*, as well as the *meaning-making processes* (facilitating a change in the sets of sets). This accentuated discontinuity, the deep rupture in a previous continuity is first acknowledged as unrecognized arrival in the myths and tales about such transitions (Propp, 1999). The new, reborn identity will reconnect to the previous one only after experiencing the discontinuity, also reflected by the social environment.

Weinreich (2004) in his theory, Identity Structure Analysis (ISA), has defined several self-states determined by the level of *diffusion* understood here as the rate of conflicted evaluations of one's important self-related entities, including one's own self-states in the varied temporal, relational, and experiential domains (such as, for example, "Currently I", "Me as a friend", or "Me when upset"). It is important to note that Weinreich uses several terms that are not considered neutral in other (e.g. clinical) frameworks. Levels of diffusion, and of its counterpoint, defensiveness, are evaluated in relation to the person's actual roles and social contexts. Low-level diffusion (defensive self-states) are often, but not always, incompatible with one's roles—just consider the differences between the role requirements of a social activist and a soldier (e.g. Saulus): the latter do not permit much ambivalence and openness to a variety of solutions. Diffusion is not identical with crisis. It expresses ambivalence but is also indicative of the person's openness to change and is adaptive when someone is transitioning between the different identity states. Weinreich (2004) identifies crisis as a self-state in which diffusion is coupled with the current self's low evaluation. Often, this is a tormenting combination involving the potentials of (self)destruction (Thompson, 2010); but may also express temporary

[2] For more details, see Chap. 2, *Transitions from a Systemic Perspective. Quantum Change and Liminality*.

surrender, a precondition for identity reconstruction. In ISA, this difference can be inferred from the overall pattern defined by the other self-positions and the related evaluations.

In conclusion, the crisis disrupts the perceived continuity of one's identity, and the life before is seen as incommensurable with the life after. Continued awareness of the previous identity elements might be tormenting, with feelings of loss, isolation, shame, guilt, helplessness, and inadequacy. Experiencing the transformative liminality of the crisis is fearful, woeful, and is both an externally (relationally) and internally conflicted state.

7.3 Suicidal Crisis and Liminal Entrapment

Stresses, traumas, and crises are common human experiences—they are normal in the sense that everyone encounters them. As I have argued, the resolution of a crisis may require personal-level and self-imposed identicide, the elimination of non-adaptive identity elements. This process is triggered by the environment and is carried out by the individual. However, this other-elicited and self-performed identicide may turn into a suicide, "an intrapsychic drama on an interpersonal stage" (Leenaars, 1996, p. 221). Sacks (1992) conceives suicide as a desperate communication attempt to find out if anybody cares. In the fantasies of the people preparing to die by suicide, the concerned others who would attend the burial would always show their sympathy and care that was missing from the individual's life. These fantasies are quite different from what happens in real life—suicide leads to complicated grief in the immediate social environment with strong and longstanding feelings of anger, guilt, and shame on the part of relatives and friends.

Suicide is motivated by impairments and slips in symbolization, and is related to the human, but nonhumane conditions. The first comprehensive explanations appear in Durkheim's (1897/2005) theory who also highlighted the relational nature of the phenomenon and pointed out the role of social integration in the process. Though altruistic suicide (Durkheim 1897/2005), self-sacrifice for the kin, especially for young close kin regularly occurs among animals, other forms of self-destruction are present only with domesticated animals as a *grief reaction*, or among wild animals in *captivity*. Self-mutilating behaviour to end physical pain or captivity is also present among animals, as well as giving up hope even when there is a real but unnoticed chance to escape. One salient example is Seligman's learned helplessness experiment (Chap. 5, *Authoritarian Discourses*; Preti, 2007; Seligman, 1972). These phenomena are closely associated with trauma-related self-harm and self-accusation in humans.

Suicide is seen as a conscious and deliberate act (Shneidman, 1986). It is conscious in the sense that people foresee the consequences of their actions, and suicide is often preceded by one's suicidal ideations (Preti, 2007; Sacks, 1992). Shneidman (1986), challenging common-sense beliefs on suicide, identified ten commonalities

Table 7.1 Shneidman's commonalities of suicide and liminal equivalents

Dimension	Commonality	Extended liminal equivalent
Purpose	Seek a solution	End liminal entrapment through self-destruction
Goal	Cessation of consciousness	Death is equivalent to recreational sleep; after waking up, a new life begins
Stimulus	Intolerable psychological pain	Psychological (spiritual) is transferred and reduced to physical
Stressor	Frustrated psychological needs	Entrapment in a liminal hotspot
Emotion	Hopelessness and helplessness	Striving for ultimate control when perceiving total loss of control.
Internal attitude	Ambivalence	Ambivalence and isolation
Cognitive state	Constriction	Constriction
Action	Escape	Arrested flight/no escape—suicide perceived as *the* escape
Interpersonal act	Communication of intention	Communication through symptoms, metaphors, and *silence*
Consistency	Lifelong coping patterns	Repetition of first order solutions. Arrested transformation in extended liminality

(Own compilation, based on Bateson, 1972*; Shneidman,* 1986*; Greco & Stenner,* 2017; *Turner,* 1969*; Watzlawick et al.,* 1974*; Williams & Pollock,* 2001)

in the process. Table 7.1 is a comparison between Shneidman's dimensions and, if liminality extends and its inherent symbolism is misunderstood, their potentially destructive liminal equivalents:

Suicide, as Leenaars (1996, p. 221) has noted, is "a multidimensional malaise". It does not have a single cause though the environment would often attribute to such reassuring but surficial causalities to the act. Durkheim (1897/2005) claimed that the same outcome, suicide could be caused either by too low levels (anomic suicide) or too high levels (altruistic suicide) of social integration. At the same time, Durkheim heavily rejected van Gennep's (1909/2019) theory on rites of passage that, eventually, could have explained for the loss of balance, extremities, and problems of social (re)integration. Lester (1994), having reviewed several clinical theories, concluded that helplessness, hopelessness, a negative view on one's future, confusion, chaos and impairments in communication, *abortive transitions* and self-blame are among the main constituents (Erdos & Javor, 2022). In Lester's (1994) evaluative study, Beck's cognitive triad on depression has proven the most relevant. This triad includes selective perception of the negative events as global-holistic, extending to all the domains of life; seeing the events and circumstances as stable-regressive, never ending but ever worsening; and construing them as internal, even if they are beyond personal control. All these are the results of learning a context of extended liminality characteristic of unprocessed traumas. The theories that Lester analysed have proven relevant in more recent evidence-based explanations (Voros et al., 2021).

Greco and Stenner (2017, p. 149) note that circles "can also become vicious. Instead of ever widening they can be ever tightening (…) our world can collapse into smaller and more constricted space-times, entrapping us into our individuality and cutting us off from our powers of action and understanding. (Greco & Stenner, 2017 p. 149). The theory of cry of pain (COP) by Williams and Pollock (2001) describes an arrested flight-no escape situation—from this perspective, entrapment in a liminal hotspot (Greco & Stenner, 2017), while being arrested in the sequel of the transition. Entrapment is a key aspect of the COP model, comprising four, interrelated factors: entrapment, hopelessness, no escape, and isolation, leading to a biologically mediated script of helplessness and its potential consequence, suicide. In such cases, one's ideas on no escape are coupled with beliefs on no rescue, and convictions about defeat. Entrapment is either conceived as internal, such as beliefs about one's own limitations, with the accompanying thoughts and the affective load of self-depreciation; or external, as the results of environmental restrictions, and toxic relationships (Erdos & Javor, 2022; Rasmussen et al., 2010). These two aspects are inseparable: what is recognized as internal is the result of internalized patterns (Ramos-Vera et al., 2024).

Double bind relations establish a context of entrapment. Smith (2002) in his ethnographic analysis on suicide focussed on the cases of Belarus and Hungary in the 1990s. He pointed out that the frequently occurring double bind settings in these two countries could play a key role in the world's highest suicide rates. Entrapment extends to all areas of human life: cognitions, behaviours, and emotional life. This is the ultimate constriction of the presuicidal syndrome: a final attempt at escape, but now from one's own tormenting consciousness of the self (Kelly, 1955; Ringel, 1976). Constriction permeates all the dimensions of experiences: space, time, and relationships. Situational constriction refers to an isolated lifeworld with no viable alternatives or meaningful activities—and the question may arise here if suicide is indeed a *deliberate choice*. Dynamic constriction denotes the accompanying feelings with the predominance of negative emotions. However, this does not equal to depression, where the lack of motivation coupled with negative emotionality is often a state in which action is *not* taken. Accordingly, entrapment has been identified as a key driver in suicide, one that is more significant than depression (De Beurs et al., 2020). What makes entrapment so critical is the sensation of being trapped in a highly stressful, traumatizing, and seemingly eternal situation with no genuine chances to escape, while experiencing abrupt alternations between liminal helplessness and surrender, and *preparedness to act*. In their study, De Beurs et al. (2020) have identified several key components and meanings, as powerlessness, a personal impression of being trapped, being in a deep hole, and the wish to run away.

The impact of the affective turmoil in an arrested transition is a significant factor. Tacey (2005) in his anthropological investigations has concluded that suicide is the result of *a failed rite of passage*. In modernity, we have learnt to understand life transformations in terms of personal crises, and the chances for ritual death and rebirth with their rich spiritual connotations have been lost (Tacey, 2005). Traditionally, ritual death as separation was not meant as "only" metaphorical (Szakolczai, 2009; Tacey, 2005). Severe physical risks have always been present in many traditional rites (Turner, 1969). Further, the metaphors we use to describe the transition, a spiritual experience temporarily opening the gates between the different dimensions of existence are *embodied,* deeply anchored in the physical environment, and are experienced by both our body and brain (Lakoff & Johnson, 1980; Lakoff, 2012b). This holds true even if with high-level abstractions, the reconstruction of the original simulations may not occur (Casasanto & Gijssels, 2015). Given the immediacy of experience, and with the strong right hemisphere domination in trauma processing, the capacity to adequately differentiate between the deeply interconnected still not the *same* physical and cultural-symbolic domains is impaired. In an arrested transition, the boundaries between the symbolic and the physical remain more permeable, bringing about a specific state of lasting psychic equivalence. With such equivalence, mental states and physical realities seem as the same and are treated as same: what is present in the mind (a fantasy or a conviction) is believed to be present in one's environment (Allen et al., 2008).

Table 7.2 shows the similarities between the psychosocial crisis and a liminal condition. Several phenomena that we tend to understand in terms of a "symptom" is integral to rites of passage as indispensable liminal phenomena. The confusing moments are resolved with the support of the wise ones and the wider community. Today's institutionalized contexts for extended or permanent liminality usually consider such conditions and behaviours as pathologies. The rigid, schismogenetic feedback mechanisms may strengthen the evolving chaotic pattern, (Horvath & Thomassen, 2008; Thomassen, 2013)—to the level of self-destruction. Both in modern and premodern social contexts, the preliminal state, separation is characterized by anxieties, grieving for the loss, and a deep internal turmoil—but the visions, expectations, aspirations, and hopes are different. The premodern is more predictable, but community support is missing when the individual is seen as a source of risk to the community. Persons at risk of suicide (e.g. when talking about their suicide ideations) were excluded from the traditional village community, as they were seen as being under the irreversible influence of Evil (Balázs, 1995).

As Voros et al. (2021) have pointed out, recent clinical conceptions on suicide (for example, Acute Suicidal Affective Disturbance and Suicidal Crisis Syndrome) rely on the classical conceptualizations by Ringel (1976), Caplan (1964), and on the COP model by Williams and Pollock (2001). Table 7.2 displays some striking parallels between these clinical notions and liminal phenomena.

Table 7.2 Crisis and the different facets of liminality

Social structure	Communitas and transformative liminality	Crisis as in liminality/extended/permanent liminality
State	*Transition—process*	*Transition/stuck in transition*
Partiality	Totality	Isolated and fragmented self
Heterogeneity	Homogeneity	Loss of identity, no-one
Structure	Communitas	Chaos, disequilibrium
Name and status	Anonymity	Perceived loss of previous identity
Status, inequality	Absence of status, equality	Status is meaningless
Sex distinctions	Sexual continence, minimization of sex distinctions	Sexuality is meaningless
Pride (self-esteem)	Humility and surrender	Self-deprecation, shame, and victimization
Care for personal appearance, status symbols, uniqueness	Disregard for personal appearance; nakedness or uniform clothing	Disregard for personal appearance
Property and wealth	Absence of property	Property and wealth are meaningless
Selfishness	Selflessness	Situational constriction
Obedience only to superior rank	Total obedience	Suggestibility; victim to manipulation; reliance on others
Specified degrees of autonomy	Heteronomy	Helplessness
Secularity	Sacredness	Search for meaning
Intermittent reference to mystical powers	Continuous reference to mystical powers	Absence of mystical powers; death seen as escape and source of transcendence
Technical knowledge	Sacred instructions	Psychiatrists as "alienists"
Speech	Silence	Silence; crisis of communication; trauma-induced symbolic breakdown, cry of pain
Kinship rights and obligations	Suspension of kinship rights and obligations	Situational constriction, reinterpretation/losses of relationships; alienation; social withdrawal
Sagacity, complexity	Foolishness, simplicity	Single, negative focus, cognitive constriction reducing the uncertainties
Avoidance of pain and suffering	Acceptance of pain and suffering as potential sources of meaning	Empty suffering; hopelessness; "repetition compulsion"
Energies needed for daily life	Enhanced energy levels	Hyperarousal, affective dysregulation, entrapment/no escape, emotional overheat ("dynamic constriction") of the liminal hotspot
Occasional reference to mystical powers	Continuous reference to, and reliance on mystical powers	None; or individual ideas on mystical powers

(continued)

Table 7.2 (continued)

Social structure	Communitas and transformative liminality	Crisis as in liminality/extended/permanent liminality
Intelligence	Foolishness	Cognitive constriction
Complexity	Simplicity	Collapse of previous complexities
Degrees of autonomy	Heteronomy	Loss of autonomy and control
Linear time	Kairotic time, temporary suspension of time	Frozen in trauma
Living (mostly) in profane spaces	Sacred space, isolation	Isolated spaces, health, and social care institutions

Source: Own compilation, based on the ideas by Erdos and Javor (2022), Eliade (1961), De Luca Picione & Lozzi (2021), Turner (1969, pp. 106–107), Sik (2023), Greco & Stenner (2017), Szasz (1995), van der Kolk (2015); Voros et al. (2021), Wiliams and Pollock (2001)

7.4 Communicating the Psychosocial Crisis

7.4.1 Helplines as Liminal Contexts

In a crisis, communication undergoes a dramatic change: the communication of crisis is a crisis in communication. Traditionally, these are the silent moments of the ritual. In the subsequent section, I will explore and illustrate the key communication characteristics by using short excerpts from a qualitative research material, the crisis calls received by an intervention helpline in the 1990s in Hungary (Erdős, 2006, 2018). This specific research, using a discursive framework, was conducted with the aim of improving crisis intervention and suicide prevention practices, following a tradition established by Harvey Sacks in the 1960s (Erdős, 2006; Kézdi, 1995; Oravecz, 2004; Sacks, 1992). More recent examples of a similar discursive approach are the works of Erdős (2018), Bloch and Leydon (2019), and Oravecz (2023).

Helplines for suicide prevention have been aiding people in a life crisis for more than 70 years now. These helplines appeared in Hungary in the 1970s (Erdős, 2006). This liminal context as a crisis heterotopia[3] responds sensitively to the transformative liminality of a psychological crisis. The conversing parties are anonymous, they do not see each other or know anything about each other's social identifiers. These liminal features liberate the caller from the usual structural limitations of everyday life and facilitate free reflections on their internal doubts and worries. Humans' flexibility to switch between the communication channels enable the conversing partners to respond to each other empathetically even if some important nonverbal cues are missing. In many ways, this context resembles the early psychoanalytic settings, where the woeful domains of the not-yet-said could open: a hidden and safe space for disclosing fantasies, projections, and secrets (Balikó, 1990).

[3] On heterotopias, see Chap. 2, *Transitions from a Systemic Perspective. Quantum Change and Liminality.*

Call-takers do not have too much control over the callers who are free to hang up at any moment if they wish—a one-sided freedom usually not granted to the call-takers (only with severely abusive calls). Due to the limited accessibility of the nonverbal channel, call-takers must learn how to focus, or even hyper-focus on the aspects of communication that may go unnoticed in a usual conversation, e.g. the metaphors or mannerisms the callers are perpetually using, or the ways the callers introduce themselves. This impression management is highly informative about the caller's internal state and motivations (Erdős, 2006; Balikó, 2000). In the excerpt below, the caller (C) at risk of suicide openly expressed her need for transcendent *ritual contents* in her very first sentences when demanding a life-saving *formula* of the call-taker (CT) in an existential crisis:

> C: Well, I don't know, finally, what, what my real problem is, but I have been struggling for months (to decide) if I should call you. My greatest problem is, I think that … in the end, you surely know why we live.
>
> CT: Uhm.
>
> C: Surely you have some kind of a formula to tell those who, who feel that (life) has no meaning.
>
> (…)
>
> C: Well, I don't know, in the end, I am not a suicide candidate, would you listen to me or at all…
>
> CT: Of course, of course. Why, what is your problem?

The call-taker responds by rephrasing the caller's original question and asks the caller to speak about the hows first. They continue by talking about the caller's life story. The caller is deeply disturbed and frightened by her unexplainable thoughts. She repeatedly uses the filling phrase "in the end", which, in this context, may also refer to suicide. Her life, from an external perspective, seems *normal* and even attractive: "in the end, I live a normal life". This discrepancy between her inner self dreading that she will "go mad", and her public self, a competent, strong, and successful businesswoman, is tormenting. She sees her life as a mere collection of banalities, lacking meaning and directionality.

Modernity does not provide us with genuine responses to similar existential crises. Other-ascribed "normality" is a source of conflicts and confusion. Thus, the existential crisis becomes an isolating and stigmatizing experience: the one who is unhappy with a normal life does not seem normal. Here, previous beliefs and values are questioned to give way to emptiness, helplessness, and pain (Erdős, 2018; Stagg, 2014). The caller's story was silenced, as everything seemed as fine as expected. In this context, however, meaning and directionality become the core questions that the caller must, and the call-taker must not, answer: the well-established principles of psychosocial counselling would exclude such direct guidance.

As the caller's story evolves, it turns out that she has fantasies, even rough plans of suicide, involving some specific details about the whens and hows. This is not surprising, as I have argued in Chap. 1 (*Living in a Dual Environment. Homo symbolicus and Languaging*) *negation* ("not a suicide candidate") does not obey the simple rules of formal logic. Instead, negation is associated with the speaker's conformity to cultural requirements to suppress such contents. Under the right hemisphere domination of trauma communication, the meaning of a negative structure changes: it is not the rationality of formal logic, but the affectivity of the crisis that is governing the person: "Not" and "suicide" are perceived as *synonyms.* The caller is considering how long life is worth living and designates the *boundary* at the age of 40, which she has already passed. She is afraid to continue her life and at the same time is afraid of death, and of the potentially debilitating physical consequences of an attempt (Erdős, 2018).

"Suicide candidate" was a contemporary and widespread term (in Hungarian: öngyilkosjelölt) designating a person who is considering suicide—so it was seen as their *fate*. It is worth noting that it took decades to challenge and change the domestic professional and public discourse on suicide: dying by suicide was first termed a "successful" suicide, and then a completed (i.e. not deficient or disrupted) suicide.

7.4.2 Verbalizing the Trauma

More than 100 years ago, Anna O., Breuer's patient, could realize that it was very useful for her to speak about her disturbing experiences and internal conflicts to a non-judgemental therapist, and named these occasions chimney sweeping (Boeree, 2009). A telling metaphor indeed, as chimney sweeps were thickly covered by soot in those days—and, metaphorically, this also happened to Breuer, an honoured doctor whose good fame was compromised by Anna's stories about their liaison (Boeree, 2009). There were no accessible cultural frames to interpret the intimacy and depths of a talking cure. Breuer terminated the treatment. Anna's temporary recovery, however, inspired Freud to encourage his patients in verbalizing what had been buried as silent stories in the domain of not-yet-said.

The meaning of hysteria is the freeze reaction itself, representing a paralysed, numb state, when the person is entrapped not in the original situation anymore but in their own body. The trauma was manifested noticeably and disturbingly through the body, in the detours of the physical symptoms that were often hard to interpret. Neurological studies revealed that the brain areas responsible for the verbal organization of the experiences in trauma survivors experiencing post-traumatic stress syndrome were relatively inactive, with a predominance of the key right hemisphere functions—strong emotions, and preparedness for physical (spatial) activities, accompanied by numbness, and an inability to travel freely in the temporal dimensions from one's memories to future visions (Levine, 2014; van der Kolk, 2015). The person seems to be struck by eternal grief over the loss, frozen in the trauma. Previous understandings on trauma mainly relied on the Freudian paradigm, but an early theory breaking away from the mainstream explanations explicitly connected the person's inability for symbolic communication to the liminal discontinuity of identity (Bonomi, 2004, p. 45):

> Kardiner contended that, when the result is a traumatic syndrome, the event does not act as a symbol, but on the contrary, it resists the work of mental assimilation, both in retrospect and in prospect. In retrospect, because it introduces a break, a discontinuity, with the previous personality; and in prospect, because the psychic elaboration of the traumatic experience is extremely difficult.

Psychoanalysts' early focus on the unconscious (dreams, imagery, physical symptoms, and the related emotions) corresponded to the recently confirmed right hemisphere dominance. While the deep traumatic experiences might be beyond verbalization, they were dedicated to translating the symptoms of hysteria into verbal contents and resolve the narrative disruption. Two questions may arise at this point: *why,* for what purpose, and *how* do we verbalize such experiences? Liberation from the trap of non-verbalness and progressing into the symbolic domain of languaging is a difficult but necessary process. Inability to verbalize the life experience is problematic in a species relating not only through nonverbal cues but also through symbols, and even building a highly complex secondary environment of these (Dunbar, 2004; van der Kolk, 2015). Without restoring the entirety of languaging capacity, and re-establishing the continuity of narrative identity, reintegration is not successful. In a study by Pennebaker and Smyth (2016), verbalizing traumatic experiences through expressive writing, a special exercise that had been introduced as a research method proved an effective way to improve one's overall health. When someone is involved in expressive writing regularly, the expressions related to cognitive processing gradually increase (Pennebaker & Seagal, 1999). This is indicative of the decreasing emotional loads, parallel to the developments in one's reflections.

In the process of verbalizing personal-level traumatic experiences, one's individual story must be matched to cultural narrative frameworks (Hänninen, 2004). Traditionally, rites provided the individuals with such symbolic frameworks, but in late modern societies, finding or selecting the appropriate one from the cultural stock of stories might be much more problematic. A prototypical example to this problem is the case of Vietnam veterans, whose experiences were highly traumatizing *and* very distant from the contemporary social realities of the American society. In modernity, a war with its seemingly "unrealistic" but very real and extensive destructions is not about heroes anymore; as Janos Szakolczai (2021, p. 114) has commented, "death is not an adventure". A war is the manifestation of a "totalitarian dystopia", the mass-level predominance of the darkest side of humankind (Horvath & Szakolczai, 2018; J. Szakolczai, 2021, p. 114). Further, no war has ever ended when the appropriate dates have been entered in our history books. The consequences of the traumas inevitably extend to several generations. Soldiers in a modern war are expected to think less, and their memories of normal life are but a distraction, a "phantom" (J. Szakolczai, 2021, p. 119). After returning home, their memories of the war become the insulated phantoms of the horrors they have experienced. Their stories could not be shared, still had their impact in their lives and in their immediate social environment.

Neimeyer (2006), when exploring the narrative disruptions in trauma-related stories, outlined three possible reasons for the resulting silence and fragmentation. The trauma leading to disorganized narratives would shatter the person's existing value system (what is required is sanctioned by the self). With dissociated narratives, the high level of traumatization prevents neurological processing and makes the experiences inaccessible. In both cases, the victims are at a loss when trying to speak about the unspeakable and they have no words to capture their lived experiences. Third, there are the stories that people would be able to tell, but their personal narratives contradict the dominant narratives of the society. Breaking the social taboos and enduring the accompanying shame—if not some severe punishment—are a major risk. Taking the risk would isolate them, or, in some societies, even their close relatives (Neimeyer, 2006). Consequently, the inner dialogue is transformed into a monologue, and the dominant narrative results in a strong and unquestionable negative coherence with its musts and must nots (Neimeyer, 2006).

In her model of narrative circulation, Hänninen (2004) has noted that the inner narrative is a debated concept. The researcher's epistemological position defines if they accept something that is entirely "inner" or would argue that every narrative is born in the moment of the conversation. In the light of the above argumentation, the lived narrative (what happened exactly) and the told narrative (what is being said about the experience) do not cover the entirety of the communication processes inherent in traumatization and crises. Though the storyline is fragmented, these internal, conflicted, and dissociated *pre-narratives* are more than mere impressions of the specific events. The vague and chaotic inner narrative exists in the domain of the not-yet-said and not-yet-reflected or pre-reflective contents of half-realities (Hänninen, 2004; Høgh-Olesen, 2024; Rober, 2002). These fragments may echo the conflicting voices of internalized others. Clear temporal organization and directionality are missing, and the fragments cannot be integrated into the continuity of identity. They exist only as potentialities in the liminal chaos, and remain private, isolating and depressing.

The tormenting inconsistencies and uncertainties may lead to social exclusion. *Alienist* was an early term for psychiatrists (Szasz, 1995). Indeed, in modernity, they are the ones who validate traumatized people's lived experiences, interpreting them as meaningful and (potentially) culturally acceptable representations. Psychiatrists are authorized to define the somewhat vague boundaries between sanity and insanity. At the birth of the profession, this gatekeeping function, upkeeping extended liminality or legitimizing the patient's marginalization, was much stronger than the doctors' responsibility to help the person utilize the transformative power of liminality and reconnect to the society. Psychiatrists were, and still are as much liminalists as alienists.

7.4.3 Temporal Perspectives

Traumatic experiences disrupt the linearity of the narrative structure: the memories are not arranged in a meaningful chain of events and experiences, following the linear orientation of everyday life. The trauma may entirely block free navigation in the temporal domains (van der Kolk, 2015). As Ringel (1976) has noted, the perception of time is deeply influenced by the person's cognitive and affective constriction. Time must be *suspended* in liminality (Salvatore & Venuleo, 2017). In the extended or permanent liminality of trauma, the person feels that the momentary is eternal—and by stepping out of this trauma-time by suicide, this is exactly what is enacted. The trauma becomes eternal as nothing can change it anymore.

A crisis is a tipping point where decisions must be made but the individual faces the situation without seeing any viable alternatives. These are to be constructed first. Noticing or construing the alternatives is contingent upon one's social resources and the successful integration of the current and the previously unresolved traumatic experiences. The crisis is a totalizing experience, and crisis time is kairotic time—the time of change when the different temporal horizons can connect, so that the person could sense the risks, and the potentialities that may not return if they are missed. The emerging, fragmented memories are painful, and the future seems unpredictable, uncontrollable, and even meaningless, with no better hopes and attainable positive visions. Past-negative and present-fatalistic temporal orientations may dominate (Zimbardo & Boyd, 2015). If some aspects of the past are seen as positive (the "golden past"), then these seem lost forever.

Studies on trauma and crisis narratives have documented that the temporal perspectives become confused and result in a temporal loop in the storyline (Erdős, 2006, 2018; Ehmann, 2002). This temporal loop, though it makes the story incoherent and difficult to follow, also establishes the connections between the experiences in the different temporal domains; thus, it paves the way to a corrective emotional experience. This may happen in the constructive intersubjective context of transformative liminality. Temporal rearrangements facilitate the escape from entrapment and proceeding towards transformation (Greco & Stenner, 2017; Stagg, 2014).

Temporality is strongly related to linear causality: what precedes an event is often seen as the cause of that event (Lakoff, 2014). Identifying such causalities grants us the illusion of control amidst the uncertainties. We may fear uncertainties more than the certainties of sufferings (De Luca Picione & Lozzi, 2021). Living under the ambiguous spell of the just world hypothesis, supposing that bad things happen to bad people only, and motivated by the wish to control the future, we are eager to identify a single cause leading to our misfortunes (Lerner, 1980). Religious conceptualizations of such misfortunes (for example, as God's will to test good people), as well as today's therapies and counselling sessions evolve around these epistemological misconceptions. In rites of transition, the problematic issue of human control was resolved via emphasizing the spiritual aspects of human existence.

7.4.4 Procedural Contents in Crisis Communication

Procedural contents, the function words orienting us in time, space, and relationships, and guiding us what to do with, and how to interpret the conceptual contents in a conversation, are almost automatically selected, and their use seems to be partly defined by one's personality and partly by the situation (Stelzer et al., 2019). Several studies have focused on pronoun use, negation, connectives, and even the use of definite and indefinite articles (Pennebaker et al., 2003, 2015). Today, these traditions (Kézdi, 1995; Erdős, 2006; Fekete et al., 2023) continue as recent discoveries in digital phenotyping under the realm of digital psychiatry (Torous et al., 2021).

Elevated use of negative structures (Kézdi, 1995; Oravecz, 2004, 2023; Voros et al., 2021) was repeatedly found in persons' texts who had died by suicide. Animals do not use negatives structures, apart from our closest genetic relatives immersed in a human environment. This is a constraint inherent in using primarily analogue signs for communication (Bateson, 1972). Animals do not die by suicide either, not having a "concept" of destroying their own selves:

> …the properties that distinguish us mostly, besides intelligence and creativity, may rest on the dark side of our nature. Humans kill their conspecifics (murder and homicide) significantly more often than any other animal species (…) suicide, or self-imposed death, seems to be quite an elusive feature of mankind, with few parallels among animals (Preti, 2007, p. 831).

Kézdi (1995) outlined an early theory, the *negative code theory* to explain for Hungary's highest suicide rate globally in the 1980s. In this theory, he connected suicide to the dominant discourse highlighting negative contents, and to the elevated use of negative structures. The Hungarian language routinely uses many of these. The double negation is the normative version. Historia Nemine, the medieval story about the ultimate liberation inherent in negation (the person named *Nobody* can do what others cannot) (Bakhtin, 1984) could not be properly translated into Hungarian as the grammatical use of "nobody", "never", or "nothing" requires an additional negative: not (for example, instead of "nobody can", "nobody cannot" is used as a correct version). This phenomenon only exists as a nonstandard dialect in English.

Interestingly, if we combine negation and reference to self, the two types of procedural contents that are characteristic of the language of suicide, the result is the rejection or annihilation of self-parts (*I+not*) or the totality of the self (*not/no+I*). In Hungarian, the personal pronouns can be expressed by suffixes only, or by adding the pronoun as well: using both is an accentuated version and frequently occurs in the language of suicide. The excerpt below is from the same caller: the connections between negation and entrapment ("caught in a cruel bind") are salient in her confused sentences. This part of the conversation is about her tormenting marital problems and her conviction that she would not be able to live alone:

> C: No, no, no, I simply know that this is what I should do, I am aware of it, but no, no, I will not be able, never in my life and he also knows this (…) Not no (any), no other solution. Either I am tolerating this throughout my life or not (…) this is, well, a kind of a cruel bind.[4]

If the speakers change the perspective, transitioning from the first person singular to the third person singular, this might result in an increased or, contrarily, decreased levels of coherence and existential mattering (Pennebaker & Smyth, 2016). Such distancing was found useful with high intensity negative experiences. However, with low intensity negative experiences, distanced reflections led to less coherence and mattering than positive reappraisal (Lau & Tov, 2023). Externalizing conversations by narrative therapists, highlighting that the problem is the problem and not the person, use this distancing exactly in the cases when the client is heavily burdened by a negative circumstance and the related negative emotions (White, 2024). Deliberately changing the narrative perspective, expressed in personal pronoun use during psychotherapy, had been a concern to neurolinguistic programming, and was also tested as a potential counselling strategy (Priest et al., 2016). The problem with this approach is that procedural contents are automatically selected. Further, the meaning of function words is also subject to change. Those who often refer to their own selves in a conversation may be overcontrolling persons but may also feel deprived of control (feel they should control or wish to control) —or they are taking some new commitments as, for example, in an oath as part of a rite.

The proliferation of negative structures and frequent references to own self do not only characterize the language of suicide: in crisis communication, such contents are higher than in the texts that disclose positive emotionality or are neutral. The frequent use of negative structures and references to self are related to the liminality of a psychological crisis and can predict suicide only if the person remains entrapped in extended liminality. The same structures may also predict the success of a rite. They are indicative of the appropriate mental state of the initiands who are transitioning between the different identities in transformative liminal settings (Kelemen & Erdős, 2003).

7.4.5 Metaphors

We express the contents that we cannot experience directly, grasp fully, are transcendent, or are social taboos through metaphors—abstractions such as time, space, transformation, spirituality, life, and death. Metaphor use requires mappings between an appropriate source domain (usually the physical environment) and a target domain (Lakoff & Johnson, 1980; Lakoff, 2012a). During major life transitions, the conventional metaphors connect us to the shared meanings of our

[4] In the original: kutyaszorító, a dog's grip or bind, a term going back to medieval times, referring to a very narrow street from where a chased dog could not escape—a *dead end*. Consider the connections to double bind, entrapment and to the root metaphor LIFE IS A JOURNEY (Lakoff & Johnson, 1980).

communities, while novel metaphors as unique and individual-level representations open the door to personally significant meaning-making and reconstruction. The rich individual connotations and high emotional loading render the reconstruction of full meaning impossible, but in-depth explorations of the idiosyncrasies and relating the personal to the cultural domain may help open the trap of a liminal hotspot, previously kept firmly closed by the tormenting feelings and symbolization errors inherent in the trauma. Transitions are captured in terms of (re)birth and death. Though we know a lot about the physiology of both the beginning and the end of life, their fundamental mysteries have not been resolved, and hopefully never will be. The beginnings and the end, however, are connected in our consciousness. Bakó (1996), in his case-level qualitative analysis, has noted that people in their suicidal ideations develop a peculiar and dangerous fantasy of *proliferation*, the continuation of life after death, usually in a better world.

Death belongs to the sacred, and has remained a strong social taboo in modernity, but without the traditional rites to tame its realities. Metaphors of death are invariably used to express the crisis experience as the separation from previous identity forms, and the unknown and insecure dimensions of liminality. Lakoff (1993, also in Lakoff & Johnson, 1980) identified several metaphorical mappings: death as (eternal) sleep, the destination of the life journey, the end of a temporal cycle such as the day (sunset, darkness), or the year (cold winter). These metaphors are conventional, powerful, and often include a script for action—for example, if one is tired of life, then they should go for a long sleep at the end of the day; if feeling entrapped, then they should find an escape as some *exit*. Importantly, in a crisis, the symbolic death of the previous identity is unavoidable. However, this "death" and the subsequent "birth" should take place in the mythic-metaphorical space and in the timelessness of a ritual (Weatherly, 2015).

Persons' metaphor use, and the deconstruction and reconstruction of metaphors parallel to transformation processes have long been considered central in the liminal context of psychotherapies. While metaphors grasp the totality of the experience with their manifest and latent contents, both the dominant pole of a construct and the one in the shadow, they may not suggest a liveable script. We do not only live and heal but may also retrogress or even die by the power of metaphors (Battino, 2002; Lakoff, 2012b). Consider, for example, Lakoff's (2012b) analysis on the first Iraqi war: the public and the soldiers sent to war were given powerful, highly affective metaphorical messages so that they would accept the necessity and rationality of the war and interpret it in the traditional narrative frameworks of a hero's story. The heroes, thus endowed with a conventional and precious identity element, were guided by a good father (the president) to save the people (the good father's children) in the whole world (Lakoff, 2012b).

The metaphors we use to designate a crisis experience are related to two types of sudden spatial movements: the first one is from the centre to the margin (McNamee, 1992, 2004). As a boundary phenomenon, the crisis separates us from our communities. A spatial boundary differentiates between the centre and the margin, the safety of our "own" habitat, and the strangeness, uncertainties, and threats of the external environment beyond the boundary. We attribute special significance to the centre, understood as our own group and our home, a safe and sacred place that must be preserved and protected, both by physical and spiritual activities (Eliade, 1961). The margin, a dwelling place for the trickster, is associated with danger (Horvath & Szakolczai, 2020).

The other basis for metaphorical mappings is rapid downward movement (Casasanto & Gijssels, 2015)—towards the underworld. Persons experiencing a life crisis often sense their entrapment as being captured in a pitfall, abyss, or whirlpool, which represent their isolation and loss of control, coupled with the images of darkness or loss of air to describe the extremely negative emotional tones of their experiences of hopelessness and despair. In the excerpt below, the caller is struggling with suicidal ideations, envisioning and assessing the potential scenes for her suicide—as the train station or her own balcony. She is complaining of not daring to use her balcony, and of sensations of derealization ("levitating"). This is a life-saving symptom, *not* to be treated prior to understanding the complexity of the case:

> C: The *abyss* is attracting me so much… so I have not entered the balcony for at least two years (…) Simply, whenever I look down, at the very moment I am having a sensation, like I have told you, that I am falling out of this world, and I can only think that only a second would be needed to step out (…) so I have got so sick of this, I cannot even tell you, sometimes I feel as if I were falling out of this world, as if I were levitating (Erdős, 2018, p. 76).

The above excerpt is a condensed description of the experiences of the entrapment in the limbo of an existential crisis. The caller is stuck at the boundary of the two worlds, unable to communicate about her condition in her close social network, for the experience is beyond the frames of ordinary life. She, however, does communicate about it in the physical symptoms of dizziness, and a choking sensation also mentioned in her call: "I had a bad choking sensation, I could feel that something was suffocating me (…) simply, I could not, not swallow but they could not find anything (…) so I got some tranquilizers". She, as other people at suicide risk often do, visited her family doctor (Luoma et al., 2002), and was complaining of vague, but, knowing her situation, highly meaningful symptoms, of the embodied meanings that clearly indicated the tormenting suppression of her story.

Metaphors are deeply rooted in the physical world, primarily, in our body. Our first experience of falling, yielding to the immense power of gravitation, is the birth experience. This is how falling, and the risks involved in transitions understood as death and rebirth,[5] are connected. Falling implies the elementary need to connect and hold on. Once the helping alliance is established, the high affectivity of the liminal hotspot giving energies for the change and the enhanced suggestibility ensuring openness to the process will turn into the lifesaving and reconstructive resources of transformative liminality.

[5] For the connection between rites of transition and Grof's birth matrices, see Chap. 2, *Transitions from a Systemic Perspective. Quantum change and Liminality.*

7.5 Conclusion

Not surprisingly, a psychosocial crisis, a notion in late modernity to describe deep changes, shares many features of transformative liminality of the archaic transition rites. What we identify as the symptoms of a psychological crisis are mainly the characteristics of liminality. Separation from the identity part that would not facilitate further growth anymore, experiencing the disorder associated with liminality, and progressing into new roles and positions, building new identities while also restoring the continuity of identity—now perceived from a more integrated and complex perspective—must occur. However, the preconditions and contexts, as well as the attributed meanings of transformative liminality are often missing, and on such occasions, the person experiencing the transition will be captured in a maximally liminal hotspot. The individual responses to crisis experiences may also involve self-destructive patterns motivated by the trauma-related psychological pain, isolation, and by the uncertainties inherent in the transition. In such cases, the symbolic death of an identity element accompanying the loss is transformed into physical self-destruction.

In the moments of a crisis, we are invariably confronted with a personal mission that is recurrent in human life. As Maruna et al. (2006) have claimed, a crisis is the rediscovery of one's world, changing meanings of the people, events, and actions. It is the hero's risky mission, reconstructing cosmic order from the perceived chaos by defining new meanings of the diffuse sensations and experiences. If successful, the explorative process may open future opportunities. The new, liberated and liberating narrative, which integrates what has already been told before and is being symbolized in the ongoing transition, could give way to the birth of a new, healthier identity (Anderson & Goolishian, 1988). The personal narratives of crisis and growth are unique and are shaped by individual experiences, but the person's meaning-making processes rely on the available cultural resources captured in the relevant stories, myths, and their central elements, metaphors.

When connecting to other members of the group and sharing one's own experiences, *Homo symbolicus* strongly relies on languaging. The internal turmoil of the crisis and the ongoing trauma-related neuropsychological processes may inhibit or radically change our attempts at verbalization. In the light of the emerging evidence, the usual question "Do you want to talk about it?" does not seem so useful, at least not under all circumstances. The mere duplication of trauma-related contents would not liberate the person from their entrapment. The question is usually reinterpreted as a promise of unconditional support—and *this* has its strong healing potentials.

Traditionally, the discursive frameworks as well as the appropriate action sequences related to a life crisis were reassuringly inherited from the previous generations—but in some cases, this could lead to permanent excommunication. Since modernity, therapy as treatment for both the body and the soul, originally understood as an art and a spiritual activity, has been transformed into a secular profession to assess and manage the extraordinary. In an era dominated by the discourses of rationality co-existing with the absurdities of permanent liminality, patterns of everyday, "normal" life cannot endow one's sufferings with meaning. This late modern condition, *empty suffering*, has become a cultural condition for mass-level mental health problems (Sik, 2023).

The crisis experience has retained the strong spiritual aspects of transition rites; but how can we interpret crisis—as a boundary of *krinein*—in an era dominated by the dissolution of boundaries and the related uncertainties? Is there a possibility for a more authentic and complex relational approach (McNamee, 2015)? The emerging questions are invariably existential-spiritual problems, and the transformation extends to the transcendent domains (Stagg, 2014). Spirituality, often misunderstood in the public discourse as some dogmatic and irrational stance, highlights the unique and the universal, the cultural and the personal in one's search for values, meaning, and purpose beyond the self. Spirituality comprises the person's ultimately significant and intimate transformative experiences (Cook, 2004). The theory of quantum change acknowledges the implications of spirituality in human life. Those experiencing the positive change describe it in terms of interconnectedness with humanity and creation, sensing the physical world as part of a more complex reality (Miller, 2004). These experiences will guide the person in their journey towards a more authentic personal identity and a fully lived life.

References

Allen, J. G., Fonagy, P., & Bateman, A. W. (2008). *Mentalizing in clinical practice*. American Psychiatric Publishing Inc..

Anderson, H., & Goolishian, H. A. (1988). Human systems as linguistic systems: Preliminary and evolving ideas about the implications for clinical theory. *Family Process, 27*(4), 371–393. https://doi.org/10.1111/j.1545-5300.1988.00371.x

Bakhtin, M. (1984). *Rabelais and his World*. Indiana University Press.

Bakó, T. (1996). *Verem mélyén. [In the depth of a pitfall]*. Cserépfalvi Kiadó.

Balázs, L. (1995). *Menj ki én lelkem a testből... Elmúlás és temetkezés Csikszentdomonkoson [My soul, leave my body... death and burial in Csikszentdomonkos*]. Pallas – Akadémiai.

Balikó, M. (1990). *Tele/pszicho/fon [Tele/psycho/phone]*. Magyar Pszichiátriai Társaság.

Balikó, M. (2000). Az impressziókeltés kommunikációs sajátosságai vokális csatornán keresztül. [Characteristics of impression management through the vocal channel]. In G. Kelemen (Ed.), *Tele-dialógus* (pp. 98–133). Pro Pannonia.

Bateson, G. (1972). *Steps to an ecology of mind. Collected essays in anthropology, psychiatry, evolution, and epistemology*. Jason Aronson.

Battino, R. (2002). *Metaphoria: Metaphor and guided metaphor for psychotherapy and healing*. Crown Publishing House.

Bloch, S., & Leydon, G. (2019). Conversation analysis and telephone helplines for health and illness: A narrative review. *Research on Language and Social Interaction, 52*(3), 193–211. https://doi.org/10.1080/08351813.2019.1631035

Boeree, G. (2009). *Personality theories. Siegmund freud*. Shippensburg University. Retrieved from: https://webspace.ship.edu/cgboer/freud.html

Bonomi, C. (2004). Trauma and the symbolic function of the mind. *International Forum of Psychoanalysis, 13*(1/2), 45–50. https://doi.org/10.1080/08037060410031052

Borsboom, D. (2017). A network theory of mental disorders. *World Psychiatry: Official Journal of the World Psychiatric Association (WPA), 16*(1), 5–13. https://doi.org/10.1002/wps.20375

Bussolari, C. J., & Goodell, J. A. (2009). Chaos theory as a model for life transitions counseling: Nonlinear dynamics and life's changes. *Journal of Counseling & Development, 87*(1), 98–107. https://doi.org/10.1002/j.1556-6678.2009.tb00555.x

Caplan, G. (1964). *Principles of preventive psychiatry*. Basic Books.

Casasanto, D., & Gijssels, T. (2015). What makes a metaphor an embodied metaphor? *Linguistics Vanguard, 1*(1), 327–337. https://doi.org/10.1515/lingvan-2014-1015

Cook, C. C. (2004). Addiction and spirituality. *Addiction (Abingdon, England), 99*(5), 539–551. https://doi.org/10.1111/j.1360-0443.2004.00715.x

De Beurs, D., Cleare, S., Wetherall, K., Eschle-Byrne, S., Ferguson, E., O'Connor, D. B., & O'Connor, R. C. (2020). Entrapment and suicide risk: The development of the 4-item Entrapment Scale Short-Form (E-SF). *Psychiatry Research, 284*, 112765. https://doi.org/10.1016/j.psychres.2020.112765

De Luca Picione, R., & Lozzi, U. (2021). Uncertainty as a constitutive condition of human experience. An extensive review of the paradoxes and complexities of sensemaking processes in the face of uncertainty crisis. *International Journal of Psychoanalysis and Education: Subject, Action & Society, 1*(2), 14–53. https://doi.org/10.32111/SAS.2021.1.2.2

Dunbar, R. I. M. (2004). Gossip in evolutionary perspective. *Review of General Psychology, 8*(2), 100–110. https://doi.org/10.1037/1089-2680.8.2.100

Durkheim, E. (1897/2005). *Suicide: A study in sociology*. Routledge.

Ehmann, B. (2002). *A szöveg mélyén [In-depth text analysis]*. Új Mandátum.

Eliade, M. (1961). *The sacred and the profane: The nature of religion*. Harper & Row.

Empson, L. (2013). My affair with the "Other": Identity journeys across the research–practice divide. *Journal of Management Inquiry, 22*(2), 229–248. https://doi.org/10.1177/1056492612446068

Erdős, M. B. (2006). *A nyelvben élő kapcsolat: egy öngyilkosság-megelőző sürgősségi telefonszolgálat beszélgetéseinek vizsgálata. [The language bond: explorations of calls of a suicide prevention hotline]* Typotex Kft.

Erdős, M. B. (2018). "… Úgy érzem, mintha kiesnék ebből a világból." A lélektani krízis átmeneti tapasztalatának narratív sajátosságai. [I feel as if I fell out of this world. Narrative characteristics of liminal experiences of the psychosocial crisis]. *Magyar Pszichológiai Szemle, 73*(1), 59–81. https://doi.org/10.1556/0016.2018.73.1.5

Erdos, M. B., & Javor, R. (2022). Entrapment and escape: Exploring the relationship between suicide and emigration in a post-communist country. *The International Journal of Social Psychiatry, 68*(8), 1636–1643. https://doi.org/10.1177/00207640211047617

Erikson, E. H. (1968). *Identity: Youth and crisis*. Norton.

Fekete, S., Fekete, J., Pótó, Z., & Lester, D. (2023). A content analysis of suicidal notes: A preliminary study in Hungary. *Suicide Studies, 4*(3), 29–39.

Garfinkel, H. (1956). Conditions of successful degradation ceremonies. *American Journal of Sociology, 61*(5), 420–424.

Gergen, K. J., & McNamee, S. (2000). From disordering discourse to transformative dialogue. In R. A. Neimeyer & J. D. Raskin (Eds.), *Constructions of disorder: Meaning-making frameworks for psychotherapy* (pp. 333–349). American Psychological Association. https://doi.org/10.1037/10368-014

Greco, M., & Stenner, P. (2017). From paradox to pattern shift: Conceptualising liminal hotspots and their affective dynamics. *Theory & Psychology, 27*(2), 147–166. https://doi.org/10.1177/0959354317693120

Hänninen, V. (2004). A model of narrative circulation. *Narrative Inquiry, 14*(1), 69–85. https://doi.org/10.1075/ni.14.1.04han

Hayward, K. (2016). *City limits: Crime, consumer culture and the urban experience*. Routledge-Cavendish

Høgh-Olesen, H. (2024). Inside the mind of the self-deceiver: Foundational issues in relation to human defences and "the unconscious". *Human Arenas. Advance Online Publication.* https://doi.org/10.1007/s42087-024-00458-7

Horvath, A., & Szakolczai, A. (2018). Political anthropology. In S. Turner & W. Outhwaite (Eds.), *Sage handbook of political sociology* (pp. 189–204). Sage.
Horvath, A., & Szakolczai, A. (2020). *The political sociology and anthropology of evil: Tricksterology*. Routledge.
Horvath, A., & Thomassen, B. (2008). Mimetic errors in liminal schismogenesis: On the political anthropology of the trickster. *International Political Anthropology, 1*(1), 3–24.
James, W. (1902/1982). *The varieties of religious experience*. Penguin Books.
Johnson, T. J., Pfenninger, D. T., & Klion, R. E. (2000). Constructing and deconstructing transitive diagnosis. In R. A. Neimeyer & J. D. Raskin (Eds.), *Constructions of disorder* (pp. 145–173). APA.
Kelemen, G., & Erdős, M. B. (2003). The role of reintegration rituals in sobriety - A comparative study on recovery and relapse. *Dynamic Psychiatry, 36*(198/199), 89–113.
Kelly, G. A. (1955). *The psychology of personal constructs. Vol. 1. A theory of personality. Vol. 2. Clinical diagnosis and psychotherapy.* W. W. Norton.
Kenneth J., Gergen Sheila, McNamee Robert A., Neimeyer Jonathan D., Raskin Constructions of disorder: Meaning-making frameworks for psychotherapy. From disordering discourse to transformative dialogue. American Psychological Association Washington 333–349
Kets de Vries, M. F. R. (2012). Conclusion: The twice-born experience. In M. F. R. Kets de Vries (Ed.), *Reflections on leadership and career development* (pp. 220–232). Wiley. https://doi.org/10.1002/9781119206477.oth1
Kézdi, B. (1995). *A negatív kód.* [The negative code]. Pannónia Kiadó.
Krohne, H. W. (2001). Stress and coping theories. *The International Encyclopedia of the Social and Behavioral Sciences, 22*, 15163–15170. https://doi.org/10.1016/B0-08-043076-7/03817-1
Lakoff, G. (2012a). Explaining embodied cognition results. *Topics in Cognitive Science, 4*, 773–785. https://doi.org/10.1111/j.1756-8765.2012.01222.x
Lakoff, G. (2012b). Metaphor and war: The metaphor system used to justify war in the gulf. *Cognitive Semiotics, 4*(2), 5–19. https://doi.org/10.1515/cogsem.2012.4.2.5
Lakoff, G. (2014). *The all new don't think of an elephant!: Know your values and frame the debate*. Chelsea Green Publishing.
Lakoff, G., & Johnson, M. (1980). *Metaphors we live by*. University of Chicago Press.
Lau, C. Y. H., & Tov, W. (2023). Effects of positive reappraisal and self-distancing on the meaningfulness of everyday negative events. *Frontiers in Psychology, 14*, 1093412. https://doi.org/10.3389/fpsyg.2023.1093412
Leenaars, A. A. (1996). Suicide: A multidimensional malaise. *Suicide & Life-Threatening Behavior, 26*(3), 221–236.
Lerner, M. (1980). *The belief in a just world: A fundamental delusion.* Springer Nature.
Lester, D. (1994). A comparison of 15 theories of suicide. *Suicide and Life-Threatening Behavior, 24*(1), 80–88.
Levine, H. B. (2014). Psychoanalysis and trauma. *Psychoanalytic Inquiry, 34*(3), 214–224. https://doi.org/10.1080/07351690.2014.889475
Levine, P. (1998). Memory, trauma, and healing. *Alternative Health Practitioner, 4*(2), 115–121. https://doi.org/10.1177/153321019800400205
Li, E., Campbell, C., Midgley, N., & Luyten, P. (2023). Epistemic trust: A comprehensive review of empirical insights and implications for developmental psychopathology. *Research in psychotherapy (Milano), 26*(3), 704. https://doi.org/10.4081/ripppo.2023.704
Luoma, J. B., Martin, C. E., & Pearson, J. L. (2002). Contact with mental health and primary care providers before suicide: a review of the evidence. *The American Journal of Psychiatry, 159*(6), 909–916. https://doi.org/10.1176/appi.ajp.159.6.909
Mair, V., Mair, D., & Liqing, Z (2009) Danger plus opportunity does not equal crisis: How a misunderstanding about Chinese characters has led many astray. *Pinyin info: A Guide to the Writing of Mandarin Chinese in Romanization.* https://pinyin.info/chinese/crisis.html

Maruna, S., Wilson, L., & Curran, K. (2006). Why God is often found behind bars: Prison conversions and the crisis of self-narrative. *Research in Human Development, 3*(2–3), 161–184. https://doi.org/10.1080/15427609.2006.9683367

McAdams, D. P. (1993). *The stories we live by: Personal myths and the making of the self.* William Morrow & Co..

McAdams, D. P. (2006). The redemptive self: Generativity and the stories Americans live by. *Research in Human Development, 3*(2–3), 81–100. https://doi.org/10.1080/15427609.2006.9683363

McNamee, S. (1992). Reconstructing identity: The communal construction of crisis. In S. McNamee & K. Gergen (Eds.), *Therapy as social construction* (pp. 186–199). Sage.

McNamee, S. (2004). Critical moments as "Transformations". *Negotiation Journal, 20*(2), 269–274. https://doi.org/10.1111/j.1571-9979.2004.00022.x

McNamee, S. (2015). Radical presence: Alternatives to the therapeutic state. *European Journal of Psychotherapy & Counselling, 17*(4), 373–383. https://doi.org/10.1080/13642537.2015.1094504

Miller, W. R. (2004). The phenomenon of quantum change. *Journal of Clinical Psychology, 60*(5), 453–460. https://doi.org/10.1002/jclp.20000

Neimeyer, R. A. (2006). Re-storying loss: Fostering growth in the posttraumatic narrative. In L. Calhoun & R. Tedeschi (Eds.), *Handbook of posttraumatic growth. Research and practice* (pp. 67–80). Lawrence Erlbaum.

Oravecz, R. (2004). Roots of discoursive suicidology. *Psihološka Obzorja / Horizons of Psychology, 13*(1), 151–161.

Oravecz, R. (2023). Az öngyilkosság folyamat-jellege az analitikus pszichoterápia szemszögéből. [Suicide as process from the perspective of analytical psychotherapy]. *Pszichoterápia, 32*(1), 15–24.

Pennebaker, J., Booth, R., Boyd, R. L., & Francis, M. E. (2015). *Linguistic inquiry and word count: LIWC2015*. Pennebaker Conglomerates.

Pennebaker, J. W., Mehl, M. R., & Niederhoffer, K. G. (2003). Psychological aspects of natural language. use: our words, our selves. *Annual Review of Psychology, 54*, 547–577. https://doi.org/10.1146/annurev.psych.54.101601.145041

Pennebaker, J. W., & Seagal, J. D. (1999). Forming a story: The health benefits of narrative. *Journal of Clinical Psychology, 55*(10), 1243–1254. https://doi.org/10.1002/(SICI)1097-4679(199910)55:10<1243::AID-JCLP6>3.0.CO;2-N

Pennebaker, J. W., & Smyth, J. M. (2016). *Opening up by writing it down: How expressive writing improves health and eases emotional pain*. The Guilford Press.

Poal, P. (1990). Introduction to the theory and practice of crisis intervention. *Quaderns de Psycologica, 10*, 121–140.

Preti, A. (2007). Suicide among animals: A review of evidence. *Psychological Reports, 101*(3 Pt 1), 831–848. https://doi.org/10.2466/pr0.101.3.831-848

Priest, A., Hollins Martin, C. J., & Bager Charleson, S. (2016). Exploring clients' responses to changing pronoun use from second person (you) to first person (I) during therapy: A constructivist qualitative approach. *Counseling and Psychotherapy Research, 16*(3), 183–192. https://doi.org/10.1002/capr.12065

Propp, V. (1999). *A mese morfológiája. [The morphology of tales]* Osiris-Századvég.

Ramos-Vera, C., Calle, D., Quispe-Callo, G., Höller, I., Forkmann, T., Ordoñez-Carrasco, J., Čopková, R., Lichner, V., Lobos-Rivera, M., Calizaya-Milla, Y. E., & Saintila, J. (2024). Sex differences in entrapment in a multinational sample: A network analysis perspective. *Frontiers in Psychiatry, 15*, 1321207. https://doi.org/10.3389/fpsyt.2024.1321207

Rasmussen, S. A., Fraser, L., Gotz, M., MacHale, S., Mackie, R., Masterton, G., McConachie, S., & O'Connor, R. C. (2010). Elaborating the cry of pain model of suicidality: Testing a psychological model in a sample of first-time and repeat self-harm patients. *The British Journal of Clinical Psychology, 49*(Pt 1), 15–30. https://doi.org/10.1348/014466509X415735

Resnicow, K., & Page, S. E. (2008). Embracing chaos and complexity: A quantum change for public health. *American Journal of Public Health, 98*(8), 1382–1389. https://doi.org/10.2105/AJPH.2007.129460

Ringel, E. (1976). The presuicidal syndrome. *Suicide and Life-Threatening Behavior, 6*(3), 131–149.

Rober P., (2002). Constructive hypothesizing dialogic understanding and the therapist's inner conversation: Some ideas about knowing and not knowing in the family therapy session. *Journal of Marital and Family Therapy, 28*(4), 467–478. https://doi.org/10.1111/jmft.2002.28.issue-4, https://doi.org/10.1111/j.1752-0606.2002.tb00371.x

Sacks, H. (1992). *Lectures on conversation Vols I & II*. (Ed. G. Jefferson). Basil.

Salvatore, S., & Venuleo, C. (2017). Liminal transitions in a semiotic key: The mutual in-feeding between present and past. *Theory & Psychology, 27*(2), 215–230. https://doi.org/10.1177/0959354317692889

Seligman, M. E. (1972). Learned helplessness. *Annual Review of Medicine, 23*, 407–412. https://doi.org/10.1146/annurev.me.23.020172.002203

Shneidman, E. S. (1986). Ten commonalities of suicide and their implications for response. *Crisis: The Journal of Crisis Intervention and Suicide Prevention, 7*(2), 88–93.

Sik, D. (2023). *Empty suffering. A social phenomenology of depression, anxiety and addiction.* Routledge.

Smith, J. A. (2002). Suicide in post-socialist countries. Examples from Hungary and Belorus. *Anthropology of East Europe Review, 20(1), 55–65.*

Stagg, R. (2014). The nadir experience: Crisis, transition, and growth. *Journal of Transpersonal Psychology, 46*(1), 72–91.

Stelzer, E. M., Atkinson, C., O'Connor, M. F., & Croft, A. (2019). Gender differences in grief narrative construction: A myth or reality? *European Journal of Psychotraumatology, 10*(1), 1688130. https://doi.org/10.1080/20008198.2019.1688130

Szakolczai, A. (2009). Liminality and experience: Structuring transitory situations and transformative events. *International Political Anthropology, 2*(1), 141–172.

Szakolczai, J. M. (2021). "Nothing new in the West": Paralleling the war rhetoric and measures of the COVID-19 pandemic with the WW1 horrors described by Erich Maria Remarque. *International Political Anthropology, 14*(2), 113–124. https://doi.org/10.5281/zenodo.5721748

Szasz, T. (1995). The origin of psychiatry: The alienist as nanny for troublesome adults. *History of Psychiatry, 6*(21, Pt 1), 1–19. https://doi.org/10.1177/0957154X9500602101

Tacey, D. (2005). Spiritual perspectives on suicidal impulses in young adults. In R. H. Cox, B. Ervin-Cox, & L. Hoffman (Eds.), *Spirituality and psychological health* (pp. 107–128). Colorado School of Professional Psychology Press.

Taylor, S. E. (2006). Tend and befriend: Biobehavioral bases of affiliation under stress. *Current Directions in Psychological Science, 15*(6), 273–277. https://doi.org/10.1111/j.1467-8721.2006.00451.x

Tedeschi, R. G., & Calhoun, L. (2004). Posttraumatic growth: A new perspective on psychotraumatology. *Psychiatric Times, 21*(4), 58–60.

Thomassen, B. (2013). Anthropology and social theory: Renewing dialogue. *European Journal of Social Theory, 16*(2), 188–207. https://doi.org/10.1177/1368431012463809

Thompson, A. H. (2010). The suicidal process and self-esteem. *Crisis: The Journal of Crisis Intervention and Suicide Prevention, 31*(6), 311–316. https://doi.org/10.1027/0227-5910/a000045

Torous, J., Bucci, S., Bell, I. H., Kessing, L. V., Faurholt-Jepsen, M., Whelan, P., Carvalho, A. F., Keshavan, M., Linardon, J., & Firth, J. (2021). The growing field of digital psychiatry: Current evidence and the future of apps, social media, chatbots, and virtual reality. *World Psychiatry: Official Journal of the World Psychiatric Association (WPA), 20*(3), 318–335. https://doi.org/10.1002/wps.20883

Turner, V. W. (1969). *The ritual process: Structure and anti-structure*. University of New York Press.

van Boeckel, J. (2011). *"When we find meaning in art, our thinking is most in sync with nature" A Review of An Ecology of Mind- The Gregory Bateson Documentary*. https://www.academia.edu/12919745/_When_we_find_meaning_in_art_our_thinking_is_most_in_sync_with_nature_A_Review_of_An_Ecology_of_Mind_The_Gregory_Bateson_Documentary

van der Kolk, B. (2015). *The body keeps the score: Brain, mind, and body in the healing of trauma*. Penguin Books.

Van Gennep, A. (1909/2019). *The rites of passage*. University of Chicago Press.

Voros, V., Tenyi, T., Nagy, A., Fekete, S., & Osvath, P. (2021). Crisis concept re-loaded?—The recently described suicide-specific syndromes may help to better understand suicidal behavior and assess imminent suicide risk more effectively. *Frontiers in Psychiatry, 12*, Article 598923. https://doi.org/10.3389/fpsyt.2021.598923

Watzlawick, P., Weakland, J. H., & Fisch, R. (1974). *Change: Principles of problem formation and problem resolution*. W. W. Norton.

Weatherly, J. (2015). The Chariot of the Hero: Myth and Metaphor in Campbell. In K. Golden (Ed.), *Uses of comparative mythology (RLE Myth)* (pp. 141–151). Routledge.

Weinreich, P. (2004). Identity structure analysis. In P. Weinreich & W. Saunderson (Eds.), *Analysing identity: Cross-cultural, societal and clinical contexts* (pp. 7–76). Routledge.

White, M. (2024). *Maps of narrative practice*. WW Norton & Company.

Williams, J. M. G., & Pollock, L. R. (2001). Psychological aspects of the suicidal process. In K. Van Heeringen (Ed.), *Understanding suicidal behaviour* (pp. 76–94). John Wiley and Sons.

Zimbardo, P. G., & Boyd, J. N. (2015). Putting time in perspective: A valid, reliable individual-differences metric. In M. Stolarski, N. Fieulaine, & W. van Beek (Eds.), *Time perspective theory; Review, research and application*. Springer. https://doi.org/10.1007/978-3-319-07368-2_2

Chapter 8
Lost in the Labyrinth of Symbols. Epiphanies as Guiding Experiences

8.1 The Birth of a Novel to Prevent Suicide

Many literary works were written about suicide, the "altruistic" form, depicted as a heroic attempt, an ultimate act to protect community members or values. Examples include lovers' extended suicide, seen as an extreme proof of "love" to continue in eternity, with such novels potentially leading to copycat behaviour known in the professional literature as the Werther effect (Schmidtke & Häfner, 1988); or suicide as a potential response to shame, guilt, and existential worries. Suicide in literature could result in a lengthy list with thousands of items, from the pieces in antiquity to contemporary works.

A twentieth-century novel by the "Hungarian Dickens", Géza Gárdonyi, entitled *Szunyoghy's Paternoster* (Szunyoghy miatyánkja, 1916/1968) was written with the explicit purpose to *prevent* suicide. Gárdonyi provides a rich description of the phenomena characteristic of presuicidal states, such as sensing entrapment, or experiencing the triad of cognitive, dynamic, and situational constriction,[1] not yet known in his era. He was informed only through his observations, experiences, reflections, and writerly intuition. His novel is an authentic description of lifelong coping strategies, of the significance of continuing bond in the grief experience, and of the redemptive potentials of post-traumatic growth (Neimeyer et al., 2014; Tedeschi & Calhoun, 2004). However, what makes the following analysis a good fit for a book about the role of symbols in the construction of liminal experiences is not these intuitions—art often predicts scientific discoveries—but Gárdonyi's unique focus on the role of *symbols* in the acts of self-destruction. For him, a firm believer in reincarnation, reason represented the counterpoint of *fantasy,* missing one's way in the labyrinth of culture by misinterpreting the symbols that should guide one's actions. The novel was written in 1913, shortly before the devastations of WWI, and

[1] For more details, see *Chap. 7, The Psychosocial Crisis as a Liminal Experience.*

M. B. Erdos, *Transitions - Liminality as Lived Experience*,
https://doi.org/10.1007/978-3-031-96007-9_8

was published in 1916. The work was motivated by an event, which the writer commented on in his diary as follows:

> 8th July 1913. A young man was found dead in the Pozsony cemetery. A gun was found beside him. A wound in his chest. A book of mine by his side and a note in pencil: This book has nearly prevented me from dying by suicide. The title of the book was not mentioned in the newspaper. As this book has nearly prevented a man from killing himself, I could probably write a book that would surely keep the lives of many: only I must make it clear that those preparing for death are disturbed by their fantasies (Z. Szalai & Tóth, 1968, p. 483[2]).

Critics argued that the novel's hero, Szunyoghy, was depicted as a victim of a *series of traumas*, probably more than any person would naturally encounter in their lives. For Gárdonyi, however, such a series was a lived reality. He lost his four young siblings as a child and then his two brothers as a young man. His father was a revolutionist in the 1848–49 War of Independence in Hungary. After the defeat, severe retaliations began. His father was rescued, but he had to hide his social identity by changing his name and place of residence. Forced paternal identicide was accompanied by frequent spatial movements—the family was moving from one place to another as his father had to change his workplace rather frequently (Gulyás, 1956). Repeated runaways and hiding one's true social identity while struggling for the continuity of personal identity are recurrent patterns in Gárdonyi's works. Gárdonyi's original name was Ziegler, a German name, possibly disturbing in the contemporary era for a firm believer in Hungary's autonomy. He named himself after the village where he had been baptized. Interestingly, he had many, about 30 pseudonyms, as a writer. He always adjusted these names to the genre and the context of his works (Garadnai, 2013; Gulyás, 1956).

As a child, he was struggling with school problems, and once he even failed in Hungarian literature. As the only surviving child in his family, he was suffering from hypochondria and chronic headaches throughout his life. His first marriage, a bitter misfit, served as a model for Szunyoghy's second marriage in the novel. His daughter had mental problems and was treated in a contemporary asylum. Towards the end of his life, he could experience love and care, finding a woman who requited his love. Later, he was sharing a home with his two sons. In consequence of the devastations and losses suffered in WWI and his impairing health conditions, he became depressed and was complaining of loss of energies. He died in 1922. One of his sons revealed that in the last few weeks of his life, he had simply refused to leave his bed (Z. Szalai & Tóth, 1968).

---

[2] In this chapter, the translations of the verbatim quotes from Hungarian into English are mine.

8.2 Fabula, Sjuzet, and Forma. Redemption Sequences

The terms fabula and sjuzet were introduced by Vladimir Propp (1999), a Russian formalist, representing a structuralist approach to narrative analysis. Fabula refers to the themes in the narrative, and sjuzet is the mode of storytelling, a summary term for the main organizing principles of the story, e.g. the chronology of the events, and the characters and places involved. The third aspect is forma, the genre (Füzi & Török, 2006; Hiles & Čermák, 2013). Propp (1999) analysed 101 folktales and identified 31 functions. These functions are described as sequels of binary constructs, for example, interdiction—violation, or unrecognized arrival—recognition (Meletyinszkij, 1999, as cited by Füzi & Török, 2006).

As for the general structure of the novel, Szunyoghy's paternoster is composed of *redemption sequences* (McAdams et al., 2001; McAdams, 2006) related to life-transforming traumas. A redemption sequence is part of generative adults' commitment stories and is associated with the narrator's enhanced levels of psychological wellbeing. Narrators describe a family blessing or special talent, and their sensitivity to others' sufferings early in life. Committed to generativity, they develop a stable personal ideology, and pursue life goals in the service of the society. Redemption sequences as narrative frames serve to transform the inescapable negative life events into positive outcomes. The redemption sequences in this novel are preceded by *epiphanies.* The hero, Daniel Szunyoghy, though emphasizing human rationality and pragmatism as the ultimate, life-saving values, remains open to these transcendent aspects when reaching a crisis in life. Presumably, as the novel has evolved, Gárdonyi's character began to live his own autonomous life, somewhat independently of the writer's original intentions, and this makes the story an authentic description of life-transforming events. Szunyoghy's development demanded more than the power of rationality.

8.3 Quantum Change and Epiphanies

Caplan's (1964) early crisis theory with its recompensation model—re-establishing a previously lost "equilibrium"—does not offer meaningful responses to the existential–spiritual questions emerging during deep transformations in life. Quantum change focuses on William James's idea on our second, and potentially additional births and rebirths in the course of life (C'de Baca & Wilbourne, 2004; *Chap. 7, The Psychosocial Crisis as a Liminal Experience*; Miller, 2004). Miller has noted that the insightful moments of quantum change result in evocative and detailed sensory memories. Unlike the flashbacks in post-traumatic stress disorder, these memories are kept as one's precious treasures, eliciting gratitude. Though these experiences are out of the ordinary and are hard to match to the cultural assets of narratives in a world appreciating rationality the most, the memories of the joyful, cathartic, and liberating experiences are firmly integrated in the person's narrative identity.

The two types identified by Miller (2004) are mystical experiences (epiphanies), and unexpected, sudden insights. The Greek word "epiphainestai" means appear or become visible—the disclosure of what has always existed but has never been recognized by the person (McDonald, 2008). An epiphany is a manifestation of a benevolent divine power, a revelation, often in the form of a specific sign (semeia), connecting the person to some transcendent quality, to the knowledge that is holistic, uniting and is beyond traditional rationalism (Szakolczai, 2017, 2024). Thus, an epiphany is a personally meaningful and insightful encounter with some benevolent supernatural quality, guiding the person towards eudaimonia, the happiness originating from living a life in harmony with one's fate (Proctor & Tweed, 2016). The subject's openness and ability to interpret the sign is crucial to overcoming the crisis and using the sign as a resource for one's personal growth. Epiphanies as transient and extraordinary mystical experiences in times of crises and uncertainties are liminal phenomena; they are complex, holistic responses to deep personal needs, indicating the presence of a personally caring higher power (James, 1902/1982; Siddiqi, 2019; Szakolczai, 2024).

Experiencing an epiphany involves the recall of previously repressed memories (McDonald, 2008), construing a bridge between one's past and present experiences. This enables the person to process what was left behind, previously seen as a mere source of fruitless "fantasies", the worries about the future. Thus, epiphanies are examples of Jungian *synchronicity*, describing an acausal relationship between two personally meaningful events that seemed to happen only by chance (Beitman, 2022). Considering this acausality, interpreting the epiphany is not an analytical but an intuitive process—a matter of sudden insight or revelation. An epiphany is not a verifiable truth, but the type of truth that is beyond cool reason. It is the truth and the reason of the heart (Szakolczai, 2017). Epiphanies are endowed with a special power, sweeping away the doubts and the darkness of liminal entrapment, and removing the barriers to personal development. Ecstatic epiphanies as prototypical liminal phenomena happen to the person in the life-transforming moments of a crisis (Siddiqi, 2019).

An epiphany can be a dream, an apparition, or a commonly occurring natural or cultural phenomenon, reinterpreted as an expressive symbol in a new, spiritual framework. Like other types of transformative liminal experiences, epiphanies are preceded by a tormenting inner chaos and the accompanying negative feelings, ideas, and states: remorse, despair, anger, depression, anxiety, alienation, loneliness, abandonment, and even suicidal ideation (McDonald, 2008). Intuitively interpreting the symbolic content and acting accordingly by surrendering to the divine powers and following their guidance contribute to one's escape from an imminent danger, to healing, and to salvation (Marinatos & Kyrtatas, 2004). As "momentary experiences of transcendence" (McDonald, 2008, p. 90), these events are unpredictable and uncontrollable but guide the person towards greater acceptance of themselves and others while putting an end to resignation and demoralization. Thus, an epiphany is illuminative about the authenticity of the self, requiring not only openness but also parrhesiastic determination and honesty. Experiencing the discontinuity of our core beliefs about ourselves and about how the world works leads to "a courageous encounter with the conditions of existence" (McDonald, 2008, p. 89).

8.4 A Redemption Story of Traumas and Escapes

Gárdonyi's novel has a double narrative frame. A young and committed detective is relating Szunyoghy's story, episode by episode as it evolves in their conversations. The detective is assigned a new task to arrest a scrounge on his escape. He is travelling in disguise, and on board the ship he meets the hero, who also uses a pseudonym. He suspects that Szunyoghy might have killed his wife, so he pretends to be utterly depressed about a broken love affair to trick him into admitting the hypothesized crime. Szunyoghy, an innocent but traumatized man, feels sympathy for the young detective and teaches him about his life to help him overcome the problems that seem to be common in their lives. His story is framed by the detective's reflective comments.

The first lesson is about Szunyoghy's paternoster, his own prayer, which he keeps saying every day: Sed libera nos a phantasia nostra ("deliver us from our phantasy") (Gárdonyi, 1916/1968, p. 450). This prayer is somewhat of a paradox by a novelist relying on his fantasy, even if he is well-known for his dedication to thorough observation and realism. In the context of the novel, fantasies are depicted as self-deceptions, the distortions of uneasy interpersonal realities; or the somewhat paranoid ideas of a person deeply entrapped in a relational problem. Fantasies may fuel the misrepresentations concerning one's own image of the self, support unattainably bright visions, or feed profound but unsubstantiated anxieties. For Gárdonyi, fantasies also involve one's involuntary, haunting memories and dreams.

This personal prayer is deeply rooted in the hero's evolving life story. Daniel Szunyoghy is the eldest son in a poor working-class family. Having experienced continual and severe physical abuse and terror at home, on one occasion he was afraid that his father might even kill him for damaging a banknote. This was the reason for his *first runaway,* a successful strategy that scared his parents and put an end to the persistent physical abuse. He turned out to be a talented pupil and his wits ensured his daily living as well as the costs of his tuition. However, one day he was falsely accused of a theft and expelled from school. This was followed by his *second runaway*. Soon the truth was discovered, and Dani was back to school, learning to distinguish between his few true friends and the disloyal fellows.

As a young man, he became the apple of his parents' eye as a student in law—God's gift, as his father proudly commented. He fell in love with a countess, a noveau riche's fiancée: "she did not look me into the eye, but, through my eyes, into my soul" (Gárdonyi, 1916/1968, p. 306). As marriage seemed impossible, strictly forbidden by the girl's father, they planned to die by suicide together, cherishing fantasies about death that would unite them forever—in a final, Romeo-and-Juliet-type union. They were determined to exchange their unbearable, lasting psychological sufferings for the brief physical pain: "a moment of pain and no more aches, neither the thought, nor the fate, neither the body, nor the soul" (Gárdonyi, 1916/1968, p. 332). On his way to meet his true love and his fate, Szunyoghy was walking through a railway station and accidentally caught sight of a wagon with two letters, SP on it. He interpreted this pervasive experience "those two letters almost shook me" (Gárdonyi 1916/1968; p. 333) as a reference to the countess' family motto: Spiro-spero (so long as I am breathing, I have hopes).

This epiphany, seemingly a small and insignificant event but with a life-saving potential through the attribution of personally significant meanings, proved a reliable spiritual guidance in the moments of utmost despair. His life was saved, but his sufferings were deep: "it felt as if an invisible hand had torn my heart into bloody shreds. I was roaming about as a walking dead whose legs, somehow, are still alive" (Gárdonyi, 1916/1968, p. 333). In this helpless state characterized by emotional numbness, he decided to leave his previous identity behind. Using a friend's name, who he had met *by chance*, he exchanged his promising career in law for one that was much more about mere survival than prosperity. He became a teacher in a small village ("in that apathetic state I thought I would go to that village in Gomor and waste my life there") (Gárdonyi, 1916/1968, p. 334).

The countess also *ran away* from home, cutting off all the connections with her family. She could find Szunyoghy by discovering a *sign*, the letters SP in a postcard message to the family, sent by Szunyoghy under a pseudonym. Having destroyed their previous social identities, they could turn on a new leaf together, working hard for the village people, teaching them, and helping them in every way they could. They deeply loved each other. Though initially they were living in deep poverty, the couple had a happy and harmonious life for a few years. "Never a shadow fell between us" (Gárdonyi, 1916/1968, p. 341).

She had unexpectedly died of pneumonia and her death was soon followed by the loss of their little son, killed in a pandemic of diphtheria.

> What is the human heart made of so that it does not break? (…) I stayed at the grave and was waiting for my soul breaking away from my body. (…) I was sitting there. Three other people, my village people were sitting beside me, the village judge and two others. They had been sitting there until the morning came, in their sheepskin coats, beside the grave on the ground. It was March. They did not speak. In the morning, I could feel that I was also covered with a sheepskin coat. I did not know when they had laid it over me. (…) Then I slept deep, and for long. Day and night. When I woke up, I could see the three men in their sheepskin coats. (…) They were silently sitting there" (Gárdonyi, 1916/1968, p. 345).

Szunyoghy thanked the people for the wake and left the village:

> I was walking and walking. I was not watching where... I decided to go as far as I could, like a rabid dog. And this was good. Other places, other trees, other faces, other talks: perhaps it was not true that Hedvig was my wife and Dani was my son. This was not true, and I was just dreaming. I am coming from somewhere, but I do not know where from. Only my eyes, they are wet (…). In the evening and in the night my fantasy brings my child and his mother to me from the grave: wherever I turn I can see them and hear them (Gárdonyi, 1916/1968, p. 347).

These deep and repeated traumas result in fragmented experiences. In the depth of the grief experience, first, there is only sensing: disrupted images and sounds.

Szunyoghy can see and hear the people talking to him, but what they are saying just does not seem to make any sense. Words are losing their meaning as life has lost its meaning. Loss of meaning extends to all areas of life, including the routine activities. The overall dissociative pattern of traumatic experiences results in depersonalization, the disintegration between the agentive I and the reflective Me ("only my eyes, they are wet") and derealization, disconnecting the person from the experience ("not true"). Impairments in communication are reflected by the short, fragmented, and unfinished sentences in these episodes. Szunyoghy's long sleep is a momentary remedy, a first aid to psychological pain—but, metaphorically, it is also a death equivalent, a temporary reunion with his deceased family members. Village people's empathetic guarding helps him survive the emotional shock. Dissociation is accompanied by a sense of extreme, self-imposed isolation. Dreams may give a temporary peace, suggesting that the loss did not happen, but he wakes up only to re-learn the terrible reality of the loss.

Walking in the physical space follows as if the physical distance could create the emotional distance from the event. Runaway as coping recurs, but with this loss, it does not bring immediate relief. To illustrate the universality of this human experience, it is worth comparing the excerpt below to Gárdonyi's work—a more recent description from the United States:

> When I ran away from home, except for the first time, I always ran away to the country. Traveling around the country was healing in itself, almost spiritual. I was trying to run away from "me," but "me" was with me all the time. I didn't really have any profound realizations while I was doing that (…) (McDonald, 2008, p. 103).

Gárdonyi uses the metaphor of a "rabid dog" to depict the risks and lethality of Szunyoghy's isolation. Avoidance of the people and places that are constant reminders of the trauma is common with persons with post-traumatic stress disorder (van der Kolk, 2015). The stigma of the liminal position, a visible or invisible mark, may render recovery difficult. In one's own community, these marks are evident, and are part of the person's traumatized and constantly reflected Me-identity.

Szunyoghy's long walk, his persisting coping strategy, seems useful in combatting trauma-related states. Indeed, walking is about healing, as the trauma is deeply located in the body, pervasively changing the patterns of thinking and feeling. Moving the body is a common element in today's trauma therapies (Shapiro, 1989; Van der Kolk, 2015). Psychological escape is manifested in physical activities. The trauma, bringing about dissociated states and fragmentation, also teaches us that we are one and inseparable: what is affecting our "mind" will also affect the "body", the two main concepts to capture the hypothesized but not necessarily precise differences in our functions and processes. Nyíri (2020, p. 13) cites Titchener (1909, p. 176) who comments on this vital connection between meaning-making and movements:

> Meaning is originally, kinaesthesis; the organism faces the situation by some bodily attitude, and the characteristic sensations which the attitude involves give meaning to the process that stands at the conscious focus, are psychologically the meaning of that process. (…) We are animals, locomotor organisms.

These deepest losses, unlike Szunyoghy's previous ones, are recurrently mentioned in the subsequent chapters of the novel and disrupt its linear composition, representing the continuity of the bond and the timelessness of the loss (Neimeyer et al., 2014; van der Kolk, 2015). While Gárdonyi highlights the role of rationality in combatting life crises, in this episode he is depicting the psychological realities of a profound trauma, extending much beyond mere rationality. In the depth of the crisis, the hero of the novel, Szunyoghy is not able to follow his own advice anymore. It is overwritten by a deeper, more holistic truth, capturing the entirety of human existence. We cannot give a rational response to the destructions and chaos of death. Szunyoghy has realized the painful limitation to his daily prayer:

> We must escape our fantasy. But this is something that we are carrying with us, don't we? With us, as a long and heavy, black spider web. This web is getting torn apart as we are leaving the place of our pain behind. (…) Finally, what is left are the pieces, winded around your heart so that no one could ever tear them off. They are the parts of your heart (Gárdonyi, 1916/1968, p. 348).

After this runaway, Szunyoghy did not tell anyone his story in the new environment, following the thanks-I'm-fine routines of everyday conversations. Traumatized persons are nonverbal (van der Kolk, 2015), and in the early phases of processing, retelling would only add to their sufferings. The cure enabling Szunyoghy to continue his life is granted by another epiphany, an encounter with a former classmate who is *accidentally* and unknowingly offering Szunyoghy a new mode for grieving. In his state of enhanced suggestibility, he is open to the idea. He is invited to an engineering position in a gold mine, but chooses to become a gold miner, a blue-collar worker instead. In his eyes, this is how he can maintain his detachment from the social environment and connect to the world of the dead:

> My soul is so much broken that I obey every word (…) My interest in his offer was raised when I could see the pale group of workers say their prayers before descending in the earth. As if they were all dead returning to their graves from the surface. What a different world – a world I have never dreamt of… (Gárdonyi, 1916/1968, p. 356).

Extreme reliance on external guidance is characteristic of people experiencing a life crisis. His friend's comments make this new way of life even more attractive, offering him an escape from the tormenting thoughts and feelings: "Upon entering the mine, the upper world disappears from the miner's mind. He forgets about himself. He is focusing on a single feeling, thought and excitement: gold" (Gárdonyi, 1916/1968, p. 357).

Szunyoghy became a successful miner, and then, as his healing proceeded, he converted into a mining engineer. Finally, he became a wealthy person planning to enter farming. After many sober years of life, one night he was drinking with his friends, and as a precaution, he put all his money in one of his boots. When he got drunk, he could find the boot most inconvenient, so he burnt it in the fireplace to wake up in the morning as an impoverished man in the depths of an existential crisis, not finding any purpose in life anymore.

> This question: 'Why do I live?' is the most murderous of all the motives chasing someone to death. A person in love can sober up. A sick person may regain hope. Those losing their

> fortune may presume working again. Those starving may find some work for daily living. A discredited person may detach himself from the rest of the world. The wounds of people losing their mate or child are healed by time. One can recover and get out of all sorts of trouble. But what if this devilish question emerges: Why do I live? For what purpose?—one cannot run away from this. One cannot hide in his work. One cannot detach himself. There is no cure for this, not even at a king's pharmacy (Gárdonyi, 1916/1968, p. 369).

His suicidal fantasy is connected to the previous trauma: "Am I a coward not to dare to greet death?" (…) You will see your father today, my blue-eyed little son" (Gárdonyi, 1916/1968 p. 375). The additional loss and the perceived inaccessibility of a new life result in a deep existential crisis. The next epiphany resolving the crisis takes place on All Saints Day, a national holiday, which is followed by the Day of the Dead. Szunyoghy, preparing to kill himself, is stopped near a cemetery by a passer-by asking for a match. Szunyoghy is asking the man about the happy singing he can overhear. He is informed that the gravedigger and his family are singing. Szunyoghy is surprised as gravediggers are the most miserable people in every village.

> Who loves his life best? (…) Everyone who loves someone – or more people. Also, those who do not love anyone, but love their work (…) a house, a garden, a bird, a dog, a cat, a rifle – for them, life is valuable. (…) the little girl in her worn-out shoes who is running so fast with a hatbox, loves the image of her future: her dream about owning a shop, having a husband and children, and lots of money (…) It is not work that makes people happy. The love of their work makes them happy. Love makes people happy (Gárdonyi, 1916/1968, pp. 379–380).

With this realization about the life-sustaining power of one's visions and hopes ("fantasy"), Szunyoghy decided to have the portrait that he had inherited from his wife repainted to resemble his late wife more. His legacy turned out to be a Rembrandt. Regaining the capital that he needed for farming, he married a young girl, a superficial woman who is attracted by appearances more than by the real values in life. She finally cheated upon him: "if marriages are tied in heaven, then she was not my wife" (Gárdonyi, 1916/1968, p. 467). After setting his garden villa on fire, Szunyoghy had disappeared, and the subsequent police investigation declared him dead. Following this identicide, he is on his way again, now to America, gently caring about a little girl and her widowed mother who he met on board of the ship, and teaching the "desperate" young man, the suspicious detective in disguise, about his life:

– …but we are looking for new connections with life.
– What if we do not find them?
– We find them, we always find them (Gárdonyi, 1916/1968, p. 469).

Table 8.1 is a summary of the hero's traumas, the responses from his social environment, and his motives, ideas, and actions to cope with the threats and pains of the envisioned, or real losses. Repeated spatial movements in his journey of life often lead to epiphanies, granting Szunyoghy the necessary and new relational-spiritual resources for post-traumatic growth.

Table 8.1 Traumas and escapes in Szunyoghy's Paternoster (own source)

Event (Trauma)	Dominant response from the social environment	Motive	Method (Coping)	Outcome
Father's regular physical abuse and brutality "I wish I died"	Father accuses Szunyoghy of wanting a revenge on him by wanting to die	Escape from father's rage	Action is not taken	No change
Causes a damage. Father's expected rage (fantasy of own predictable death based on a previous event—father had brutally killed their own dog)	Mother predicts father's rage	Escape from father's rage	First runaway, spending a night in the meadow	No punishment; receives care
Falsely accused of a theft and expelled from secondary school	People turn their back on him, shame and beat him	Restore one's honour	Second runaway, making concrete plans to kill himself; or choosing a non-professional career	Epiphanies. 1. Openness for a potential turn in his career. 2. The thief is arrested, and his good fame is restored. 3. New position: a private tutor in his future wife's family
As a young adult, falling deeply in love with a countess, Hedvig. The lovers would rather die than let anyone separate them	His love is accepted but must be hidden from the rest of the world	United in love forever	Concrete plans of extended suicide	–
Hedvig is forced to marry another man—they agree to meet at a cross and kill themselves	Kept as secret	United in love forever	Planning the method and the exact date	Epiphanies: 1. Seeing a sign that refers to Hedvig and hope (SP). 2. Meets a former friend and borrows his position and identity as a village teacher

(continued)

Table 8.1 (continued)

Event (Trauma)	Dominant response from the social environment	Motive	Method (Coping)	Outcome
Hedvig's death	Not mentioned	Not mentioned	Not mentioned	The trauma continues
His little son's death	Strong support by the village people to prevent his suicide	To cease consciousness	Runaway without a purpose; giving up his identity	Epiphany: meeting a friend from his "life before" who does not know about his loss
Loss of fortune	Not mentioned	Finds no meaning in life	Hang himself	Epiphany: 1. Meeting a stranger on the spot. 2. His legacy from his wife is a Rembrandt
His second wife's disloyalty	None—kept as secret	To stop being used in a relationship	Runaway to the New World (the Americas); a pretended deadly accident to hide his true social identity	Meeting a widow who resembles his first wife. Expressing generativity and care for the widow and her child

The repeated runaways, the escapes from the threats, and painful memories as spatial, physical movements are complemented with changing positions in the relational sphere. Throughout the story, physical movements facilitate significant encounters and life-transforming epiphanies. In the moments of quantum change, the continuity of identity is disrupted, and the person is dragged by the whirlpool of the crisis experience. In these moments, the previous meanings and values concerning ourselves and our relations are shattered. The discontinuity of identity is acknowledged in the archaic rites of passage, and is often accompanied by external markers as, for example, changing one's name. These permanent or temporary markers represent the external responses of the witnessing community to the deep identity disruptions. Importantly, rites unite the mental and the physical domains, creating space both for one's activities and reflections. Rites tackle the totality of the experience, and by doing so, they repair the breakdown of symbolic functioning. It takes time to connect the new meanings and values to the previous ones and rebuild continuity with the painful storms of the past. For Szunyoghy, continuity is finally established through generativity and love. The hero's experiences eventually make him not only stronger but also a more caring person as he is progressing in life.

Though Gárdonyi wrote this novel more than 100 years ago in an Eastern European country, its theme is independent of the cultural context. A recent film, The Dreamseller (2016) by Monjardim and Bueno, shown a century after the publication of Gárdonyi's novel, begins with a scene in which a homeless person, wandering in the city and living the life of marginalized people, saves a psychiatrist from dying by suicide. His strikingly honest and wise comments and questions help the people around him find meaning in life. This film, focussing on the societal and cultural changes that have made many human lives miserable in the twenty-first century, is guiding us from an utterly competitive lifeworld towards genuine care, and depicts how deep trauma, guilt, and sufferings can lead a person, an *outcast* of the dominant society, to live a fulfilling life in the service of others. The hero, previously a successful businessman, teaches the people around him how to live an authentic life, and by focussing on human values, realize their potentials of eudaimonic happiness.

References

Beitman, B. (2022). *Meaningful coincidences: How and why synchronicity and serendipity happen*. Simon and Schuster.

Caplan, G. (1964). *Principles of preventive psychiatry*. Basic Books.

C'de Baca, J., & Wilbourne, P. (2004). Quantum change: Ten years later. *Journal of Clinical Psychology, 60*(5), 531–541. https://doi.org/10.1002/jclp.20006

Füzi, I., & Török, E. (2006). *Bevezetés az epikai szövegek és a narratív film elemzésébe. [Introduction into the analysis of epic texts and narrative films]*. Bölcsész Konzorcium.

Garadnai, Z. (2013.08.05.) *Hogyan lett Ziegler Gézából Gárdonyi Géza? Magyar Nemzeti Levéltár. [How did Géza Ziegler transform into Géza Gárdonyi?]* https://mnl.gov.hu/mnl/ol/hirek/hogy_lett_ziegler_gezabol_gardonyi_geza

Gárdonyi, G. (1968). Szunyoghy Miatyánkja [Szunyoghy's paternoster] In Gárdonyi, G., *Ábel és Eszter. Kisregények 1905-1913*. (pp. 247–471) Szépirodalmi Kiadó.

Gulyás, P. (1956). *Magyar írói álnév lexikon: A magyarországi írók álnevei és egyéb jegyei. [Encyclopaedia of Hungarian writers' pseudonyms: pseudonyms and other characteristics]*. Akadémiai Kiadó.

Hiles, D., & Čermák, I. (2013). Narrative psychology. In C. Willig & W. Stainton-Rogers (Eds.), *The sage handbook of qualitative research psychology* (pp. 146–162). SAGE Publications.

James, W. (1902/1982). *The varieties of religious experience*. Penguin Books.

Marinatos, N., & Kyrtatas, D. (2004). Conclusions epiphany: Concept ambiguous, experience elusive. *Illinois Classical Studies, 29*(1), 227–234.

McAdams, D. P. (2006). The redemptive self: generativity and the stories Americans live by. *Research in Human Development, 3*(2-3), 81–100. https://doi.org/10.1080/15427609.2006.9683363

McAdams, D. P., Reynolds, J., Lewis, M., Patten, A. H., & Bowman, P. J. (2001). When bad things turn good and good things turn bad: Sequences of redemption and contamination in life narrative and their relation to psychosocial adaptation in midlife adults and in students. *Personality and Social Psychology Bulletin, 27*(4), 474–485. https://doi.org/10.1177/0146167201274008

McDonald, M. G. (2008). The nature of epiphanic experience. *Journal of Humanistic Psychology, 48*(1), 89–115. https://doi.org/10.1177/0022167807311878

Miller, W. R. (2004). The phenomenon of quantum change. *Journal of Clinical Psychology, 60*(5), 453–460. https://doi.org/10.1002/jclp.20000

Monjardim, J, & Bueno, L. (2016). *The Dreamseller*. (Film). Filmland International.

Neimeyer, R. A., Klass, D., & Dennis, M. R. (2014). Mourning, meaning, and memory: Individual, communal, and cultural narration of grief. In A. Batthyany & P. Russo-Netzer (Eds.), *Meaning in positive and existential psychology* (pp. 325–346). Springer Science+Business Media. https://doi.org/10.1007/978-1-4939-0308-5_19

Nyíri, K. (2020). Suppression, depression, pictorial pressure: The road from Freud to Arnheim. In P. Aczél, A. Benedek, & K. Nyíri (Eds), *How images behave.* (pp. 13–23.) Hungarian Academy of Sciences – Budapest University of Technology and Economics.

Proctor, C., & Tweed, R. (2016). Measuring eudaimonic well-being. In J. Vittersø (Ed.), *Handbook of eudaimonic well-being* (pp. 277–294). Springer International Publishing/Springer Nature. https://doi.org/10.1007/978-3-319-42445-3_18

Propp, V. (1999). *A mese morfológiája. [The morphology of tales]* Osiris-Századvég.

Schmidtke, A., & Häfner, H. (1988). The Werther effect after television films: new evidence for an old hypothesis. *Psychological Medicine, 18*(3), 665–676. https://doi.org/10.1017/s0033291700008345

Shapiro, F. (1989). Eye movement desensitization: A new treatment for post-traumatic stress disorder. *Journal of Behavior Therapy and Experimental Psychiatry, 20*(3), 211–217. https://doi.org/10.1016/0005-7916(89)90025-6

Siddiqi, B. (2019). Existentialism, epiphany, and polyphony in Dostoevsky's Post-Siberian Novels. *Religions 10*(1), 59. https://doi.org/10.3390/rel10010059

Szakolczai, Á. (2017). Permanent (trickster) liminality: The reasons of the heart and of the mind. *Theory & Psychology, 27*(2), 231–248. https://doi.org/10.1177/0959354317694095

Szakolczai, A. (2024). An epistemology of revelation. *Religions, 15*(9), 1126. https://doi.org/10.3390/rel15091126

Tedeschi, R. G., & Calhoun, L. (2004). Posttraumatic growth: A new perspective on psychotraumatology. *Psychiatric Times, 21*(4), 58–60.

Titchener, E. B. (1909). *Lectures on the experimental psychology of the thought-process.* Macmillan.

van der Kolk, B. (2015). *The body keeps the score: Brain, mind, and body in the healing of trauma.* Penguin Books.

Z. Szalai, S., & Tóth, Gy. (1968). Gárdonyi Géza kisregényei. Utószó. [Géza Gárdonyi's short novels – an epilogue] In G. Gárdonyi (Ed.), *Ábel és Eszter. Kisregények 1905–1913.* (pp. 473–486). Szépirodalmi Kiadó.

Chapter 9
Dialogue and Transformative Liminality

9.1 Dialogue as Good Communication

The threatening and destructive atmosphere of permanent liminality is only one facet of liminality. As Buechner et al. note (2021, p. 242):

> …liminal space (…) need not be only a place of loneliness and discomfort, of rootlessness, a zombie-like half-life of not belonging anywhere, but it also can be a place of possibility and readiness, a place to step out from, a place of "yes/and," reflecting an integration of multiple realities and potential unity. One way to describe this phenomenon is captured in the term "no-where" to "now-here."

Transformative liminality is a potential context for healing, reaching a positive synthesis, in which the acute ambiguities and uncertainties are resolved and gain new meaning. The process, rescuing us from the futile rumination over the past events and from the constant worries about envisioned future risks, facilitates our liberation from fruitless sufferings and opens a road towards personal integrity. Liminality is enacted through transformative dialogue (Gergen et al., 2001), a specific genre with its rich potentials to reconnect us to the social world of here and now.

The original Greek word, dia+logos (through+word/meaning) yields various interpretations. When used in the sense of sharing or transferring meaning, it is translated simply as "conversation". In the Socratic, argumentative form, dialogue is understood as a way of finding the truth and morality through logic by testing one's own and other people's assumptions (Zappen, 2004). In this conception, dialogue is built in an asymmetric context, between a person who knows more about the truth while pretending to be ignorant, and their conversing partner, who thinks of themself as the knowledgeable party while being ignorant. For example, Plato's Euthydemus (2008) is a piece about the logical consequences of mistaking the signifier for the signified, the linguistic label for the entity it refers to. To summarize Bakhtin's interpretation on Socrates, Zappen (2004) has noted that dialogue does not only serve the purposes of persuasion but it is also a way to express our shared

M. B. Erdos, *Transitions - Liminality as Lived Experience*,
https://doi.org/10.1007/978-3-031-96007-9_9

responsibility for our ideas, words, and actions. In this perspective, dialogue is both about knowledge and critical reflections, and about the morals associated with knowledge. This tradition has generated many different forms that may qualify as dialogue in business or politics, for example, the bargaining orientation, the negotiating orientation, or the mediation orientation (Gergen et al., 2001). These interactions are mainly targeted at finding a common denominator—an important goal—but, unless the speakers are immersed in the liminal moments of a *transformative dialogue*, their core meanings of high emotional–relational significance will neither be enriched nor reconstructed in the process.

Logos has a further layer of meaning: it refers to the order of the universe as the word (principle) of God.[1] Thus, dialogue is related to spirituality, divine wisdom, and creative powers. In the Christian tradition, logos is often identified with Jesus who symbolizes *redemption*. The spiritual aspects of dialogue recurrently appear in the classical and contemporary interpretations. In this sense, dialogue is about positive transformation and creation, and as such, is part of the sacred, and its community manifestation, the ritual. Dialogue involves the momentary dissolution of previous boundaries. It is strongly connected to humans' creative potentials through the construction of shared social realities (Penman, 1992). Dialogue is a communication context, in which people's caring, collaborative, and constructive capabilities are strongly intertwined and freely manifested. Penman (2012) has emphasized that the openness of the dialogue is fundamentally different from the egocentrism of the debate, which is targeted mainly at defending one's own beliefs and persuading the other party. Dialogue acknowledges the diversity of values and perspectives that people bring into the conversation and rebuilds the social contexts for empathetic communication. Thus, dialogue is good communication—a relationally responsive language use focussing on people's lived experiences and the unique meanings they attach to these (Gergen et al., 2001; Penman 2012).

9.2 Addressing Life's Ultimate Questions

In a version of the medieval Grail romance, a piece of the Arthurian legends, Percival, a noble but naive knight, proud of his good manners and recently acquired knowledge of refined court etiquette, misses to ask a redemptive question that could liberate Anfortas, the Fisher King from his longstanding sufferings caused by an incurable wound. Anfortas is the guard of the Holy Grail, Jesus's chalice from the Last Supper filled with his blood that was collected by Joseph of Arimathea after the crucifixion. It is a vessel for the forgiveness of sins. Through its mystic healing power, the Grail is keeping Anfortas alive but cannot cure him, a sinner not yet forgiven. The gift of eternal life turns into a pernicious curse. His, and his people's sufferings will continue until the knight chosen by the Grail brings him salvation.

[1] "By the word of the Lord the heavens were made" as in Psalm 33:6.

This will also end his service as a protector of the Saint Grail. *Anfortas is stuck between life and death*: he cannot transition either to a healthy state in his world, or to the other world until the knight the Grail chooses arrives and proves that he sincerely feels for the sufferer by asking the long-awaited question of compassion.

Percival is the chosen one. However, he is not ready to meet the knightly challenge of care, mercy, and empathy yet. Brought up in seclusion in the forest and dressed up as a *fool* by his mother to protect him from the threats of knightly life that had killed his father, he was not yet prepared to perform his life's most important spiritual mission. However, as the hero who was born to possess the gifts of ultimate grace, he cannot escape his fate. An epiphany, an encounter with the knights from Arthur's court connects him to the contemporary structures of the court and formally establishes his position in the medieval social order. His education begins, and as part of his lessons, he is taught not to ask potentially irrelevant, inconsiderate, and annoying questions. He follows the rule mechanically without understanding its true meaning: caring for others. At this point, he is but an *imitator* of a genuine knight. He is not dressed up as a fool anymore, but in a sense, internally, he is still one. His shadow, the fool inside could teach him the lessons of humility and true concern for others, only if he were listening to it.

His automatic and merciless politeness almost proved fatal. In this specific context, it was interpreted as a sign of cruel indifference and a total absence of empathy. He was chased away from the castle that disappeared in the mist, not to be found again until the chosen one has learned his deeper lessons. Percival's desperate efforts to find the Grail for the second time proved abortive. Finding the Grail is beyond human control. Anfortas' castle is covered in the mist and is disclosed only at a kairotic moment. After many years of living the life of a knight errant, serving those in need and thus proving his penitence and ability to care, Percival is given another chance. Having learnt through sacrifice how to be a true knight, he can finally ask the redemptive question that brings salvation not only to the Fisher King but to Percival himself. Both escape the limbo of extended liminality and reach their new statuses: Anfortas can gain absolution, and Percival can prove that he is worthy of his holy mission, the Grail's service.

This story is illuminative of the inherent potentials of a transformative dialogue with a suffering person. The will and the aptitude to support the person and consider their needs is not enough. Formal education, and pre-reflective, limited life experiences are not enough either. What is needed is learning through a series of transformative liminal experiences to prepare one for a special type of connectedness that is beyond the ordinary pragmatics of social behaviour. Though the journey involves trials and sufferings, the status is not achieved through one's efforts or performance only but is granted in the intersubjectivity of the encounter. "The Thou meets me through grace - it is not found by seeking" (Buber, 1958, p. 17).

This deep, authentic, and primary relationship, the encounter between the I and Thou involving the person's whole being is at the centre of Buber's philosophy of dialogue as the ultimate source of meaning in life, represented in the famous quote: "All real living is meeting" (Buber, 1958, p. 17). Communication is a continuous process—it lasts so long as we live. Maintaining self-centredness, a permanent focus on one's own self, is a detachment from the fundamental human condition: hearing the other and the sharing of lives (Risser, 2019). The I must remain open for the communion, and such openness involves surrender to the powers of intersubjectivity (Buber, 1958). Buber argues that the relationship determined by the primary word I-Thou is a transformative, liminal, and transient phenomenon, happening on the boundaries, in the in-betweenness of intersubjectivity. He illustrates this intersubjectivity by breathing, our vital connection with the environment, momentarily and repeatedly dissolving the boundaries between the self and the environment. The I-Thou relationship is one of the primary patterns or primary *words* (logos) that humans are involved in.

The other type, I-It relationship is brought about by our constructive abilities and symbol use: here, care and communion are exchanged for instrumentality, objective reflectivity, and agency. I-It patterns are the types of relationship we are involved in for most of the time. These patterns are embedded in, and are predominated by social positions, structures, object symbols, and technological advances. The primacy of I-It, when extended too far in the domain of close human relationships, is accompanied by fruitless instrumentality. As Cooper (2003) has noted: "in the I-It attitude, I distance myself from the other and survey, study, measure and observe him or her. The other becomes something apart from me, something to which I direct my attention and from which I extract knowledge" (Cooper, 2003, p. 135). Thus, I-It establishes the processes that we consider *progress* in late modernity, while I-Thou is about the authenticity of relationships, (inter)personal meaning, and a touch of transcendence. In a third variant, monologue disguised as dialogue, the participants do not enter the emerging intersubjectivity but follow the mere formalities of the genre instead (Cooper, 2003). Here, genuine openness, mutual acceptance, emotional involvement, and relational reflectivity are exchanged for an attractive lip service only, as the focus is solely on one's own self. The other's role in the relationship is reduced to meeting one's needs (Gergen et al., 2001).

In his first attempt, young Percival does not allow himself to be immersed in sympathy, not to mention empathy, but is guided by his worldly ambition to become a "perfect" knight and gain appreciation and fame for his knight-appropriate behaviour. This deep but self-centred, monolithic, and externally driven desire, and the accompanying, non-reflected automatisms in his behaviour characteristic of novices wanting to be worthy of full recognition in their field of study cause him to fail. Percival, with his automated perfectionism, is acting in the I-It domain of clear boundaries, rules, and structures, excluding any other interpretations or the deeper meaning of the encounter. In this domain, objectifying and segregating relationships prevail. Contrastingly, in the dialogue, ideas are deeply anchored in the conversing parties' lived experiences of transformative liminality. Thus, the participants in a dialogue are struggling to leave behind the abstract, distancing, intellectualizing, and judgemental positions (McNamee & Moscheta, 2015). This takes genuine courage, as people are used to assessing each other according to their social roles and obligations shaped by the roles and requirements of the social structure, but do not relate to each other with the entirety of their selves: "The primary word "I-It" can never be spoken with the whole being" (Buber, 1958, p. 54.) The Fisher King as a sinner needs mercy, but forgiveness will not come from the rules. It can originate only from care and empathy that warriors must also learn, or else limitless destructions will follow.

Both the I-Thou and I-It relationships are inherent in human nature. I-Thou relationships cannot be sustained for long, as such liminal intensities and the dissolution of boundaries are characterized by the concentration of energies and high affectivity, in the sense of both high-level, impulsive, and chaotic emotionality, and intense receptivity (as being affected) (Greco & Stenner, 2017; Stenner, 2017; Turner, 1969). I-It requires paradigmatic thinking, rationality, and logic, while the transcendence of I-Thou is expressed through multi-layered narrative fractures, images, and embodied metaphors to approximate and capture the holistic transformative experience. Buber warns us that the proliferation of instrumentalities, flourishing in I-It relationships and characteristic of certain historical era, undermines the ultimate values of human existence. In the uninterrupted realms of I-It, the privacy and alienation of the I and the institutionalized It will dominate (Buber, 1958). However, neither type of primary relationships—the I-Thou of intersubjectivity and the I-It of objectification—can ever completely disappear. One may predominate over the other, but the supressed pole is always there in the shadow, ready to emerge. This alternation is the intersubjective manifestation of the macro-level shifts between communitas and structure described by Turner (1969).

9.3 A Dialogue on Dialogue

In 1968, Martin Buber and Carl Rogers, the two prominent authors who have significantly contributed to our contemporary notions on dialogue, were invited to share their ideas and comment on each other's conceptions. Their notions bear much resemblance. Both scholars have emphasized the totality of experiences, involving one's cognitions, emotions, and intuitions, freely manifested in the dialogue with its strong potentials to confirm the entirety of the other person's unique being. Rogers emphasized the role of empathy and unconditional positive regard, the unconditional acceptance of Thou when entering the intersubjectivity and the now-here of the I-Thou relationship. Gergen et al.'s (2001) suggestion, affirming the other by accepting that their experiences and feelings are different from ours, is how we can put this absolute principle into practice. Rogers also identified a third prerequisite for transformative dialogue: *Congruence* establishes harmony between one's constructs on the self and their experiences: "relevant experiences flow freely into awareness and are symbolized accurately (…) incongruence means that important experiences are denied" (Lux, 2010, p. 278). Congruence as authenticity is freedom from any psychological defence that confuses human interactions and constitutes inconsistencies between one' evaluations of their genuine developmental needs and the goals they envision—a freedom from delf-deception.

However, there were some salient differences between the two scholars' ideas, potentially, a consequence of the major differences in their life experiences. Having witnessed World War I, Buber held a different notion on human nature, seen as essentially good by Rogers and corrupted only by unfortunate life circumstances (Lux, 2010). For Rogers, dialogue in psychotherapy is an important key to self-actualizing, while Buber claimed that dialogue was not possible without spontaneity and mutuality between the partners, and this could not happen in psychotherapy. The discussion between Buber and Rogers, moderated by Maurice Friedman ("Dialogue between", 1960), resulted in a long and fruitful correspondence between the two renowned thinkers. Even so, there were several disruptions in the conversation. Friedman was Buber's friend, and this might have created, at least initially, a sense of imbalance in the situation. Rogers was a representative of contemporary psychology that was on its highway to gain strong professional monopolies as the scientific field dedicated to explaining human behaviour, with its underlying complexities of human traits, motives, affects, and cognitions. Buber's overall influence was strong in several disciplinary areas, including psychology. The conversation starts with Rogers' somewhat lengthy introduction, meant as an apology, of his first question:

> (…) the first question I would like to ask you, Dr. Buber, may sound a trifle impertinent, but I would like to explain it and then perhaps it won't seem impertinent. I have wondered, How have you lived so deeply in inter-personal relationships and gained such an understanding of the human individual, without being a psychotherapist? (…) ("Dialogue between" 1960, p. 208).

In his response, Buber explained that as a young man he had indeed studied psychiatry for three semesters but had not seen the contemporary therapeutic relationship as a genuine dialogue. Mutuality of the experience, an important aspect of dialogue (Cissna & Anderson, 1994) was entirely missing from such relationships. The use of labels (diagnoses), the strict hierarchy between a knower, the therapist, and a not-knower, the patient, as well as therapists' contemporary role conception—catalysts that largely remain unchanged in the process—excluded such moments:

> (…) change if possible something in the other, but also to let me be changed by him. At any event, I had no resistance … put no resistance to it (…). I cannot be so to say above him and say "No! I'm out of the play. You are mad" ("Dialogue between", 1960, p. 209).

Buber continued by relating the traumatizing events of World War I and the loss of his close friend who had been brutally murdered right after the war. His description reveals a deeply traumatizing, somatic-level experience:

> I was compelled to imagine just this killing, but not in an optical way alone, but may I say so, just with my body. And this was the decisive moment, after which, after some days and nights in this state, I felt "Oh, something has been done to me" ("Dialogue between", 1960, p. 210).

Buber proceeded with his experiences during World War I: "cannot say it in another language, it was really a living with those people. People wounded, killed in the war". Rogers responded to him by using his therapeutic technique, nondirective mirroring, which, in this context, seemed bit of a misfit, and was immediately followed by an invitation for spatial rearrangements—potentially, to resolve the transient uneasiness appearing not only in the spatial, but also in the relational domain:

> Carl Rogers: You felt their wounds.
>
> Martin Buber: Yes. But feeling is not sufficiently strong—the word feeling.
>
> Carl Rogers: I'm going to make one suggestion, even though it interrupts us a little. I can't face the mike and face you at the same time. Would you mind if I turned the table just a little? (Moves table) (…)
>
> Maurice Friedman: While he's changing, I want to admit that Professor Rogers' question reminded me of a theological student from a Baptist seminary who talked to me about Professor Buber's thought, and when he left he said, "I must ask you a question. Professor Buber is so good. How is it he's not a Christian?" (Laughter) ("Dialogue between", p. 210).

Friedman, sensing the slight disturbance in the conversation, was responding with a second story (Arminen, 1998), a humorous reflection relieving some of the tension but not fully resolving the confusion. The statement put Rogers into the position of a student—a useful one when someone is involved in a dialogue for knowledge construction. This was a lively and spontaneous conversation, but was it a dialogue? Several assumptions behind Buber's and Rogers's approaches to dialogue were rather different. Rogers concentrated, most importantly, on the phenomenology and function of dialogue: help people develop their uniqueness through unconditional acceptance provided by the therapist. For Buber, dialogue, as an ontological basis for human existence, is a fundamental and primary relationship, and cannot be a "means" of anything. If it is, then it is but a monologue disguised as dialogue, targeted only at the cognitive domain: "two or more men, meeting in space, speak each with himself in strangely torturous and circuitous ways and yet imagine they have escaped the torment of being thrown back on their own resources" (Buber, 1958., p. 37).

The I-Thou dialogue is about liminal experiences and is a transient liminal experience itself. Thus, it leads to transformations, enriching the participants' current understandings and interpretative frames, opening and grounding future possibilities in an altered semiotic chain (Relio & Salvatore, 2024). The next sections in this chapter focus on this specific feature, the deep transformative power anchored in the transitory intersubjectivity of the totality of the I-Thou relationship.

9.4 Born in Care—Born in Dialogue

Buber has claimed that in the beginning there is the relation. This idea is echoed in Gilligan's theory of the ethics of care (Gilligan, 1993; Okano, 2016). Here, I do not interpret care as a counterpoint to justice by contrasting women's voice to men's: Parsifal is a man who must learn sensitivity and care to become a whole person and a true knight. Rather, I would like to emphasize that the predominant ideology of globalization unilaterally focuses on limitless competition, and in this social Darwinist framework, the concept of care is expelled into the shadow.

Several studies have confirmed that learning a dialogical and caring pattern, a turn-taking responsive to the interactional partners' developmental needs and mental states begins with birth, if not earlier. For example, in-phase and anti-phase synchronies between the mother and the infant prepare the human baby for such turn-takings in communication, which are sensitive to the context and the interactional partner's needs (Ohmura et al., 2023). An early theory by Baldwin (1896) focused on the role and processes of adaptive imitation and social cooperation. How do we learn socially appropriate and meaningful, conventional units of communication, such as gestures or the components of languaging used in one's own culture? Baldwin's circular reaction, both an evolutionary mechanism and an individual-level learning process, is a series of refining imitations (Cahan, 2003). The proto forms of our sophisticated symbolic achievements are initiated by the learner, the infant, who actively and spontaneously produces some vocalizations or gestures that are similar to, but not yet identical with a culturally meaningful variant. For example, they are moving their hand in a way that resembles waving; or they are saying baa-baa, interpreted by the proud Turkish parents as the baby's meaningful word and motivated use of their vocalization for "daddy" and by the proud Hungarian parents for "baby". Through a series of transformative imitations, governed by the environmental responses received from significant others, babies gradually learn to approximate the culturally appropriate variant and learn to connect the signifier to the signified. The attentive, and in the fortunate cases, also enthusiastic and caring environment will tirelessly support this matching process and repeat the raw product in a more refined form. The baby, sharing humans' exceptionally strong imitation tendencies will quickly learn the symbol through the constant, strong reinforcements: adults' encouraging attention and smiles. Such learning takes place in a dialogue involving the participants' whole selves—the caretaker's thoughtful, relationally focused, and *underplayed* self and the baby's emerging self in the intersubjective domain (Budwig, 2000). Our mirror neuron system, active both on perceiving and performing a specific activity, facilitates this process as early as in the first year of life (Acharya & Shukla, 2012).

Mentalization theory (Fonagy et al., 2002) has some further implications for the early development of our dialogical capacity (Erdos, 2006). Fonagy et al. (2002) focused on the development of the self and identified different communication patterns in the infant-caretaker dyad, resulting in learning healthy versus unhealthy modes of the management of emotions and relating to others. If the caretaker can sensitively identify the baby's actual affective state (e.g. happy, relaxed, angry, frightened) while mirroring the state by using the same category *and* marking the state, indicating that this is not their own emotion but that of the infant, then the child will gradually learn to appropriately identify and manage their own emotions. Importantly, affects motivate semiosis, and affects are signs to be interpreted (Salvatore et al., 2021).

However, mistakes might, and do occur in the process. If correction is fast enough then this is not a major problem—rather, it may teach the baby that the quality of the relational contents in communication must be closely and constantly monitored, and corrections are necessary and possible. Tronick and Cohn (1989) have concluded that in the mother–infant interaction, often seen as the prototype of an ideal and harmonious relationship, continual corrections are needed—and these adjustments occur so rapidly that they are hardly discernible without a thoughtful, moment-by-moment analysis of the videotaped interactions. There are the cases though, when the caretaker is not able to respond adequately to the baby's emotional needs and such corrections are mostly missing. They may use an incongruent, false category, for example, mirror a "happy", positive state instead of the "anxious", negative one. Should this be a permanent pattern in the interaction, the baby will neither be able to identify and differentiate between their own emotions, nor appropriately recognize other people's emotions. Inadequate parental mirroring might be the result of some direct traumatization, or of the more indirect transgenerational transmission of the trauma's possible consequences: the suppression of negative emotions or being flooded by these emotions. Learning and naming a variety of emotional states while also anchoring these in the body are the first steps in most therapies offered for recovering people who had developed serious problems in emotional regulation (Csaszar et al., 2024).

A different problem may occur if parental mirroring is categorically congruent but is not appropriately marked. Here, marking refers to slight differences to designate *reflective* communication in mimics, gestures, and vocalizations. If the caretaker's signals are the same as the infant's own signals, then the caretaker is not empathetic but sympathetic, for example, by responding to the child's anxiety with clear signals of their *own* anxiety (Fonagy et al., 2002). This is a symmetrical (schismogenetic) communication pattern, though the baby would need a complementary response to soothe their anxiety. The caretaker's calming response to the baby would be a non-symmetrical dialogical pattern, responsive to the infant's *needs* where the tensions experienced could be soon followed by a relief. In the cases where sympathy prevails over empathy, plain affective symmetry is dominating over empathetic complementarity, and the caretaker's agentive self responds instead of the reflective self, the baby will learn that their negative emotional states are limitless, dangerous, and per se unmanageable. They are simply flooded by these emotions and, consequently, experience loss of control over their feelings (Fonagy et al., 2002).

The resulting experiences about these early and non-restored mismatches are very similar to the experiences of being entrapped in a liminal hotspot (Stenner, 2017). Sharing the same emotions within a community is inherent in a rite of transition—but extending the liminal phase and being stuck in that phase is utterly destructive. The very base of empathy is momentary sympathy, a non-reflected affect, but what we can see in adequate mirroring is the outcome of the caretaker's interpretative and reflective processing: empathy. Categorically congruent, marked mirroring is not only present in the nonverbal communication of emotions: it is the basic relational-dialogical pattern extending into the realm of symbols (Erdos, 2006).

9.5 The Dialogical Self

The idea that our self contains multiple I-positions, established by our experiences of primary relationships, is not an entirely new one. Van der Kolk (2015) quotes Rumi, the thirteenth-century poet and philosopher, who, in his poem, *The guest house,* drew a parallel between our life and a guest house populated with various persons, occasionally arriving, leaving, and then perhaps returning. Van der Kolk (2015) continues by referring to William James who asserted that we have as many selves as many relationships. Berne (1968) in his early transactional approach, the adult-parent-child model defined three major self-positions that roughly corresponded to the earlier Freudian notions, the tripartite structure of our personality: the id (child) governed by the hedonistic pleasure principle, the ego responsible for adapting to realities (adult), and the superego with its strict, inflexible rules and unattainable morals (parent). Their functions, such as resilient adaptation facilitated by the adult, hard-and-fast rules in times of a major threat non-reflectively applied by the parent, and the strong affectivity and energies of the child are clearly distinguished. In Berne's model, the predominance of the respective functions is characteristic of both the triggering situation and the experiencing person's role interpretation, the results of their socialization. Mead's (1934) seminal theory differentiates between the I in an agentive role, and Me, the reflected self (or selves) in one's web of relationships as interpreted by the individual.

The introduction of these theoretical self-components predicted further elaborations on the nature of the human self. We identify and counter-identify with the many different traits of significant others, internalizing their characteristic and relatively stable responses to specific situations. These identification processes continually occur, and repeated revisions of their results take place in liminal moments. Hermans (2001) has described our personal guest house, the dialogical self, by connecting Bakhtin's (1984a, 1984b) notions on polyphony and dialogue with James' theory on the "I", the self as knower representing continuity, distinctness, and volition, able to process our experiences and a source of personal identity. This "I" is contrasted with the self as known, extending, and connecting to external entities ("me/mine"). The dialogical self is defined as the "dynamic multiplicity of relatively autonomous I-positions in an imaginal landscape" (Hermans et al., 1992, p. 28; Cooper, 2003). In possession of our symbolic and narrative potentials, we can alternate between these positions in parallel with the changes in life events, situations, and relationships.

Cooper (2003) has connected Buber's distinction of the two primary words, I-It and I-Thou, to Hermans' notion on the dialogical self. In this conception, the internal encounter between the I-positions is characterized by the unconditional confirmation of these unique I-positions (I-I form). This experience is not about (con) fusion but about revelations and acceptance: for example, it happens when people suffering from a previous trauma acknowledge their wounded I-positions. The boundaries between the different I-positions do not merge entirely in healthy relationships: "each of the I-positions maintains a certain individuality, and do not fuse with, overlap into, or contaminate others" (Cooper, 2003, p. 133). The other form, I-Me is specified by some degree of rational detachment and objectification—a potential source for diminished wellbeing, if permanently maintained. Temporary detachment and objectification are necessary and useful: in a study by Pennebaker and Smyth (2016), changing the narrative perspectives between the I and Me (e.g. referring to I by a general pronoun) were a successful strategy to cope with traumatic experiences. Interestingly, mothers also refer to themselves by using the culture-specific general pronouns in their interactions to nurture their children's emerging selves (Budwig, 2000). This finding supports Michael White's (2024) therapeutic technique of externalizing conversations: objectifying a disturbing I-position first and rejecting or embracing it only after thorough explorations.

How can we address the influence of the cultural resources giving a frame to our autobiographies in this conception? If the interpretations of our individual experiences remain detached from these resources, then liminality will be prolonged. Further, we prioritize certain voices through our personal evaluations, and differentiate between novel, liberating, and constructive voices, and the destructive ones that sustain chaos only, but do not lead to creation and integration. Consequently, a manager should be employed in Rumi's guest house, a master self that is not a mere victim of the hegemonic powers but is able to govern all these voices and establish the singularity of the self through reflectivity in the context of this polyphonic organization (Brown, 2013). The master self or manager self is working for integration, coordination, and the resolution of intrapersonal conflicts. Clearly, there is a difference between the polyphonic-dissociated and the dialogical self. The dialogical self requires the resolution of self-destructive intrapersonal conflicts through continual reflections on the different I-positions. This capacity is shaped early in life, as Vygotsky's studies on the development of inner speech may indicate. Inner speech is initially external (relational) and involves the imitation and internalization of others' voices (Cooper, 2003).

Weinreich (2004) in his identity theory (Identity Structure Analysis, ISA, also in Chap. 1. *Living in a Dual Environment. Homo symbolicus and Languaging*), relying on Kelly's (1955) personal construct theory and repertory grid technique, suggested the general term "entities" to capture the domains of persons, symbols, and objects—anything relevant for the I, together with one's reflected selves (Me-s), and the emotionally significant "mine" positions. These entities, including our own agentive selves in the different temporal domains as current, past, or anticipated future selves, and the exploratory selves shaped by recurring situations (for example, relaxed, tense, or out-of-self I-positions) are continuously evaluated by the reflective self. Meta-perspectives of the selves indicate how important others see the self, according to that person ("I think that others see me as…"). ISA pays special attention to the alternating evaluations of these self-positions, the conflicts and ambivalence between these positions, and the manner people resolve the conflicts. These processes are embedded in a relational network of one's significant others and are sensitive to situational changes. There are some distinguished positions in the model, such as the ideal and contra-ideal selves serving as the benchmarks for one's evaluations (Weinreich, 2004). Weinreich's model resolves several dilemmas raised by the theory of the dialogical self and provides a rich description on the related self-processes (rather than structures). ISA has a linked framework software, Ipseus, where the entities and constructs relevant for the specific investigation are identified by previous qualitative studies that focus on participants' discourses (e.g. Erdos et al., 2024; Javor et al., 2022; McNeill et al., 2019; Saunderson, 2002). Without the manager self, giving one's responses to an ISA/Ipseus instrument, such studies would hardly be possible. Weinreich's model is sensitive to the important aspects of continuity and change in the master self or metaself. In this view, identity as the image of our self is a reflective framework for the construction of the dialogical self.

9.6 Symmetry and Complementarity

In the previous section, I have referred to Fonagy et al.'s (2002) conception, who asserted that symmetric versus complementary patterns pertained to the development of our mentalizing skills, comprising self-awareness, momentary mindfulness, and relational reflectivity. From this perspective, complementary communication patterns seem useful in fostering one's development, while the symmetrical ones do not—at least not at first sight, and not with the negative emotions early in life. Naturally, what is beneficial in adult–infant interactions might not be extrapolated to adult–adult communication; and what works well to soothe negative emotionality might not be useful with positive emotions, in which we sympathetically immerse and simply enjoy the experience.

Buber (1958) highlighted the importance of reciprocity in dialogue, requiring at least transient symmetrical positions. Are these two different views contradictory or reconcilable as the two aspects of the same complexity, a dialogical process? In a focused study by Watzlawick et al. (1968), permanent symmetry was identified as a competitive pattern, a tit-for-tat type of interaction, leading to escalating conflicts between the conversational partners. The couple studied by the researchers were fighting for the right of primacy to tell their common story. They were guided by the desire to win the game, disorienting them from the actual topic with an enhanced, still fruitless focus on the relational aspects of the ongoing communication. Responsiveness to the partner's needs was entirely missing from the permanently symmetrical pattern. However, rigid complementarity was not a solution either, as no new knowledge or insights could result from this stable, safe, and nonchallenging pattern. In such cases, one of the speakers is taking the lead, and the other, either utterly submissive or simply indifferent, adopts an anything-goes stance, approving whatever is being said. The same negative results of the two opposing strategies are explained by the rigidity of feedback mechanisms, schismogenesis, with its enhanced polarization and the resulting ruptures of identities (Bateson, 1972; Horvath & Thomassen, 2008; Szakolczai, 2015; Thomassen 2013). The best results, understood both as meeting the goals of the interaction and partners' satisfaction with their relationship, were achieved through alternating between these two basic patterns, symmetry, and complementarity, adapted flexibly to the actual needs and positions of the conversing partners. This was neither one's triumph over the other, nor surrender to them, but genuine collaboration to reach a common goal, in this case, building a joint narrative (Watzlawick et al., 1968). Development is based both on the safety of complementarity and the challenges inherent in symmetry. Symmetry allows for sympathetic involvement, and combining the two patterns, symmetry and complementarity flexibly transform this into empathy.

Arminen's (1998) study on 12-step fellowship speeches, which, formally, seem to be monologues as the speakers do not take turns like they would in a common conversation, is illuminative of a key point in the dialogue. In his conception, the dialogic relationship is established through reflective mirroring in the storytelling: speakers constantly refer to each other's previous stories, showing that they have deeply internalized these, adding them to the stock of stories for future use in their own storytelling. Arminen, when studying these *second stories*, emphasized that each story determines the positions for the next speaker, but these positions do not define the theme so much as the emotional contents and attitudes. Speakers establish symmetry through the conversational rules, the emerging themes, and the personal appraisals, while they also introduce complementarity by adding new elements to all these. "Your story" can become "my story" only when the persons' lived experiences behind these stories are constructed as somewhat similar, facilitating an encounter with the other as a cognitive–affective–embodied whole (Cooper, 2003)—this is the modus operandi of traditional transition rites. Arminen (1998, p. 227) commented on a case from his own professional context when the thematic mapping of the second story was appropriate, but the speakers' roles, emotions, and experiences differed significantly. The mismatch was interpreted by the first speakers as questioning the core values brought into the conversation and resulted in a counter-encounter: mutual embarrassment, and the termination of contact.

Mirroring through languaging and symbol use is not a rational–logical issue. The second story as a notion echoes Rogers' idea on nondirective mirroring. If treated mechanically, as a mere technique (simply repeating some of what the client has said), it can become a source for misunderstandings and relational failures instead of the targeted, ever-deepening understandings. We also repeat verbatim what we have just heard when it does not make too much sense for us, or we have doubts about the validity of the statement. Thus, repetitions can also be annoying and distancing. They can reflect genuine interest only if they are coupled with the appropriate communication cues indicating the listener's emotional reflections. To decide what, when, and exactly how should be mirrored is part of the art of building a second story. Mirroring is a momentary but deep involvement, when your story indeed becomes my story, and your concern is also my concern (Erdos, 2006).

Recent research results on mirror neurons have confirmed Rogers's idea about the depth, intensity, and *reciprocity* experienced in a therapeutical session. The encounter extends deep into the somatic level (Rasmussen & Bliss, 2014; Kodama et al., 2018). For example, Gernert et al. (2023) have confirmed that the synchrony of certain physiological markers during psychotherapy predicts symptom reduction. A study on heart rate synchrony in counselling by Kodama et al. (2018) uncovered the physical aspects of the shifts in complementarity and symmetry, representing a strong alliance with alternating leader–follower roles between the therapist and the client. Psychotherapists are not catalysts only: reciprocity in communication was present at the deepest, heart level:

> Overall, the therapist tended to lead the client in terms of heart rate synchrony (55.69% and 44.31%, respectively). In Phase 1, the therapist's ratio (48.31%) was slightly lower than the client's ratio (51.69%), while in Phase 3, the therapist's ratio (52.12%) was higher than the client's ratio (47.88%). Although the ratio differences during these phases were subtle, interestingly, in Phase 2 the therapist's ratio (58.66%) was relatively higher than the client's ratio (48.31%). (Kodama et al., 2018).

The turn-takings, also expressed in the changes in heart rates, involve both complementarity with a leader and a follower, and, in the moments of flexibly changing the roles according to the communicating partners' needs and goals, moments of symmetry. Therapists' claim, that they do not only use their knowledge (therapeutic techniques) but also their whole being to induce and facilitate change, seems substantiated.

Seltzer and Seltzer (2004) analysed moments of liminality emerging in psychotherapy. The consolidated, inflexible, and constricted meanings guided a widow towards suicide to follow her late husband into death. Using ethnographic conversation analysis as a method, authors explored the key transformative moments of a therapeutic session where the monologue of the suicidal person is questioned by the therapist's "not-knowing" stance and undisguisedly expressed confusion. This is an open attitude, accepting and encouraging the emerging alternatives to already existing beliefs during the conversation. Dialogical moments are a prerequisite for reflexive inquiry and establish a zone both for self-reflexivity and relational reflexivity (McNamee, 2004). Self-reflexivity involves stepping out of the comfort zone of objectification and engaging in the shifts between the I-I and the I-Me, while relational reflexivity includes alternating between the primary relations of the I-Thou and the I-It.

In the above case, the guest therapist invited to join the intervention appears as an outsider in the continuity of the sessions. She is representative of a social institution as a therapist, and at the same time, possesses the liminal characteristics of a stranger, potentially introducing new perspectives to promote the transformation. Paradoxically, her specific knowledge is the creative use of her not-knowing position, the power to question the taken-for-granted, the dominant story inviting the patient to die by suicide (Seltzer & Seltzer, 2004). She understands how the traditions of ordinary life could be a barrier to the resolution of an extraordinary situation, demanding the redefinition of the situation—like in Percival's story. Everybody would know and deeply understand that widows mourn, and if isolated, are at risk of suicide. This cognition is more latent but is also present in the Western world, and was expressed openly in the relatively recent, but now illegal, practice of sati, widows' ritual sacrifice (assisted, required, or even forced "suicide") in India.

In our culture, psychotherapists as "alienists" (Szasz, 1995) are authorized to constantly monitor the web of meanings that occasionally entrap people. An additional external perspective is useful to challenge and overwrite the monolithic meanings. Therapy requires stepping into a context of transformative liminality to put an end to the widow's entrapment between life and death, and to her self-imposed social isolation. Help involves breaking the taboos, and asking targeted, but not necessarily "polite" questions about the taken-for-granted social realities. When directly questioning about the ownership of the pills that the widow had already used and wanted to take in the future to die by overdose, the guest therapist got a bit confused while searching for the appropriate wording of the question. The pills, strong pain killers, were used by the patient's late husband in the terminal phase of cancer. The patient treated these as her legacy, confusing the boundaries between her late husband and herself. Such enmeshment is typical of one's entrapment in liminality. Her will to keep the pills was informally approved by her environment, though formally (legally) she did not even have the right to do so. To redefine the boundaries, separation from the key meaning, suicide as a means of being united with the deceased husband, and its signifier, the pill, was essential, and this involved entering a chaotic state to break the epic of a golden past (Seltzer & Seltzer, 2004). "The guest therapist opens by presenting herself as a stranger so puzzled by the meanings encountered in this situation that she has to laugh at her own confused attempt to find words to describe them" (Seltzer & Seltzer, 2004, p. 368).

The analysis focused on the process of liberating alternative voices, other than the dominant and destructive one. Prioritizing someone's unquestionable truth, monologism, will prevent the co-construction of a more adaptive framework for the continuation of life. Seltzer and Seltzer (2004) utilized Bakhtin's (1984a, 1984b) seminal idea about the role of two opposing forces that shape meaning-making and meaning consolidation in communication. Centripetal forces consolidate, homogenize, and finalize meanings, as words of supreme tradition. In the epic built mainly on centripetal forces, the past is seen as a reservoir of ultimate positive values and a distance is established from the contemporary realities seen as meaningless or shallow as compared to this golden past. This rigid pattern provides the frameworks for a monologue, and the transformation of meanings is not a possibility. Contrastingly, centrifugal forces ensure openness and the representation of diverse perspectives. Carnivalesque genres and humour open the possibilities for the construction of new meanings and the renewal of the somewhat "exhausted" previous forms (Eliade, 1961), the rigid hierarchy of complementarity. Thus, the multiple-voiced novel represents a contrast to the epic by its polyphonic structure, in which new meanings evolve through dialogue and reflections. What was already there but existed only in its potentialities is now unfolding (Bakhtin 1981; Seltzer & Seltzer, 2004). In the specific case, a premature negative coherence has been formed, while the person should still be in the limbo of the transition. Here, dialogue is a means to help her accept the chaos and grief involved in the transition and tolerate the affective load of the transition without giving up hope.

Psychotherapists must gracefully balance between order and chaos, therapy as a social institution, and the moments of liminality expressed in the therapeutic process. Radical presence, holding "one's own ground *while* being open to the other's orientation" (McNamee, 2015, p. 377, italics belong to the author) is established in liminality and goes counter to the claims by the therapeutic state with its monolithic institutional structures and conservative, rigid identity definitions. Participants enter the liminality of therapy and then return to the stability of institutional order, now in the possession of a new interpretive framework—in the above example, one by which a widow can continue her life, detach herself from the world of the dead, and join the community of those living in the neighbourhood.

Utilizing the chaotic, spontaneous, egalitarian, and even humorous moments of the therapeutic dialogue, not conforming to participants' previous expectations, are at the centre of postmodern approaches (White, 2024; Tarragona, 2008). Acknowledging the multiplicity of the dialogical self is central to diverse therapeutical applications, as this is how innovative moments can be introduced to challenge and reconstruct the stories people live by (Gonçalves et al., 2012; Razzaque, 2019; Viou & Georgaca, 2023).

9.7 Dialogue and Creativity

If rigid complementary patterns between the parties consolidate the hierarchies and the existing meanings, finally leading to a monologue—disguised, or not even disguised as a dialogue—then, in such settings, our transformative and creative potentials are curbed. This was a main concern expressed by the physicist David Bohm (2014), who demonstrated his preference for equity in the cold war context in the United States. Consequently, he had to leave the country. He believed in the transformative power of dialogue, in which people could collaborate freely to develop a new idea. His group technique to initiate dialogue to solve scientific problems evolved around the temporary dissolution of hierarchic relationships by introducing special rules to the conversation. He proposed the suspension of the initial screening of the emerging ideas, and of the judgements concerning other participants' ideas. These judgements are the results of our previous assumptions shaped by the usual hierarchic frameworks in everyday life. In a Bohm-dialogue, anyone could freely join an emerging idea and make their further contributions. These rules ensure that everyone can confidently enter and participate in the conversation, and the emerging ideas undergo a spontaneous evolutionary process in the temporary, transformative liminal context. This safe milieu for transformative dialogue is not identical with today's precarity, associated with permanent liminality in the neoliberal academic context. Acknowledging incompleteness (Penman, 1992, 2012): that there is no, and can never be any final knowledge as science is about "re-search", is an important point here. This liberates the participants from the unnecessary and contraproductive constraints of authority and hierarchy, the "ennobling discourse" (Bakhtin, 1981, p. 427), establishing privileges, but not renewal, for the participants.

The space for the construction of new knowledge through genuine dialogue opens in transformative liminality. It facilitates the emergence of a shared flow experience characterized by the participants' high-level involvement, concentration, and the joy of creation (Csikszentmihályi, 1990, 1996). On such occasions, positive energies are released in a safe and appreciative environment. The altered relational focus on participants' unique competencies and the suspension of judgements, encouraging creativity, have proven useful in organizational and community development projects: Appreciative Inquiry (AI) is a guide to dialogical languaging, highlighting that people's actions are guided by their language use (Cooperrider & Whitney, 2000). Language use *is* action, and semiosis is anchored in people's lived experiences. Transformative dialogue leads to positive action in times of change. There remains, however, one important question for future studies: how could the results of these precious moments of transformative liminality, should they occur, be utilized, and built into today's proliferating societal contexts of permanent liminality?

9.8 The Power of Dialogue

We are evolutionarily prepared for dialogue, in the sense that languaging is inseparable from our social-relational skills and creativity, central to the human behaviour complex (Csányi, 2000). We are practising these dialogical patterns even when we are alone. We envision the potential responses of the people around us: "…the voice of the other is always implied in the original spoken voice: this is the basis of dialogicality" (Sundet, 2010, p. 86). We have developed not only the potentials but are also governed by the innate need to enter a personal dialogue with internalized others. We instinctively mirror each other's gestures and word use, marking these as our internalized responses. We can respond to each other's stories with a second story that thematically, and in terms of values and attitudes is similar to the story we have just heard to maintain and strengthen our relationships (Arminen, 1998). Through these actions, we constantly develop our mentalizing skills, leading to ever-deepening understandings of the people around us and of ourselves. Taking an autobiographical stance, we keep building and constantly renewing our own narrative identities through the external and internal dialogues—both on personal and on group levels.

Dialogicity as meaning-making requires temporary immersion in liminality, but the transient nature of the experience is crucial here. Trying more of the same will not lead to deeper involvement in dialogue. If the temporary is transformed into an extended or permanent quality, then the original dialogical pattern, now fuelled by rigid feedback mechanisms, transforms into an inflexible pattern, and will finally collapse. Shifts between the renewing forces of chaos and the reconstruction of cosmic order in a miniature of human interactions are central to dialogue, a basic pattern to promote our personal development. This is the communication aspect of humans' efforts to adapt the personal constructs and stories we live by to shared realities, either by expanding, reframing, or consolidating the previous frameworks. From time to time, we must choose between the reassuring and perhaps illusionary safety and stability ("it has always been so and worked very well") and the adventurous, and potentially risky expansions ("this seems so much different now and perhaps I have been wrong…") (Kelly, 1955). Involvement in these continual hermeneutic circles demands a dialogue and leads us to personal, lived discoveries about the awesome complexities of human life.

The question if we can maintain and develop our strong human and humanizing potentials inherent in dialogicity in our era is a disturbing one. Now we seem to focus more on sensing and immersion in a constant flux of enhanced experiences and adopt ready-to-use, e-convenient schemes while fiercely competing for the remnants of Earth's resources. Will we take the intense pains of building self-reflectivity and relational reflectivity? How can we cope with the new challenges of late modernity without the transformative and creative power of genuine dialogue? Can we afford any further losses in our dialogical capacity, a human survival mode shaped by our biological and cultural evolution? Dialogue is hope: "…if life is to be sustained, hope must remain, even where confidence is wounded, trust impaired" (Erikson, 1964. p. 115). Hearing the other is also about healing the other and ourselves, the I and the Thou, from the recurring, extended disruptions of human existence.

References

Acharya, S., & Shukla, S. (2012). Mirror neurons: Enigma of the metaphysical modular brain. *Journal of Natural Science, Biology and Medicine, 3*(2), 118–118. https://doi.org/10.4103/0976-9668.101878

Arminen, I. (1998). *Therapeutic interaction: A study of mutual help in the meetings of alcoholics anonymous*. The Finnish Foundation for Alcohol Studies.

Bakhtin, M. (1981). Forms of time and of the chronotope in the novel. In *The dialogic imagination* (pp. 84–258). University of Texas Press.

Bakhtin, M. (1984a). *Rabelais and his World*. Indiana University Press.

Bakhtin, M. (1984b). *Problems of dostoevsky's poetics*. University of Minnesota Press.

Baldwin, J. M. (1896). A new factor in evolution. *American Naturalist, 30*(354–355) 441–451; 536–553.

Bateson, G. (1972). *Steps to an ecology of mind. Collected Essays in anthropology, psychiatry, evolution, and epistemology.* Jason Aronson.

Berne, E. (1968). *Games people play: The psychology of human relationships*. Penguin.

Bohm, D. (2014). *On dialogue*. Routledge.

Brown, C. S. (2013). Overcoming the master self through the cultivation of a dialogical self-identity. *Dialogue and Universalism, 23*(3), 83–93. https://doi.org/10.5840/du201323334

Buber, M. (1958). *I and Thou*. Charles Scribner's Sons.

Budwig, N. (2000). Language, practices and the construction of personhood. *Theory & Psychology, 10*(6), 769–786. https://doi.org/10.1177/0959354300106004

Buechner, B., Ritter, A., & Spann, R. (2021). Embracing endless liminality: Improvisation and the "Practical Mystic". In V. Bentz & J. Marlatt (Eds.), *Deathworlds to lifeworlds: Collaboration with strangers for personal, social and ecological transformation* (pp. 242–260). De Gruyter. https://doi.org/10.1515/9783110691818-015

Cahan, E. D. (2003). James Mark Baldwin: The natural and the good. *Developmental Review, 23*(1), 9–28. https://doi.org/10.1016/S0273-2297(03)00003-0

Cissna, K. N., & Anderson, R. (1994). The 1957 Martin Buber-Carl Rogers Dialogue, as Dialogue. *Journal of Humanistic Psychology, 34*(1), 11–45. https://doi.org/10.1177/00221678940341003

Cooper, M. (2003). “I-I” and “I-me” transposing Buber’s interpersonal attitude to the intra-personal plane. *Journal of Constructivist Psychology, 16*(2), 131–153. https://doi.org/10.1080/10720530390117911

Cooperrider, D., & Whitney, D. (2000). Exploring appreciative inquiry. *Journal of the World Business Academy, 14*(2), 69–74.

Csányi, V. (2000). The ‘human behavior complex’ and the compulsion of communication: Key factors of human evolution. *Semiotica, 128*(3/4), 243–258. https://doi.org/10.1515/semi.2000.128.3-4.243

Csaszar, F., Erdos, M. B., Ellis, R., Kelemen, G., & Javor, R. (2024). Novel psychoactive substance use and psychological trauma: A multimethodological analysis. *Substance Use & Misuse, 59*(12), 1722–1730. https://doi.org/10.1080/10826084.2024.2369181

Csikszentmihályi, M. (1990). *Flow: The psychology of optimal experience*. Harper Perennial.

Csikszentmihalyi, M. (1996). *Creativity. Flow and the psychology of discovery and invention*. Harper Collins Publishers.

Dialogue between Martin Buber and Carl Rogers. (1960). *Psihologija* (3), 208–221. https://www.jstage.jst.go.jp/article/psysoc/3/4/3_1960.208/_pdf/-char/ja

Eliade, M. (1961). *The sacred and the profane: The nature of religion*. Harper & Row.

Erdos, M. B. (2006). *A nyelvben élő kapcsolat: egy öngyilkosság-megelőző sürgősségi telefonszolgálat beszélgetéseinek vizsgálata. [The language bond: explorations of the calls of a suicide prevention hotline]*. Typotex Kft.

Erdos, M. B., Karpati, T., Rozgonyi, R., & Jávor, R. (2024). Identity structure analysis: a potential framework for process and outcome evaluation in psychotherapy. *Mental Health and Social Inclusion, 28*(5), 699–717. https://doi.org/10.1108/MHSI-06-2023-0071

Erikson, E. H. (1964). *Insight and responsibility*. W.W. Norton.

Fonagy, P., Gergely, G., Jurist, E. L., & Target, M. (2002). *Affect regulation, mentalization, and the development of the self*. Other Press.

Gergen, K. J., McNamee, S., & Barrett, F. J. (2001). Toward transformative dialogue. *International Journal of Public Administration, 24*(7–8), 679–707. https://doi.org/10.1081/PAD-100104770

Gernert, C. C., Nelson, A., Falkai, P., & Falter-Wagner, C. M. (2023). Synchrony in psychotherapy: High physiological positive concordance predicts symptom reduction and negative concordance predicts symptom aggravation. *International Journal of Methods in Psychiatric Research, 33*(1), e1978. Advance online publication.. https://doi.org/10.1002/mpr.1978

Gilligan, C. (1993). *In a different voice: Psychological theory and women’s development*. Harvard University Press.

Gonçalves, M. M., Cunha, C., Ribeiro, A. P., Mendes, I., Santos, A., Matos, M., & Salgado, J. (2012). Innovative moments in psychotherapy: Dialogical processes in developing narratives. In M. Märtsin, B. Wagoner, E.-L. Aveling, I. Kadianaki, & L. Whittaker (Eds.), *Dialogicality in focus: Challenges to theory, method and application* (pp. 173–192). Novinka/Nova Science Publishers.

Greco, M., & Stenner, P. (2017). From paradox to pattern shift: Conceptualising liminal hotspots and their affective dynamics. *Theory & Psychology, 27*(2), 147–166. https://doi.org/10.1177/0959354317693120

Hermans, H. J., Kempen, H. J., & Van Loon, R. J. (1992). The dialogical self: Beyond individualism and rationalism. *American Psychologist, 47*(1), 23–33. https://doi.org/10.1037/0003-066X.47.1.23

Hermans, H. J. M. (2001). The dialogical self: Toward a theory of personal and cultural positioning. *Culture & Psychology, 7*(3), 243–281. https://doi.org/10.1177/1354067X0173001

Horvath, A., & Thomassen, B. (2008). Mimetic errors in liminal schismogenesis: On the political anthropology of the trickster. *International Political Anthropology, 1*(1), 3–24.

Javor, R., Erdos, M. B., & Ellis, R. (2022). Drifting, not driving. Identity structure analysis to explore entrepreneurial identity. *Vezetéstudomány-Budapest Management Review, 53*(5), 2–15. https://doi.org/10.14267/VEZTUD.2022.05.01

Kelly, G. A. (1955). *The psychology of personal constructs. Vol. 1. A theory of personality. Vol. 2. Clinical diagnosis and psychotherapy*. W. W. Norton.

Kodama, K., Tanaka, S., Shimizu, D., Hori, K., & Matsui, H. (2018). Heart rate synchrony in psychological counseling: A case study. *Psychology, 9*(7), 1858–1874. https://doi.org/10.4236/psych.2018.97108

Lux, M. (2010). The magic of encounter: The Person-Centered Approach and the neurosciences. *Person-Centered and Experiential Psychotherapies, 9*(4), 274–289. https://doi.org/10.1080/14779757.2010.9689072

McNamee, S. (2004). Critical moments as "Transformations". *Negotiation Journal, 20*(2), 269–274. https://doi.org/10.1111/j.1571-9979.2004.00022.x

McNamee, S. (2015). Radical presence: Alternatives to the therapeutic state. *European Journal of Psychotherapy & Counselling, 17*(4), 373–383. https://doi.org/10.1080/13642537.2015.1094504

McNamee, S., & Moscheta, M. (2015). Relational intelligence and collaborative learning. *New Directions for Teaching and Learning, 143*(143), 25–40. https://doi.org/10.1002/tl.20134

McNeill, C., Erskine, A., Ellis, R., & Traynor, M. (2019). Developing nurse match: A selection tool for evoking and scoring an applicant's nursing values and attributes. *Nursing Open, 6*(1), 59–71. https://doi.org/10.1002/nop2.183

Mead, G. H. (1934). *Mind, self, and society: From the standpoint of a social behaviorist*. The University of Chicago Press.

Ohmura, N., Okuma, L., Truzzi, A., Esposito, G., & Kuroda, K. O. (2023). Maternal physiological calming responses to infant suckling at the breast. *Journal of Physiological Sciences, 73, no. 3*. https://doi.org/10.1186/s12576-023-00860-w

Okano, Y. (2016). Why has the ethics of care become an issue of global concern? *International Journal of Japanese Sociology, 25*(1), 85–99. https://doi.org/10.1111/ijjs.12048

Penman, R. (1992). Good theory and good practice: An argument in progress. *Communication Theory, 2*(3), 234–250. https://doi.org/10.1111/j.1468-2885.1992.tb00041.x

Penman, R. (2012). On taking communication seriously. *Australian Journal of Communication, 39*(3), 41–63.

Pennebaker, J. W., & Smyth, J. M. (2016). *Opening up by writing it down: How expressive writing improves health and eases emotional pain*. The Guilford Press.

Plato. (2008). *Euthydemus*. (trans: Jowett, B.). The Project Gutenberg EBook of Euthydemus. https://www.gutenberg.org/files/1598/1598-h/1598-h.htm

Rasmussen, B., & Bliss, S. (2014). Beneath the surface: An exploration of neurobiological alterations in therapists working with trauma. *Smith College Studies in Social Work, 84*(2-3), 332–349. https://doi.org/10.1080/00377317.2014.923714

Razzaque, R. (2019). *Dialogical psychiatry. A handbook for the teaching and practice of Open Dialogue*. Omni House Press.

Reho, M., & Salvatore, S. (2024). Redefining meaning: A micro-genetic model of the constitution of experience. *Integrative Psychological & Behavioral Science, 58*(3), 828–835. https://doi.org/10.1007/s12124-024-09849-5

Risser, J. (2019). Hearing the other: Communication as shared life. *Journal of Applied Hermeneutics, Article, 8*, 1–17. https://doi.org/10.11575/jah.v0i0.68707

Salvatore, S., Palmieri, A., Cordella, B., & Iuso, S. (2021). The decay of signs' semiotic value: A cultural psychology interpretation of the contemporary social scenario. *Culture & Psychology, 27*(4), 539–561. https://doi.org/10.1177/1354067X211027276

Saunderson, W. (2002). Women, academia and identity: Constructions of equal opportunities in the 'New Managerialism'–a case of 'Lipstick on the Gorilla'? *Higher Education Quarterly, 56*(4), 376–406. https://doi.org/10.1111/1468-2273.00226

Seltzer, M., & Seltzer, W. J. (2004). Co-texting, chronotope and ritual: A Bakhtinian framing of talk in therapy. *Journal of Family Therapy, 26*(4), 358–383. https://doi.org/10.1111/j.1467-6427.2004.00289.x

Stenner, P. (2017). *Liminality and experience. A Transdisciplinary approach to the psychosocial.* Palgrave Macmillan.

Sundet, R. (2010). Therapeutic collaboration and formalized feedback: Using perspectives from Vygotsky and Bakhtin to shed light on practices in a family therapy unit. *Clinical Child Psychology and Psychiatry, 15*(1), 81–95. https://doi.org/10.1177/1359104509341449

Szakolczai, Á. (2015). Marginalitás és liminalitás [Marginality and liminality]. *Regio, 23*(2), 6–29.

Szasz, T. (1995). The origin of psychiatry: The alienist as nanny for troublesome adults. *History of Psychiatry, 6*(21, Pt 1), 1–19. https://doi.org/10.1177/0957154X9500602101

Tarragona, M. (2008). Postmodern/poststructuralist therapies. In J. L. Lebow (Ed.) (2008). *Twenty-first century psychotherapies: Contemporary approaches to theory and practice.* (pp. 167–205.) John Wiley & Sons Inc.

Thomassen, B. (2013). Anthropology and social theory: Renewing dialogue. *European Journal of Social Theory., 16*(2), 188–207. https://doi.org/10.1177/1368431012463809

Tronick, E. Z., & Cohn, J. F. (1989). Infant-mother face-to-face interaction: Age and gender differences in coordination and the occurrence of miscoordination. *Child Development, 60*(1), 85–92. https://doi.org/10.2307/1131074

Turner, V. W. (1969). *The ritual process: Structure and anti-structure*. Aldine Transaction, University of New York Press.

van der Kolk, B. (2015). *The body keeps the score: Brain, mind, and body in the healing of trauma.* Penguin Books.

Viou, M., & Georgaca, E. (2023). "Their voice becomes my voice": Understanding the development of the dialogical self through the internalization of voices in group psychotherapy. *Theory & Psychology, 33*(4), 577–596. https://doi.org/10.1177/09593543231176254

Watzlawick, P., Bavelas, J. B., & Jackson, D. D. (1968). *Pragmatics of human communication: A study of interactional patterns, pathologies and paradoxes*. Faber & Faber.

Weinreich, P. (2004). Identity structure analysis. In P. Weinreich & W. Saunderson (Eds.), *Analysing identity: Cross-cultural, societal and clinical contexts* (pp. 7–76). Routledge.

White, M. (2024). *Maps of narrative practice*. WW Norton & Company.

Zappen, J. P. (2004). *The rebirth of dialogue: Bakhtin, socrates, and the rhetorical tradition*. State University of New York Press. https://doi.org/10.1353/book4821

Index

M. B. Erdos, *Transitions - Liminality as Lived Experience*,
https://doi.org/10.1007/978-3-031-96007-9

www.ingramcontent.com/pod-product-compliance
Lightning Source LLC
Chambersburg PA
CBHW070223210825
31307CB00063B/134
9783031960062